ALSO BY BERNARD COOPER

*Guess Again*

*Truth Serum*

*A Year of Rhymes*

*Maps to Anywhere*

# The Bill from My Father

*A Memoir*

BERNARD COOPER

*Simon & Schuster*

New York   London   Toronto   Sydney

SIMON & SCHUSTER
Rockefeller Center
1230 Avenue of the Americas
New York, NY 10020

Chapters of this book have appeared in the following publications:
"First Words" and "The Bill from My Father" (under the title "Mine")
in *Los Angeles* magazine; "Winner Take Nothing" in *GQ, The Best
American Essays of 2002,* edited by Stephen Jay Gould, and *The Man I Might Become:
Gay Men Write About Their Fathers,* edited by Bruce Shenitz. The chapter entitled
"The Bill from My Father" was performed on *This American Life.*

This is a work of nonfiction. However, certain names and details of the
characters' lives and physical appearances have been changed, and some events
have been altered or combined for the sake of narrative continuity.

For information about special discounts for bulk purchases,
please contact Simon & Schuster Special Sales at
1-800-456-6798 or business@simonandschuster.com

*Designed by Kyoko Watanabe*

Manufactured in the United States of America

10  9  8  7  6  5  4  3  2  1

Library of Congress Cataloging-in-Publication Data
Cooper, Bernard.
The bill from my father : a memoir / Bernard Cooper.
p. cm.
1. Cooper, Bernard, 1951—Family. 2. Cooper, Bernard, 1951—Childhood and youth.
3. Authors, American—20th century—Family relationships. 4. Authors, American—
20th century—Biography. 5. Gay men—United States—Biography.
6. Fathers and sons—United States. I. Title.
PS3553.05798Z4625 2006
813'.54—dc22                    2005044503
[B]

ISBN-13: 978-0-7432-4962-1
ISBN-10:    0-7432-4962-3

# Acknowledgments

Thanks to Sloan Harris (who encouraged me to put it all together) and Margaret Marr at International Creative Magicians for their astonishing sleight of hand. Steady momentum for this project was provided by Geoff Kloske, one of the country's largest exporters of midnight oil. Steven, Kathryn, and Eliza at the Steven Barclay Agency have been invaluable in allowing me to meet writers and readers I might not otherwise have had the pleasure to know.

Where would a writer be without trusted early readers? I was lucky enough to see this text through Jeff Hammond's X-ray eyes. Tom Knechtel's gently rustling pom-poms bolstered my spirit without disturbing the neighbors. Glen Gold and Alice Sebold were instructive and loving and just plain fun. Two chapters in this book were shaped with a set of precision tools belonging to Kit Rachlis at *Los Angeles* magazine. Amy Gerstler, amazing poet, turned the manuscript pages WITH THE POWER OF HER MIND ALONE! I could not have started, finished, or written the middle part of this book without Jill Ciment's friendship and long distance calling plan, or without Atsuro Riley's full-color diagrams of the universe.

My story only touches upon those of my sisters-in-law, Nancy and Sharleen, who have my deepest gratitude. Rabbi Bob Barruch performed a fact-checking mitzvah. Benjamin Weissman performed a high dive while lighted on fire. Other superhuman feats were performed by Michael Lowenthal, Kimberly Burns, and Laura Perciasepe.

This book was completed with generous support from the National Endowment for the Arts and from the Brian Miller Fellowship.

# Contents

The Bill from My Father

# First Words

"I scratch," said my father. "Itch it!"

I'd asked if he knew what his first words had been. Instead of *ball* or *mama,* he blurted his earliest misunderstanding, his voice so plaintive an imitation of his childhood self I almost leaped out of my chair and asked him where it scratched.

The two of us were sitting in the living room of his Mediterranean house in Hollywood, the house in which I grew up and where my father now lived alone. During my boyhood, the room had been used to receive my parents' guests, a progressively rarer occurrence over the forty years of their marriage, and especially since my mother's death. The pillows, as always, were plumped, if musty. Knickknacks lined the shelves of the breakfront. A broad mahogany coffee table gleamed at our knees. This was the largest room in the house, its acoustics muted by wall-to-wall shag, the once-white fiber aging into ivory.

*Itch it.* Eighty years had passed since he made that jumbled plea to his parents, but when he tilted his head in recollection, sunlight from the bay window glinted in his horn-rimmed glasses, his brown eyes lit with the expectation that his need was about to be relieved—all it would take was accommodating fingers. I could almost feel his prickling skin and see him arch his back like a cat.

"But what you'd meant to say was, 'I itch, scratch it'?"

"Of course that's what I meant to say! I was just a kid, for Christ's sake. I got the words all turned around."

A microphone was propped atop the coffee table, and I nudged it closer to where he sat. I couldn't ask my father a question without his taking it as a challenge. He'd rightly have said the same of me. For as long as I could remember, our communication had been a series of defensive reflexes. No scholar could interpret a text with more care than we'd devoted to parsing each other's remarks, searching for words that might be tinged with insult. *I didn't mean you look tired in a bad way. I heard you the first time. What's with the face?* Such was the idiom in which we spoke. Not surprising, we didn't speak often, and when we did, it wasn't for long.

I'd been raised to assume that my father's history was a place forever out of bounds, a mythical city. His refusal to mention his past was as elemental as his olive skin, as inbred as his restlessness, as certain as his gloom at the first drops of rain. My father wouldn't talk. Oh, he rambled all right, joked and cajoled, but talk it was not. He blustered about the price of gas. He rhapsodized about the steak he ate for dinner, where it fell on the spectrum from rare to well done. But for all his chatter, he remained aloof. It was almost as if he hadn't existed before I was born, as if his history began the moment I perceived him, a blurry face floating above my crib and cooing musical nonsense. I'd lain there wide-eyed and made him happen, and so he was mine as much as I was his.

A tirelessly inquisitive kid, I'd often asked about his life before me. Where had he grown up? How had he met my mother? What did my three older brothers, Robert, Ronald, and Richard, do for fun when they were my age? He'd answer without elaboration— *Atlantic City. . . . At a friend's apartment. . . . Horse around*—his terseness a warning that I'd have to content myself with whatever tidbits he parceled out. My father wasn't evasive so much as skilled at the illusion of candor. You asked, he answered. He routinely used the fewest words. Further questions were impertinent.

Our current conversation was more of the same.

"What other things do you remember from when you were little?"

"Taffy."

"Taffy?"

"Saltwater taffy."

"Tell me more."

His expression said, *Taffy is taffy, for Christ's sake. What's to tell?* He was dressed in a khaki polyester jumpsuit, the official uniform of his retirement. The zipper ran from neck to crotch, enabling him to slip in and out of it with a minimum of effort, like a quick-change artist who donned the same costume again and again. The position of the zipper served as a barometer of his mood. When tugged low, it exposed a gold chain nestled in his silver chest hair. My father had an eye for the ladies, and he, in turn, gave them something to see: a wedge of tanned and manly skin. When pulled high, the zipper signaled his wish to withdraw, to go about his business unnoticed, the khaki fabric a camouflage that allowed him to merge with the background. That day in his living room, the jumpsuit was zipped as high as it would go.

He leaned forward in the wing chair and cleared his throat. "It was delicious, that taffy. Sticky and sweet. I bought it on the Atlantic City boardwalk. They made it with ocean water, which they got right there from the beach. In buckets, or something. That's why they called it 'saltwater' taffy. Now do you see?" He stared intently at the tape recorder while he spoke, as if the machine was not only recording the things he said but listening. When his hearing aid suddenly shrieked with feedback, he fiddled with its tiny dial until the sound sputtered and finally died. Then he blinked at me, speechless.

"Anything else?" I hadn't quite figured out how to narrow down my questions, how to prod him on. He drummed his fingers on the arm of the chair. What I didn't know about my father could have filled a book.

The idea to write a book about him had been suggested a few days earlier by an editor at a publishing house in New York. She phoned me at home one afternoon, introduced herself, and said she'd come across an essay I'd written about my father in a small literary review, one of my first appearances in print. She asked if I'd read a recent best-selling memoir about a writer's relationship with his father, and when I told her I had, she proposed I write a version of that book for her. "But with your dad," she added as an after-thought, "instead of his."

It worried me that this editor (I hadn't yet published a book, and like a duckling that follows the first thing it sees, I'd begun to think of her as *my* editor) had such a definitive vision of the final product. Was what she really wanted this other author's book, but typed by me? She sensed my hesitation and tried to entice me with her blithe tone. *I'll provide the front and back cover,* she seemed to be saying. *All you have to do is hand me the pages!* Then came the flattery, which worked like a charm since I react to praise of any kind with a Pavlov-ian devotion to the person pouring it on. At some point money was mentioned—not all that much, but a larger sum than I'd ever dreamed of being able to earn from my writing and one that I pic-tured piled before me, a mound of cash.

I wanted to say *yes,* but I wasn't sure whether I could coax from my father enough stories, anecdotes, hazy recollections, or random chat to carry on a dinner conversation, let alone fill an entire book. How could I write a book about a man whose mystery was ever-present, whose mystery confirmed his being as a shadow confirms the person who casts it? What if trying to write it only revealed how little I knew, less a biography than a chronicle of noncommunica-tion? What if I began it but couldn't finish? By saying *yes,* I'd prob-ably end up proving to my father that his son was a bungler, undeserving of his trust all along. No wonder he hadn't shared very much! Not knowing about him was my fault!

"Are we thinking it over?" the editor asked excitedly.

"Are we ever," I said.

On the other hand, it would be foolish to refuse her offer because . . . well, because money was involved, but also because the rest of my family was gone forever and Dad was all I had left, though I wasn't sure what constituted "all." Or "Dad" for that matter. I knew so little about him that I wasn't even sure what I didn't know. It both-ered me that I was more familiar with the personal history of a local

TV station's silver-haired newscaster after reading a profile about him in the Sunday paper (his parents came from Ireland and he majored in journalism at UC San Diego) than I was with the personal history of the man who raised me, ate at our table, paid our utility bills, and slept in the same bed as my mother. Were we father and son, I sometimes wondered, or merely strangers who answered to those terms? Writing the book would require us to spend time together for a series of interviews, and if I posed the questions just so, these forums for measured revelation, with their civil rules of back and forth, might be just what I needed to get to know him.

I told her I'd give it a try.

The next day I called my father and explained that a publisher in New York wanted me to write a book about him. Writing was a hobby as far as he was concerned, a fine if inexplicable pastime like jigsaw puzzles or model planes. He believed I'd someday give up my literary ambition and "find myself," which is to say find myself working at a legitimate job. I'd been teaching freshman composition at a local college for five years, and when I first told him that my course load consisted of three classes a week, his eyebrows bunched together and he said, "You only work three days a week?" In fact, I had two classes on the same day, so I was on campus *two* days a week—a clarification I didn't make. I considered explaining how much time I spent preparing lectures and grading stacks of exhaustingly foggy essays and how difficult it sometimes was to see the novels and poems and short stories I loved become little more than tributaries draining into the Mighty Syllabus. But there would have been no point in arguing. Nothing short of building a pyramid with my bare hands would have struck my father as a line of work more strenuous than his own. This might have been understandable had he worked on an assembly line or a construction crew and found his son's bookishness lazy and effete, but we're talking about a lawyer who'd glided downtown each weekday morning in a white Cadillac, his fingernails buffed to a high gloss, his briefcase embossed with interlocking letters, *ESC,* for Edward Samuel Cooper. My father worked hard, and I saw in our occupations a number of similarities—rows of books lining our shelves, hours spent presenting a story—whereas he saw none.

"The publisher might pay me good money," I told him. I thought the financial angle would make a good impression, though the "might," I realized at once, had been a strategic mistake, proof of my dubious business sense.

"When did you want to stop by?" he asked.

And that was that. Not, *Who's the publisher?* or, *Why a book about me, of all people?* Not even, *How much money do you think you might make?* His sheer incuriousness could be infuriating, but I wasn't about to alienate my subject by getting angry at him, at least not before I'd extracted a few anecdotes and cashed the check for my phantom advance. We made a date for the following day. Three P.M. sharp.

In all fairness to my father, I have to admit that I was also relieved by his lack of curiosity because it meant I didn't have to tell him about my essay in the literary review. In it I'd mentioned—alluded to, really—his marital infidelities, and I didn't think his anger would be appeased by my trying to explain that (1) I hadn't written about him to air a grievance, or (2) I took it as a rule of human nature that sexual longing propels people in all sorts of unexpected, not to mention extramarital, directions, or (3) the tone in which I portrayed him was sympathetic and forgiving. He didn't need my sympathy or my forgiveness, and I wasn't up to an elaborate fan dance of self-justification.

The truth, or one sedimentary layer of it, was that my father didn't know I knew about his various affairs. Worse, if he asked me how I'd found out about them, I'd either have to make up an excuse or tell him that I'd learned of them one day when I came home from high school. I stepped through the back door to find my mother standing in the middle of the kitchen, waving above her head what appeared to be a white flag. She muttered what sounded like, "He's a heel," or, "He'll get his." I set my schoolbooks on the counter and walked closer, resisting the impulse to touch her because she seemed too feral to be consoled. It was four o'clock in the afternoon, but she still wore the bathrobe she'd put on that morning, balls of Kleenex stuffed in a pocket. Without saying a word, she thrust toward me what I realized wasn't a white flag after all but a pair of my father's boxer shorts. I took them automatically, as if I'd been handed a glass of milk. Then she folded her arms across her chest. The bearer of a terrible patience, she waited to see what I'd say or do.

I rubbed my thumb across the cloth, assessing it by touch as I'd seen her do with bolts of fabric. The cotton had been thinned by frequent bleaching. The elastic waistband had lost its snap. With those observations, I'd pretty much exhausted every detail of my father's boxers, except for the obvious blotch my mother alleged was lipstick. I finally forced myself to examine it while keeping my expression as blank as I could. The stain was reddish (though the popular shades of lipstick at the time were tropical pinks and orangy corals) and not so definitively kiss-shaped that it could be inter- preted, beyond a doubt, as an imprint of lips. It streaked across the placket toward the crotch, a sight as otherworldly as a comet. I'd long ago realized that my parents must have had sex at least four times during their marriage because they gave birth to me and my three brothers, but I couldn't bring myself to picture them doing the deed, which would have made it hard to look at them ever again without picturing it. I found it easier, relatively speaking, to imag- ine an unfamiliar woman performing oral sex on my father, because she'd be a faceless stranger instead of my mother, whose hazel eyes were bright with fury, her hot breath wafting toward me.

Studying my father's underwear in her company seemed too odd and intimate an occurrence to actually be happening. Light seeped through the kitchen windows, dimming into that nameless phase between late afternoon and early dusk. The wall clock ticked. The refrigerator shuddered. Cotton spilled over my open hands. I felt as if I'd entered a dream—my mother's or mine, it was hard to tell—in which a taboo had been dredged from the unconscious. I had to gather the will to speak, carefully, the way one gathers shattered glass. When I suggested, half in earnest and half to get the whole thing over with, that it might not be lipstick at all but strawberry jam, my

mother kept repeating, "Strawberry *jam?*" She wanted someone—
even her son—to verify the evidence and share her outrage.

Perhaps she thought my remark was a way to defend my father
or convince her that she'd jumped to the wrong conclusion, when
what I'd meant to do was protect both of my parents (and myself)
by making that stain a petty mishap, soluble in soap and water. Until
that day I'd been one among a high school full of teenagers who
believed that adults lived largely in a world of convenient illusions,
yet all it took was my mother chanting *"Jam?"* to make me see that
it was I who was holding on to the illusion that my parents' marriage was a good one, and furthermore, that thinking anyone could
live a life exempt from such illusions was the biggest and most common illusion of all.

Had my father known I'd written about—or alluded to—his
infidelity, he certainly wouldn't have let me interview him for a
book. And so I kept quiet about why the editor from New York had
called me in the first place.

The tape made a faint hiss as it spooled from reel to reel, like
the sound of waves breaking in the distance. "Tell me more about
the boardwalk, Dad." He sat back in the chair and closed his eyes.
He folded his age-spotted hands in his lap and sighed because
remembering was work. From within the depths of recollection my
father asked, not unkindly, "What do you want from me? Seagulls or
something?"


Until he retired, at the age of seventy-five, my father worked on the
top floor of the Continental Building, twelve stories of weathered
brick in downtown Los Angeles. A frosted-glass door stenciled with
his name and profession stood at the end of a long, dimly lit hallway,
which made it seem like a door of last resort. He specialized in
divorce law. Even as a child I sensed that our family's prosperity bore
some connection to the dissolution of human relationships, the
money in my father's billfold payment for a grim yet necessary service: unburdening people of each other. In the 1950s, two decades

before California's no-fault divorce law, a couple needed to prove they had reason to be granted a divorce, that in fact they had no recourse but to seek one, and so my father became adept at inflaming his clients' sense of betrayal, at making their perfectly ordinary spouses seem insufferable and cruel, the couples' love a blunder from the start. By the time I was old enough to grasp what he did for a living, my father had earned a reputation for handling cases whose tawdry details often made it into the pages of the *Los Angeles Herald Examiner*. He collected his clippings in a black scrapbook that lay atop our coffee table. I'd mull over those strips of newsprint for hours, trying to decipher the how and why of love gone wrong.

*The Case of the Baking Newlywed* told of Mrs. Beverly C. Cleveland, a woman who cooked continually during the first ten days of her marriage, filling the couple's small refrigerator with an uneaten banquet of pies and roasts and casseroles. Had I not read otherwise, Mrs. Cleveland would have struck me as a typical, even ideal, homemaker, since cooking was a skill that husbands seemed to covet in a wife. What had Mrs. Cleveland done that was any different from what my mother, and my friends' mothers, and the mothers on TV did every day of their lives: chop, mash, fry, whip, grate, freeze, and reheat? I imagined the Clevelands' warm apartment perfumed with simmering dinners. According to my father, however, Beverly Cleveland's culinary marathon was a ploy to avoid her "wifely obligation." In the article he referred to Jake Cleveland as his "kissless client," whose "connubial crisis" was due to the couple's ten-day "hellmoon," the hellish specifics of which weren't mentioned in print. The newspaper photograph showed Mrs. Cleveland wincing from the glare of a flashbulb and raising a hand to shield her face from the camera—a mug shot of shame itself.

At ten years old I was too young to articulate, but not too young to sense, that somewhere beneath this case lay Beverly Cleveland's avoidance of sex, or at least of her husband. Jake Cleveland hadn't been photographed for the article and I couldn't help wondering if he was ugly. No matter if he was the Creature from the Black Lagoon; the verdict fell in his favor, and this put his wife on par with the thieves and forgers and other criminals whose pictures also appeared in the *Herald*. "Don't be an idiot," said my father when I asked if there were laws about cooking too much food, and if mother could get arrested for it.

While thumbing through the scrapbook, I could never quite decide whether my father acted as an agent of fairness, or of petty revenge. Just being in the position to make such a decision gave me a heady sense of omniscience, since my father—who laid down the law in our house—was suddenly subject to my judgment, instead of the other way around. I mean omniscience literally, for in trying to determine whether my father's livelihood was noble or corrupt, I sometimes envisioned his cases as though I were floating invisibly near the courtroom ceiling, up where lightbulbs hummed in their sockets and the California flag drooped from its staff. Below me, an avuncular, black-robed judge sat in a kind of private balcony and watched as my father and another attorney tossed blame back and forth like a hot potato.

Another headline read, *Case of "the Captive Bride" Ends in a Blaze of Poetry.* Here, my father defended the right of a Mr. and Mrs. Nunez to keep their sixteen-year-old daughter, Florence, virtually locked in her bedroom until she turned eighteen, forbidding her to live with her husband, Peter Ramos, with whom she'd eloped. To prove his devotion, Peter stood on the sidewalk outside the Nunez house day and night, reciting the love poems he wrote for Florence, which he read loudly enough for her to hear through the walls. Worried that his clients might have to listen to lovesick couplets for the next two years, my father applied for a restraining order that would, if not silence the poet, keep his verse at a distance. "The boy won't let up with the moon and June," was how he put it to the reporter. "Peter may be standing on a public sidewalk, but he's no better than a peeping Tom, what with the way he's invading my clients' privacy."

Peter, however, saw nothing but nobility in his persistence. Florence was his muse as well as his wife, and his longing never flagged in her absence. He hired Arthur Marcus, an attorney who, in a semantic counterattack, dubbed Peter "the banished groom" and claimed that Florence was being "held captive" against her will. (I imagined her in a prison cell with a vanity table and canopy bed). Mr. Marcus immediately summoned Florence to appear in court, where she could testify to Peter's honorable character and prove herself mature enough for marriage.

Dad answered the writ of habeas corpus with a poem of his own:

> *The court lacks jurisdiction*
> *To make an order stern,*
> *The paper filed by Peter*
> *Requires no return.*
> *And all the allegations*
> *Including sigh and cry*
> *Each of them now Florence's*
> *Parents do deny.*
> *And for the further answer to*
> *This impassioned plea*
> *We would remind rash Peter*
> *That he should clearly see*
> *A child of sixteen is too young*
> *To claim a mate for life*
> *Without consent of her guardians, thus*
> *Can only lead to strife.*

My father could moon and June with the best. The marriage was annulled.

Because he was such a laconic man at home—his all-purpose grunt meant yes and no, hello and good-bye—it astonished me to read about the verbal acrobatics with which he so often bent the law to his whims. How else but through supernatural powers of persuasion could he have made a boy's love poem seem like a brick hurled through a window, or argue that a freshly baked pie was the cause of a husband's sexual deprivation? Apparently, if Dad insisted the grass was blue, he leadeth you beside blue pastures.

The marital conflicts I read about in my father's scrapbook weren't much different from the fights that broke out every day on the baseball diamonds and jungle gyms of my elementary school playground—"Cheater!" "It's *my* turn!" "Stop looking at me funny!"—but enriched and twisted beyond all proportion. Was wedlock simply a larger playground? Were lawyers bullies paid by the hour?

I overflowed with questions in those days because I was certain the world operated according to some hidden system that, sooner or later, an adult would explain in the same patient way that Mr. Wizard, the science teacher who hosted an after-school TV show, explained the wonders of water displacement or the magic of static electricity. That adults were wiser than children wasn't just a homily as far as I was concerned but a belief more tolerable than the prospect that both children and adults were as dumb as rubber balls. Because if no one knew how or why things happened, then no one could stop bad things from happening or make good things happen—a human helplessness I was hard-pressed to accept. Although my father may not have given me the answers I sought, I felt sure he possessed them, just as he possessed a knowledge of the law and would one day give me his grudging guidance.

Only once did he take my future in hand, hoping to impart a lesson for my betterment. I would have soaked it up in a second had I understood what the lesson meant. He called me into the living room one Friday after coming home early from court. He'd propped our Bell & Howell projector on the coffee table, the reels threaded and ready to spin. Across the room, balanced on a wobbly tripod, stood the home-movie screen, its gritty opalescent surface sparkling in the afternoon light. Dad's hands were clasped behind his back, his shoulders squared.

Before entering the room I had to remove my shoes because the carpet was still new and my mother, who hadn't yet discovered clear plastic rug runners, was determined to get her money's worth of pure, untrammeled, glamorous white. My father wore black dress socks—men's *hosiery,* they were called in the department stores—and his feet looked as dark as holes in a snowdrift.

"Your father," he announced, "wants to show you something."

This was the first time I'd ever heard him refer to himself in the third person, and it piqued my interest, implying as it did that my father was out of the room and the man standing before me was not who I assumed. But who else could he be? I was a late child, fifteen years younger than the youngest of my three brothers—all of whom had moved away from home by the time I turned ten—and my next thought was that Dad was going to tell me he wasn't my father but my fourth and oldest brother. What had happened to my real father wasn't clear in the fantasy, which came over me so fast there wasn't time to account for his whereabouts. I figured he must be out there somewhere, happy and unharmed.

"Why are you looking at me like that?" my father asked.

"I don't know."

"Well," he said, "have a seat."

The couch (my mother called the color *salmon,* my father, *lox*) was so plush that it took me a moment to sink down to solid matter. Meanwhile, my father walked toward the picture window, each padded footfall adding to the hush. Even under normal circumstances, closing those drapes was something of a ceremony, for they were heavy as bedspreads and printed with a pattern of mortar and bricks. When Dad pulled the cord, bricks swooped together like the halves of a wall and the room went dark.

Light shot from the lens of the projector and burrowed through the room. It flickered over the furniture and gave the dark a restless depth. I watched dust motes whirl and collide in the beam, and this bright turmoil, this erosion of countless powdery grains, was proof of a fact I knew all along but hadn't grasped until that moment: the world was being ground to bits. I was still transfixed when I heard my father tell me to snap out of it and pay attention to what was on the screen.

In a wood-paneled office, a stout black woman sat across a desk from a white man, whose bony hands were folded atop an ink blotter. A pen holder slanted in his direction, and next to it a name plate identified him as a judge. His lips moved nonstop, but the film was silent and I couldn't make out a word he was saying. All the while he stared into the camera with the unnatural expression of a person who'd been told to act natural and not stare into the camera. The woman paid respectful attention, leaning forward once or twice in a futile effort to interrupt. She clutched under one arm a leather-bound book that was either a Bible or a volume of the *Encyclopaedia Britannica*. On the desk beside her lay an overstuffed purse.

The judge was still yammering when the purse, without so much as a twitch of forewarning, stood up, wavered on two spindly legs, and walked toward him, though "walked toward him" suggests that the purse had a particular destination, whereas its halting progress was more along the lines of two steps forward, one step back. For a moment I wondered whether it was a marionette, though I couldn't see strings, and besides, who in their right mind would make a marionette that looked like a staggering handbag? No, the purse's sense-lessness hinted at the possibility that it once possessed sense and now was trying to get along without it. This was animal motion, too reflexive with muscle and nerve to be anything inanimate.

The judge's mouth stopped moving when the scruffy whatever-it-was lurched into his line of vision. He gave it a wary, sidelong glance, ready to react should something unexpected occur, which, considering what had occurred already, would have to be inconceivably strange. That's when the camera slowly zoomed in, moving as if it, too, were an animal, a predator hunting its unsuspecting prey. It slid between the woman and the judge, intent on the mound in the middle of the desk. Feathers slowly came into focus. Wings bristled as the creature breathed.

"What is it?" I whispered.

"Watch," said my father.

He had been a witness to the actual event, but because I didn't know this yet, his *Watch* was like a magic command that caused what happened next to happen. A stump emerged from the thing's right side, which until that point had looked identical to its left. The stump pivoted toward the camera and paused long enough to reveal its severed end. A tunnel of tendon and pearly bone led inside the creature's body, the sight no less gruesome in black-and-white. The woman's fingers descended into view, holding an eye-dropper by its rubber bulb. She squeezed until a bead of clear liquid glistened at its tip, then angled it toward the cavity. The stump strained upward.

The idea of watching the creature being fed made me speechless, queasy. How much closer would the camera zoom? What kind of contractions would swallowing involve? That blind, groping, hungry stump was the neediest thing I'd ever seen. Leaving the room was out of the question; my father would view my retreat as rudeness, or worse, as proof that I was a delicate boy unworthy of paternal wisdom. I couldn't have fled anyway; sunk in the possessive depths of the couch, I could barely move.

The droplet wobbled.

"Sugar water," said my father.

Not until later that night, after unsuccessfully begging myself to please stop thinking about the gaping wound, did I realize that *sugar water* referred to the solution in the eyedropper. At the time, however, my father might as well have said *spoon clock* or *hat bell* for all the sense his comment made.

The pendulous droplet fell into the stump. Then another and another. For all that creature knew it had started to rain, and the rain tasted sweet. As the woman doled out the final drops, words scrolled up the screen:

> There is hope for you too
> when you see how divine power
> keeps Lazarus alive!
> Mrs. Martha Green's decapitated fowl
> lives to become
> THE MIRACLE CHICKEN!
> This 20th century wonder brings a possibility
> of new life and new healing
> to an army of believers.
> It's all TRUE!
> This movie is AUTHENTIC!

The woman's purse was a headless chicken. I might have uttered this fact aloud since it came as such a great, if short-lived, relief. My father had used the phrase "like a chicken with its head cut off" to describe all manner of frenzied activity, applying it to bad drivers and harried salespeople and even to my mother, who cooked dinner in a state that could be described either as motherly gusto or stifled rage. Every time I heard the expression, I pictured the figurative chicken running around a barnyard in circles and spurting a geyser of blood before dropping dead in the dust. Dropping dead *forever,* I should add, because it never occurred to me that a chicken might survive its execution, give hope to humans, and star in a film. Wasn't a head indispensable?

Dad towered beside the projector, his figure awash in flickering light. He loosened his tie and unbuttoned his collar. "There's your old man," he said, pointing to the screen.

A crowd dressed in Sunday finery milled around the front lawn of a clapboard house. People stepped aside to let my father pass, a sea of hats parting before him. Mrs. Green trailed in his wake. She cradled Lazarus in her arms, careful not to let the bird be jostled and also not to hide it from view. Making his way through the crowd, Dad cast frequent backward glances to make sure Mrs. Green and her bird were behind him. Photographers jockeyed to get a good shot. Reporters frantically scrawled on their notepads. Men and women craned their necks, some letting children straddle their shoulders to get a better look.

> Mrs. Green refuses to hand Lazarus over to the S.P.C.A.
> despite a court order from Judge Stanley Moffatt.
> Her attorney, Edward S. Cooper, claims the bird is
> "an act of providence
> for the benefit of all mankind."

The throng of spectators, two or three people deep, waited behind a listing picket fence as my father escorted Mrs. Green into a yard overgrown with blooming hibiscus and bougainvillea. She seemed at home there, so I supposed the yard was hers. It may have been an effect of the grainy eight-millimeter film, but this ramshackle Eden glowed with an ancient, paper-thin light, as if the screen had turned to parchment. It wouldn't have surprised me if one of the bushes had burst into flame and spoken in a holy baritone.

My father carried his monogrammed briefcase by his side. He and Mrs. Green walked to a small table that had been set up on a patch of grass. They glanced nervously at the camera, humbled by the expectant crowd. Black and Caucasian faces looked on, soldiers in an army of believers. Mrs. Green gazed almost sorrowfully at the bundle in her arms. Hesitant to let it go, she inhaled a bracing, duty-bound breath, then gingerly lowered the chicken onto the table. Its feet dangled like scrawny tassels, and once his legs touched the table top, they buckled without a hint of resistance.

I'd learned over the years to heed my father's impatience as one would a storm warning, and watching him stand there on-screen, I recognized signs of impending anger as he glared at that motionless bird. A prominent vein bulged on his forehead. His grip on the briefcase tightened. I could almost hear him thinking, *Of course this would happen. What did I expect? Just when things were going my way, fate sticks out its leg and trips me.* He and Mrs. Green stood side by side and I thought I saw him nudge her with a silent ultimatum: *Do anything you have to do, but get that goddamn poultry to move! You want people thinking this is some kind of hoax?* I felt the weight of his briefcase in my hand, his hot collar encircling my neck, his heart thumping inside my chest. "What if it doesn't move?" I asked. Meaning if it didn't, would we both be ashamed?

He looked worried in the movie but not in real life. He smiled faintly and crossed his arms. "That bird's as alive as I am," he said.

Silent concern rippled through the crowd; a few people used their hats as fans or consulted hefty, gilt-edged Bibles. Mrs. Green patted her forehead with a hankie. The twentieth-century wonder looked about as wondrous as a feather duster.

What were my father and Mrs. Green to do? They couldn't rouse it by snapping their fingers or waving their hands in front of its face. Maybe they could communicate to the bird through touch, the way Annie Sullivan had tapped the word *water* on Helen Keller's hand. Of course, it wouldn't look good if my father and Mrs. Green started poking at the chicken; you can't badger a miracle to happen and then expect people to marvel when it does.

I gasped when the chicken sprang to its feet, wings thrashing the air. Feathers bristled when it stretched its stump. The camera pulled back as if rearing in fear and astonishment. People in the background flung up their arms in a mute *hallelujah*. Mrs. Green's unbounded joy caught my father off guard; he swayed in her embrace, eyeing the chicken over her shoulder. Big letters bellowed from the screen:

Cock-A-Doodle-Do!

My father's high, delighted laughter rose over the sound of the projector. "Is that chicken something?"

"Rooster, you mean?"

"Chicken," he corrected, annoyed that I might have missed the big finish, might have been distracted when water turned to wine.

"Chickens don't crow," I told him.

"What?"

Tricky business, repeating a statement that belonged, I realized too late, in the "back talk" category. I scrambled to match oinks and tweets and moos with the appropriate animal, only to discover that the correspondences were more debatable than I'd realized. My rooster remark sounded arrogant now, and possibly untrue. "Do roosters crow?" I found myself asking.

The projector lit my father's face from below. His chin and brow were islands of light, his eye sockets deep, unreadable. "Supposing a chicken doesn't crow," he said. "Then this one's more of a miracle."

\*   \*   \*

"Remember the headless rooster?" I asked.

My father leaned toward the microphone. "Chicken," he insisted, then sat back in his chair.

"But the chicken supposedly crowed, Dad. And chickens—I'd stake my life on this—don't crow. They cackle. Or cluck?"

The querulousness in my voice, and the irritation in his, had been preserved for thirty years.

"Look," he said, "if the client says a chicken crowed, the chicken crowed. Mrs. Green heard it. So did half the people who were at the press conference that day. Maybe they were in a religious state. That kind of thing has never happened to me personally, so I wouldn't know. All I know is that Mrs. Green buys the chicken from a local butcher, takes it home for dinner, puts a pot of water on the stove, and when she goes to pluck the thing, it stands up and starts strutting around the kitchen like this was just another day on the farm. She's standing there gawking when a voice comes out of nowhere and tells her to name the bird Lazarus, and she hollers, 'Praise the Lord.'" Here my father lifted his arthritic arms as high as he was able, the jumpsuit stretching taut across his belly. "She gets on the phone to call her friends, who call their friends, and so on, and pretty soon people are showing up at Mrs. Green's house in droves, lining up just to get a look at the thing. Being your enterprising type, she starts charging admission. Can you blame her? She sees a brass ring and she grabs it. That's America.

"Eventually the S.P.C.A. gets wind of what's going on and Stanley Moffatt, the San Bernardino District Court judge, summons her to appear in his chambers and calls what she's doing 'a sideshow' or some such prejudicial remark he had no business making. He orders her to hand Lazarus over to the county veterinarian for 'the advancement of science,' whatever the hell that means. Mrs. Green hired me to keep the S.P.C.A. from taking her faith away, was what it amounted to. My job was to prove that the animal was happy, that keeping it alive wasn't your usual cruelty like chaining a dog to a tree or letting a horse go without oats. What we had here was a case of the government interfering with an individual's religious freedom, a clear breach of the Constitution."

He straightened his back, regal in his wing chair. "I ask you," he said, pounding the chair's upholstered arm, "would Mrs. Martha Green be on the wrong side of the law if she was charging money for people to see a chicken with *two* heads, or if she was selling fried chicken dinners? Would a judge order her to cease and desist, to surrender her property, under those circumstances? She might need a business permit, but that's a moot point because the S.P.C.A. got involved, not the small business bureau. The woman believed she was doing something good, and I believed she believed it. The bird went ahead and died not long after Moffatt's ruling, but even dead it meant a lot to people."

"Okay," I said, afraid to interrupt a story that spilled forth with uncharacteristic ease. All the while, the shiny strand of magnetic tape was saving his speech for posterity, every word awaiting transcription. There might be a book here after all, I guardedly told myself, and it struck me that the editor from New York—*my* editor— possessed the gift of literary foresight. How many other careers had she influenced with her deceptively offhand suggestions?

I composed my face into what I hoped was a receptive expression. *Go on,* it invited him. *I've waited a long time to hear you talk. A lifetime, precisely.*

My father paused. "What's with the face?"

I touched my cheek to see if the attentive face I felt from the inside was the one that showed. It wasn't, but I'm pretty sure it had been before Dad asked.

"If she'd told me Lazarus was a goddamn camel and he recited the Gettysburg Address, I would have done my best to back her up, and there would have been witnesses coming out of the woodwork to say they heard him with their own two ears, and the next day there'd be a headline in the *Herald:* '*Camel Quotes Lincoln.*' That's the kind of world we live in. Don't kid yourself and think it's not. I did what I needed to do to win. I heard what I had to."

"Makes sense," I said.

"For Christ's sake, if you don't believe the chicken crowed, I'll prove it! It's written in print!" His defensiveness took me by surprise until I realized that at that point in our visit, and in my tenure as his son, sense was relative. He'd caught a hint of equivocation in my eager agreement. His joints cracked as he rose to his feet. "I've still got my file on the case. Say whatever you want about your old man; he keeps good records. That scrapbook's in here, too." He reached into each of the cubbyholes lining the breakfront's desk, searching for the key that opened the drawers at its base. His hand came back empty again and again. "The key's got to be here somewhere." He lifted a pile of mail to see if the key was underneath. Weeks' worth of bills were sloughed to the floor.

"I'll take your word for it, Dad. Really. Sit down and tell me more."

He patted the pockets of his jumpsuit. Nothing. "A key doesn't just get up on its own and walk away."

A long pause during which the two of us considered the possibility that, yes, a key isn't supposed to do something so rash, but it might anyway. That's the kind of world we live in.

Next on the tape come woody *thunks* accompanied by the rattle of brass latches that won't give up their grip; my father tested the drawers to see if any were unlocked. Mother had called this massive piece of furniture a "conversation piece," though I'm sure my father's tirade against it—"Goddamn Fort Knox!"—wasn't the kind of conversation she'd had in mind. He lowered himself onto his hands and knees and began combing through the matted shag to see if the key had fallen nearby.

I pushed myself out of the couch—as enveloping as ever—and brought the tape recorder closer. I let the microphone dangle from my arm, near enough to pick up his voice but not so near that it might cause him to become self-conscious. I'd begun to understand the documentarian's paradox: the witness alters the event he's observing by the act of observation. If I hadn't been there pressing him to remember the past, my father would be sprawled contentedly on the couch, tossing salted nuts into his mouth and watching *Wheel of Fortune.* Instead, he was scrounging for a key while I hovered over him. The khaki jumpsuit clung to his body and made him look like a plump, ungainly baby, though his neck was creased with an old man's wrinkles and his breath came hard. I switched off the tape recorder and set it on the desk. "Dad," I said, holding out my hand, "let me help you up."

My father looked up from the flatland of the carpet. The sight of me seemed to strike him like a blow. His forehead furrowed, his face grew pale. I was the only son he had left. Bob had died of Hodgkin's at twenty, Richard of colon cancer at thirty-one. At the age of fifty, Ron's heart stopped. With each death my father cried his son's name, and without the son to nod in recognition, those cries continued to carry on the air, never quite fading.

My father refused my outstretched hand. He wouldn't have

taken my brothers' hands either, had they been there to hold them out. The man's dominion had always been simple: *we* were indebted, never the other way around. Worse, then, when the son who offers assistance is the last, a dark-eyed composite of heirs long gone, compliant sons who'd asked fewer questions, learned by example, and followed him into the field of law. Whatever thoughts they harbored toward their father, they kept them quiet as sons should. Silence was a kind of respect. They'd never think to write a book—pages, he'd suspect, of evidence against him. Yet there I stood, the son who'd been spared. A watchful boy unlike the others, yet too much like the others to bear.

He practically climbed the brass latches in his determination to get up on his own. The breakfront shuddered with his weight, porcelain courtiers and crystal aperitif glasses chiming on the shelves above him. With majestic effort, he managed to stand. He grabbed the tape recorder off the desk and shoved it into my hands.

"What did I . . . ?"

"A son doesn't help his father up."

"A son . . . ?"

"A son doesn't help his father up."

"What does a son do?"

"A son helps his father look for the key. Now get out of my house."

When I was a boy, misbehaving in the Cadillac's backseat, my father would suddenly swerve toward the curb, lurch to a stop, and order me to get out in some unfamiliar part of town. "You can live *here*," he'd announce, not bothering to look around and see where we were. It was elsewhere, of course, and any place that wasn't home illustrated elsewhere's disadvantages. The streets, if they were peopled, were peopled by strangers. Awnings cast their scraps of shadow. Buses roared past and spewed exhaust. "Ed, please," my mother would groan. While my father brooded behind the wheel, I'd grip the door handle and consider making him sorry with an act of flagrant obedience: I'd disappear into the city and lose myself faster and more irretrievably than he could banish me. I'd beg for food, live in

Griffith Park, make the clothes on my back last forever. I'd survive outside his good graces, without his money and without his love. But the plush seat was comfortable, and the idling car rocked like a cradle, and soon the world was slipping past the window as the Cadillac merged with traffic.

"Get out of my house," he repeated, pointing toward the front door.

While the walls still enclosed me and the roof hung overhead, I peered into my father's face, the face I'd always studied to see if I was good or bad, right or wrong. The face by which I took my measure.

I should have helped him look for that key. I should, for once, have used my powers of observation to a practical end. What lapse of consideration, what selfishness, prevented me from hunkering down and searching with him? Those drawers were crammed with artifacts, evidence of his history. Wasn't that what I'd come for?

*A son doesn't help his father up.* His words reverberated in the sudden flood of sunlight as I opened the door, on the flagstone walkway that led to the street, as I started my car. They had about them a biblical ring, as if an eleventh and ultimate commandment had somehow escaped my attention till now.

My literary mission was a bust. The tape recorder (I'd probably never use it again and couldn't take it back because I'd lost the receipt) lay on the passenger seat along with a cassette that chronicled a few sound effects produced by the living room furniture, an account of a headless, supposedly crowing chicken, and what my father claimed were his first words—perhaps the last I'd hear from him.

I was thirty-three and still living in the neighborhood in which I'd grown up, fifteen minutes away from my father's house. Stucco apartment buildings had risen on lots where postwar bungalows once stood. Billboards for safe sex and neon signs for businesses like the Tanning Institute had started to crowd the eastern end of Hollywood Boulevard. The streets where my father threatened to leave me as a child—*See how long you last*—had become the ones in which I lived, and driving through them that day seemed like fresh exile. I resolved, as before, to fend for myself, and swore his absence wouldn't matter. *Mr. Divorce* my mother had called him, her sarcasm having clarified, over years of marriage, into a feeling as strong as love. How quickly I'd thought of an alibi when she'd handed me his boxers. My innocence was as laughable as his.

While stopped at a red light, I reached a verdict: the man was a bastard. But no sooner had the light changed, no sooner had I stepped on the gas, than I remembered how, at Sunday breakfast, my father would heap mounds of strawberry jam onto slices of rye. One for me and one for himself, again and again till the two of us were bursting. He'd excavate an entire jar, down to the dregs, where the spoon struck glass. When my frugal mother clicked her tongue, he'd pat the empty chair beside him. "What do the pennies matter in the end? Who are you saving your pleasure for?" She'd glance at us uncertainly, then sit as if she'd been waiting all her life to plunge into that very chair, to squander food after years of scrimping. He'd hand her a slathered slice of bread, careful not to spill one glossy drop, though now and then a dab of jam—I saw it happen—would fall into his lap.

# My Father's Jumpsuit

A month after my father kicked me out of his house, and through a series of circumstances I'll explain momentarily, I ended up wearing his khaki jumpsuit to a garden party that took place on a warm July afternoon. Embedded in the polyester were whiffs of his minty soap and cologne, phantom clouds of talcum powder, plus a musky odor that was all his own. While I drank rum punch and shook people's hands, I inhaled pungent blasts of Dad.

In olfactory terms the jumpsuit overwhelmed me, but in fact I stood a good a foot taller than my father and the fit was snug. My wrists jutted from the sleeves and the pants legs ended above my ankles. Ordinarily, I'd never wear a polyester jumpsuit in public, or in private for that matter, especially one as uncomfortable as this. It's misleading to call polyester a fiber since the word implies a weave of separate threads through which air can circulate, whereas the sticky sensation of actually wearing it is like being wrapped in what Webster's defines as "a thermosetting polymeric resin used in the manufacture of plastic." Just scooping a mound of potato salad onto my plate caused me to perspire as though I'd rolled a boulder uphill. I could feel my pores dilate and my cheeks flush and I understood what it might be like to be an arthritic old man whose slightest physical effort exacts, for all the world to see, a price in sweat and breathlessness.

While I dabbed at my forehead with a napkin, Monica, a colleague of mine who taught a seminar called "A Feminist History of Film" and who always wore jeans and running shoes to school, walked up to me—was it really her?—in a miniskirt. I could tell from her uncharacteristically sheepish demeanor that she felt as if she was in one of those dreams where you discover you're in public without your pants. Which essentially she was. She teetered, unbelievably, on a pair of high heels. "Do not speak a word of this to my students," she pleaded, "or I'll never be able to quote from *The Second Sex* again." She took a swig of punch and asked what I was teaching that term.

The previous night I'd read John Cheever's "Reunion" in preparation for my class "American Literature Since 1950." The story's teenage narrator, who hasn't seen his father in three years, goes to meet him at Grand Central Station, where the man is already fifteen minutes late for an hour-long stopover between trains. "My father," thinks the son, "was my future and my doom." I had to catch my breath before I could move on to the next sentence. The phrase was so powerful, it seemed to be mulling me over rather than the other way around. Was every son destined to slip deeper into his father's fate the more he resisted it?

I told Monica that my class was reading Cheever and quoted the line from "Reunion." I also told her the jumpsuit came from my father's closet and that wearing it caused a suffocating but instructive empathy. Monica nodded knowingly. She explained that she'd decided to shave her legs in order to wear the miniskirt and had bought a package of disposable pink "women's" razors knowing perfectly well they were really blue "men's" razors sold for the same price but aimed at female consumers. Her inability to rebel and buy the blue ones instead of the culturally permissible pink ones represented, she believed, a significant lapse for a Marxist-feminist such as herself. "All of which is a way of saying," she said, "that as I stand here in a skirt and talk about shopping, I've become my mother."

At that, we clinked our cups of punch.

The realization that one is growing older comes to most of us, if we're lucky, in bearable increments; that way, the full cargo of mortality doesn't sink the boat, so to speak, but is brought on board in the form of manageable hand luggage. One year you develop an almost erotic fondness for the warmth of a hot water bottle tucked between cold sheets; the next, you and your friends devote an entire dinner conversation to the benefits of dietary fiber and, less appetizingly, its effects. But that afternoon, while sipping rum punch and quoting John Cheever, I wasn't simply poised on the cusp of age or cringing youthfully at its imminence. I was officially and forever an adult, and the owner of my costume was my future and my doom.

Here's how I came to be wearing the jumpsuit. My father and I hadn't spoken to each other since the incident in his living room. His absence nagged me, and the pangs grew worse instead of better as the days went by. It wasn't as if we saw each other often, and as he himself might have put it, "Built on bedrock our relationship was not." Yet I missed him all the same, or missed the enigma of him. Where was my place in the world if not in opposition to my father? Like a bat who navigates by echolocation, I was lost unless I asked him a question and heard him ask a question back:

*How are you, Dad?*

*How should I be?*

During the month we weren't speaking, I was beset by a series of Dad sightings, all of which turned out to be false alarms. They began the day he demanded I leave his house. In fact, they began on my drive home. I'd stopped at the supermarket to buy myself a calming bottle of beer, and as soon as I passed through the turnstile I saw him bent over a freezer case and peering inside. Because I'd sped away from his house with great haste—it was as if I'd been catapulted back into the world from the force of his slammed door—I couldn't imagine how he'd managed to arrive there before me. His face was lit from below by those lights they have inside freezer cases so you can read the labels on cans of concentrated orange juice and boxes of Popsicles, and this harsh arctic light, along with the vapors wafting around him, made it seem, for one mythic instant, that my father had thawed from a block of ice. The sight of it so disarmed me that I almost forgot we'd had a fight not ten minutes ago, if you could call what had taken place between us a fight.

I held my breath and approached him, prepared to say something conciliatory, though I wasn't sure what. I reached out to tap him on the shoulder and when he turned toward me with a puzzled look, I realized that this elderly stranger bore only a general resemblance to my father: bald head, thick glasses, portly torso. And herein lies a clue to why this sighting was the first of many; since most men of my father's age have lost their hair, wear corrective lenses, and are padded by fat, the number of individuals onto whom I could, and did, project my father was exceedingly large. These misrecognitions weren't the kind I could laugh off or back away from without embarrassment, but lapses that caused me to make an illegal U-turn in one instance and in several others to wave dramatically as I ran toward an old man who probably thought he was about to be attacked. I should add that I'm usually quite keen when it comes to identifying a celebrity or political figure who whizzes by for a millisecond as I'm pressing the remote control. But how could I continue to trust my knack for facial recognition when a huge portion of the geriatric male population had become, overnight, dead ringers for my father?

Dad now inhabited Los Angeles in a broad, metaphysical sense, and his ubiquity made it impossible for me to go a day without thinking I'd seen him pumping gas into his Caddy or walking through the automatic doors of the local post office. I couldn't go a day, in other words, without dwelling on our estrangement, without replaying his edict that I leave.

My father had been the dumper and I the dumpee, and it's common knowledge, at least for the son of a divorce attorney, that the dumpee of the couple usually has a harder time with the breakup.

"Listen to the terms you're using to describe the situation," insisted a psychotherapist. "Dump. Couple. Breakup. These terms should tell you something." The psychotherapist also happened to be the man I'd been living with for two years, the partner I'd kept awake long after his bedtime with questions about where things had gone wrong between my father and me. Brian was the very picture of attentiveness and professionalism, poor guy. He lay beside me in the dark, stifling yawns and only occasionally turning to check the dial of our bedside clock.

"Are you saying I have some kind of homosexual fixation with my father?"

"No," he said. "That's what you have with me. I'm saying that the words you're choosing indicate an unusual intensity of feeling."

"I'm not *choosing* the words. They're spoken in the heat of the moment."

"I use the word *choosing* because it helps give the . . . the speaker a sense of control over his emotions."

"You were going to say *patient,* weren't you? Helps give the *patient* a sense of control."

"Absolutely not!" said Brian. Then wearily, "I was going to say *client.*"

His remark sobered me. I stroked his arm and promised not to act like an analysand.

"Does that mean I can go to sleep?"

I said yes and meant it. I settled back and closed my eyes. But questions about my father were like those trick birthday candles that burst back into flame a second after you blow them out. I sat up and asked, "Do you think it's more complicated for a homosexual man than a heterosexual man to have a conflict with his father because there's some kind of—I don't know—libidinal underpinning?"

"No."

"Because, believe me, I am not attracted to my father, either consciously or unconsciously."

"Technically, you wouldn't know if you were unconsciously attracted to him because you wouldn't be conscious of it."

"Well," I said, plumping the pillow, "I'm not." With my receding hairline and deepening crow's-feet, I was well on the way to looking like my father, so the more I protested the possibility of his attractiveness, the more, in effect, I protested my own. All of which wouldn't have been so uncomfortable if the psychotherapist to whom I'd been protesting hadn't also been the man I hoped would want to have sex with me as I grew old. Yet if Brian found me attractive as I aged, perhaps he also considered my father an attractive older man, a notion that made me a little squeamish, not to mention Oedipally competitive. I was about to come right out and ask Brian to rate my father on a ten scale, but it suddenly seemed crucial that thoughts about my father's physical desirability not be dwelled upon by either Brian or me while the two of us lay together in bed. And so I changed the subject, or more accurately, leapt to a subset of the same subject. "What was that whole thing with the key about, anyway? I keep hearing him tell me, 'A son doesn't help his father up.' It barely makes sense—just enough to drive me crazy."

"Maybe you should call him and talk about it."

"What would I say? 'Sorry I tried to help you off the floor, Dad. I've seen the error of my ways and next time I'll leave you there'?"

"Look, if the reason the two of you aren't speaking doesn't make sense, then the reason you contact him again doesn't have to make sense, either. If nothing makes sense, act accordingly."

While I considered Brian's advice, he began to take deep, oblivious breaths. His jaw went slack, the muscles of his face released from the tension of waking life and its many necessary expressions. Repose must be a particularly welcome state for Brian since his job requires him to look as if he's not only listening to, but is actually interested in, other people's problems, an especially daunting task when it's almost midnight and the problems are mine. I loved how sensible he could be. I also loved how insensible he could be, and I watched him sleep for several minutes before I drifted off.

Brian was right; I probably didn't need a pretext to phone my father and reestablish contact. Nevertheless, a pretext was handed to me a few days later when Lynn, an old girlfriend with whom I'd been romantically involved in college, called to tell me that she and her lover, Monica, the aforementioned film historian, were going to throw a party based on *The Stepford Wives,* a movie from 1975 that Monica had shown in her feminist film seminar. The movie, from a novel by Ira Levin, is set in the picturesque fictional suburb of Stepford, Connecticut, where the husbands are carrying out a plot to turn their independent modern wives into ideals of passive, anachronistic womanhood. The transformations are achieved by way of outpatient operations whose details are vague, but after the surgery, each wife possesses an unflagging, almost robotic good cheer and a predilection for elaborate hairdos and frilly dresses. The men hope to regain their rightful place in the households and communities of a misguided liberal America, whose cities, their scheme suggests, are choking in the smoke from burning bras.

As for the party, Lynn told me that she and Monica each planned to play the role of perfect hostess to the hilt. "We're going to serve Cheez Whiz on Ritz crackers and walk around like we're anesthetized," she said enthusiastically. Lynn gave me the date and time of the party and urged me to dress in the repressive spirit of Stepford. Years after its release, the movie had remained for many people of my generation a deliciously sinister parody of the rigid middle-class conventions of grooming and behavior into which we'd been indoctrinated as children and which we found stifling as adults. Our early years were spent desperately trying to conform to those conventions and our later years were spent desperately trying to escape them. The party's premise was a battle cry of irony, especially considering that the guest list consisted almost entirely of Lynn and Monica's lesbian-feminist friends, who thought of skirts and high heels as hobbling devices invented by men to limit a woman's physical agility and fetishize her helplessness. "By the way," Lynn added, "since Brian has to see clients that day, you'll be the only guy at the party." A few of Lynn and Monica's friends were staunch separatists who avoided contact with men and who smoldered with unspoken accusations whenever I walked into the room, as though, by being a queer Jewish adjunct teacher with a crummy income, I was a minion from the world of male privilege who'd come to rob them of their civil rights. When I suggested to Lynn that my presence might make her separatist friends uncomfortable, she said, "You have to understand that they're not reacting to you as an individual, they're reacting to your penis, so there's really nothing for them to be threatened by."

"Oh, thanks," I said. "You always know how to make me feel better."

"You know what I'm trying to say. They're really sweet people underneath all that swagger."

As soon as I hung up, my father's polyester jumpsuit sprang to mind. It wasn't as apt for the party's theme as, say, a Dacron leisure suit would have been, but borrowing it gave me the excuse I needed to call him and make amends. I dialed 662-6806, seven numbers imprinted forever in the Rolodex of memory.

My father picked up after a single ring. "What the hell do you want?"

I hadn't said hello, so his vehemence threw me off guard. "How did you know . . . ?"

"Oh, it's you. Hello."

"Who were you expecting?"

"Some nut from the phone company."

I pictured the mound of unopened bills on the breakfront desk. Someone from the phone company had gotten on his bad side, and I thought this might leave room on his good side for me. "There's something I've been wanting to talk about, Dad."

"It's your dime."

"About what happened in the living room . . ."

"What happened in the living room?"

Either (a) he didn't remember our altercation or (b) he remembered but was acting as if he didn't because feigning ignorance would make this potentially unpleasant phone call easier on us both. I followed Dad's lead and opted for amnesia, starting the conversation from scratch.

"I was wondering if I could borrow your jumpsuit."

"Sure. When did you want to come pick it up?"

"I just need it for a day, is all."

"Okay."

"I'll bring it back dry-cleaned."

"I said okay, didn't I?"

"I know you wear it a lot and I don't want to deprive you of . . ."

"Of clothes? You think that's my only clothes? Don't be ridiculous. I got a closet full. You really like to make things difficult, don't you?"

"Things *are* difficult, don't you think? I'll never get used to it."

He laughed a bitter, commiserating laugh. "If I had a nickel for every pain in the ass I've had to put up with," he said, "I'd be a rich man with a sore ass."

"The phone company's on your case these days?"

"Why should I pay for calls I didn't make?"

"Have you disputed the charges?"

"Every time they call. And believe me, they don't let up. I'd get an unlisted number if I didn't have to pay them to get it. You should hear the way they twist things around! They connect me to this person and that person until I don't know whether I'm coming or going. I'm keeping track of how long they've put me on hold and I'm going to take them to court and charge them for every minute of it, with interest. Don't think I won't."

"Bureaucracy."

"You can say that again."

Back and forth we batted life's hassles. If we both insisted the world was unfair, then we both lived, for a while at least, in the same world.

"I'll be there in an hour," I said.

I must have been even more eager for a reunion than I realized, for recollection entirely bypasses my hanging up the phone and getting dressed and driving to his house, setting me smack in his upstairs bedroom. Mother had carpeted the master bedroom in the same white shag as our living room, the wallpaper flocked with white fleur-de-lis. In keeping with the decor, Dad stood before me clad only in a pair of boxers, and though the sight of them reminded me of the lipstick incident, I refused to give the memory a crimson inch.

My father often remarked on the anatomical landslide of his aging body, but that afternoon he didn't appear at all modest about the excess flesh of his chest and belly or the creases in his skin. Throughout my boyhood, I'd reassured myself that by the time I grew up, medical science would find a cure for aging just as it had for polio, and if the cure was delayed, I'd have myself cryogenically frozen until an antidote to death had been invented. Now, as an adult, I pitied the rationalizations of that boy, yet I looked at my father stripped to the waist and tried to tell myself that a strict regimen of exercise and diet might spare me from the effects of age— a deceit that had itself grown old, too feeble to soothe me.

Dad chatted about this and that just to hear the sound of his own voice, and after all these weeks of our not speaking, I listened just to hear the audio portion of fatherhood. "You don't need anything besides the jumpsuit, do you? Money or something?" When I told him no, he jokingly asked if I could loan *him* a twenty.

He swung open his closet door. The odor of mothballs wafted from its dim interior, where a small, high window admitted a single shaft of light. The closet seemed as separate from the outside world as a sanctuary, the air inside it a muffled, secret substance. Dad flicked a switch and the bare lightbulb revealed a museum of suits, an archive of ties in every width and color, the leathery husks of at least a dozen shoes. His khaki jumpsuit hung from a hook, looking limp and dejected without my father to give it life.

"Try it on," he insisted.

In the spirit of locker room camaraderie, I stripped to my Fruit of the Looms, dipped my feet into the puddle of polyester, and tugged upward. Once I'd stuffed myself inside the jumpsuit, my father appraised me, or rather, gazed at me and appraised himself. "I'm getting a little thick around the middle," he said. "But you're still pretty thin. I should lay off the potatoes."

"Potatoes don't make you fat."

"This," he insisted, grabbing a handful of loose flesh from his stomach, "is a potato."

"It's maybe the butter you put on it, not the potato per se."

"Potato persay?" He adjusted his hearing aid. "Turn around and let me get a look at you!" He made a stirring motion with his index finger.

"It kind of binds," I said, rigid as a stick figure.

"What are you talking, binds? It looks wonderful! How about we go out and I'll buy you one of your own? We'll get some lunch and then stop at the Big and Tall on Western. They got them in any kind of color. Leisure suits, too. You point and I'll pay; it's as simple as that. Whaddaya say?"

"That's really generous, Dad, but I'll probably only wear it once."

"And to where will you wear it?" He couldn't stop smiling at the sight of me: Daddy's simulacrum. In our rush to reestablish contact, he hadn't bothered to ask why I wanted to borrow his jumpsuit, and I hadn't bothered to think he might.

"To a party at Lynn's."

"Oh? What kind of party is Lynn giving?"

"Just a . . . party party."

His smile died.

Not until I was stuffed into the jumpsuit and facing its now distrustful owner did it occur to me that I would react exactly the same way had my father come over to my house, borrowed a pair of jeans and a T-shirt, squeezed into them while I stood there in my underwear, and then informed me that he was off to what he didn't have the chutzpah to admit (but my sixth sense whispered) was a costume party. How far would he go in assuming my identity? Would he toss off my stock phrases and pet expressions? Would he give a mock lecture on John Cheever to a bunch of other parents, who, dressed like their offspring and guzzling rum punch, laughed their heads off and egged him on? If this sounds paranoid, let it be known that as a boy, I'd mimic my dad to the delight of those kids in our neighborhood who'd been fathered by oddballs, which is to say every kid on the block. And later, when my red-eyed fellow potheads mumbled about their uptight folks, I'd freak them out by asking, as Dad, if they planned to spend the rest of their lives dancing through the daisies.

To this day I can conjure my father's voice at will—the soprano notes of pleasure, the rumble of disgust, the singsong Yiddish equivocation, the elastic *Oy* and rasping *Eh*. It's not uncommon for me to answer one of Brian's questions as my father would (with another, more imploring question), or to blurt an opinion about a movie or current event by stepping deftly, if I do say so myself, into and out of Dad's persona. This is not a talent on my part any more than being possessed by the spirit of Napoleon Bonaparte would be a talent; you're either the mouthpiece for a dead emperor or you're not. It's a neurochemical condition like Tourette's, all helpless tic and lurching verbiage. Anyway, watching my father dash off to make light of me at a costume party would be even worse if I'd just told him how wonderful he looked.

My intent hadn't been to disguise myself as my father so much as to disguise myself as the type of man who would wear a polyester jumpsuit. But the syllogism, had I stopped to give it thought, went roughly thus: A Stepford husband would wear a polyester jumpsuit; my father wears a polyester jumpsuit; therefore, my father is a Stepford husband. This logic insulted his sartorial taste, his very style of husbandry. By asking to borrow my father's clothes, I'd asked the subject of my caricature to contribute to his exaggeration.

I unzipped the zipper a couple of inches to make breathing easier, and there it was, the requisite accessory—chest hair only slightly darker than my father's. He leaned against the dresser, its glass top reflecting fleur-de-lis like huge but motionless snowflakes. Despite or perhaps because of his boxers he looked absolutely nude. So nude that my being clothed might as well have been the result of my having stolen the jumpsuit right off his back, or of his having sacrificed it for the sake of my warmth. This could have been the last jumpsuit on earth, and it wasn't big enough for both of us.

Dad glared at me over the rims of his glasses. "What's Brian going as?"

I considered: *Brian's going as his father, too.* But the truth provided a better evasion. "Brian can't go. He sees clients that day."

"So what you're telling me," said my father, crossing his arms, "is that some people actually work for a living."

"Is your father still pissed?" asked Monica.

We'd planted ourselves beside the buffet table. In the center there rose a three-tiered punch bowl Lynn had rented for the party. Rivulets of peach-colored punch trickled over its crystal rims, the constant watery burble almost as soothing as the booze itself. Muzak wafted from outdoor speakers, renditions of old standards so plod-ding and homogenized they were unidentifiable.

"Things are okay for now," I told Monica. My father had given up on his cross-examination, finally amused to see a younger ver-sion of himself standing in his bedroom and stammering excuses; how could he stay mad when his past was trying to appease his pre-sent? I left his house with the jumpsuit tucked under my arm.

Lynn was chatting with a trio of lesbian separatists who wore matching gingham shifts with lace trim. All that cool, roomy cotton seemed to cause them as much discomfort as polyester caused me. They couldn't stop tugging and plucking at the fabric.

Lynn excused herself from the group and sauntered toward me and Monica with a fake-dainty walk. The silver platter she held in her arms had been picked clean of everything but crumbs. She kissed Monica on the lips, a masterpiece of perfunctory suction. "Hello, darling," she said in what was fast becoming the afternoon's obliga-tory robot drone. She turned to me. "Why, Mr. Cooper, you cut quite a figure in that jumpsuit." Lynn and I had lived together for three years before we both came out—drove each other out, as we liked to say—and in all that time she rarely wore makeup, so it was a shock to see her batting a pair of false eyelashes. She bent toward me and inhaled, closing her spidery eyes to better place the scent. In her own voice she said, "You even smell like your father. Is it Old Spice?"

"Very old. And what do you mean, 'even'?"

"I mean you kind of look like him in that getup."

By now I was determined to replace every drop of lost perspira-tion with rum punch, and after a few more gulps I found myself woozily resigned to the family resemblance. My father, after all, was the only living member of the immediate family left for me to resemble.

Lynn and Monica and I glanced around the yard at women

arrayed in summery ensembles, several wearing wide-brimmed hats, their outfits accessorized with costume jewelry or tiny clutch purses that matched the sherbet colors of their shoes. The guests had gone to great lengths to dress as the kind of women their mothers had hoped to be, or to dress as the kind of daughters their mothers had hoped to have. Some milled about the flagstone patio, talking and laughing and nibbling hors d'oeuvres. Others congregated beneath the shade of an oak tree whose enormous gnarled branches seemed to take root in the sky. The gathering could have passed as a lesbian Stepford, or a chimerical cocktail party dreamed up by a restless husband in a John Cheever story, a man who knew his wife both too little and too well, and who longed to spend an idyllic day in the company of alluring ladies.

I refilled my cup of punch and lurched away from the buffet table to mingle with the crowd. The lawn felt more topographically complicated than it had when the party started. One gregarious, white-gloved guest commented on the jumpsuit. When I told her it was my father's, she asked if he was a skydiver or a gas station attendant. "He's a retired attorney," I said. I tried not to think about my tongue, which had become a little numb and stubborn. "He wears it every day because he can wake up and just jump right into it"— here I damply snapped my fingers—"ready to sit around the house and relax in front of the television without having to fuss with buttons or waste a moment deciding what to wear. And you don't have to iron the thing. Ever. It holds its shape, which is more than you can say for most of us. Thanks to this one-piece, stain-resistant, wrinkle-free article of clothing, my father now has time in abundance, and he'll have it in greater and greater abundance until he possesses eternity itself!"

"Wow," she said, fingering her pearls. "That's some jumpsuit."

# Who's Been
# Sleeping in My Bed?

The jumpsuit was still at the dry cleaner's when my father called to tell me he'd developed a mysterious medical condition overnight. "I couldn't sleep a wink," he said. "The sheet felt heavy as a goddamn anvil on my big toe!" By morning, the toe was swollen and shiny and so painful he could barely take a step without moaning out loud. I suspected that his ailment was gout, a disease I'd have known nothing about had I not just read an essay on Sylvia Plath's poem "Daddy" in preparation for my class on American literature since 1950, and learned that the lines "Ghastly statue with one gray toe / Big as a Frisco seal" were a reference to her father's chronic gout. So, while I had my father on the phone, I looked up *gout* in the dictionary, read him the definition to see if it rang a bell, and when I came to "an inflammation characterized by exquisite tenderness," he shouted, "That's it! It's exquisite!"

His physician, Dr. Graham, considered it a particularly debilitating attack and suggested that, until the pain and inflammation subsided, my father hire a live-in nurse to help around the house. Impressed that I'd arrived at the same diagnosis as his doctor, Dad asked if I could be there to advise him when he "tried the new nurse on for size," or what the home-care service more prudently called "the patient/provider intake session."

The interviewee, a short, sturdy woman with a brassy stack of teased hair, arrived right on time. She wore a pantsuit whose pants were neatly creased, and this, along with a purse slung like a duffel bag over her shoulder, gave her an air of almost military preparedness. Dad and I greeted her at the front door and immediately started talking at the same time, flustered by the fact that this unfamiliar woman wasn't simply here to visit, but possibly to live. When we found the presence of mind to invite her inside, she strode through the foyer in silent white shoes, assessing the house with the keen eyes of a person who'd worked at hundreds of different homes and had learned how to sum up, with a single glance, the lives led inside them.

Once she'd settled into the living room couch, Betty Schaefer fished a notepad from her purse and began asking my father questions about his blood pressure medications and their side effects. She proposed a diet low in animal fat and dairy products, telling us how high levels of uric acid in his bloodstream had caused crystal deposits to form around the joint in his big toe. "Gout used to be called 'rich man's disease,'" she explained, "because only people like kings could afford the foods that cause it." My father smiled. *Crystals, kings*— gout was now a badge of honor as well as a goddamn anvil. Betty laid out a plan for his convalescence that made a strict regimen of Indomethacin, bland food, bed rest, and diuretics sound as rejuvenating as a tropical cruise. Dad shot me a glance that meant: *As long as there are nurses like her in the world, people walking around in bodies are better off.* And as we both realized but would never admit, having Betty there to offer assistance and enforce the doctor's orders would keep us from becoming more touchy with each other than we already were.

The second my father told her she was hired, Betty dashed out the door and rummaged through the back of a yellow station wagon parked in our driveway. She returned with a pair of aluminum crutches that enabled my father to hobble around the house with-

out putting pressure on his swollen toe. Even when it came to simple tasks, however, the crutches hindered as much as they helped,
making him as awkward as a man with six limbs. It quickly became
apparent that the less my father could do on his own, the more stubborn he'd become. Instead of telling one of us he was thirsty, he'd
thump through the kitchen on his crutches, teeter at the sink, and
draw himself a glass of splattering tap water. If Betty and I made a
move to help, he'd shoo us away with such an emphatic wave of his
hand, he'd nearly lose his balance. He must have worried, I realize
in retrospect, that unless he kept a stranglehold on health, he'd begin
a quick, precipitous slide toward a life of dependence. But back
then, as I watched him fill a glass to the brim, his forehead bunched
in concentration, all I saw was misplaced pride. Why had he hired a
nurse, I wondered, if he was so determined to fend for himself?

This question became all the more pressing when I visited him
a few days later. Betty had taken a break to watch *This Is Your Day,* a
weekly show in which Benny Hinn, a placidly evangelical man in
heavy stage makeup, laid hands on a steady stream of sick and
injured audience members, each more telegenically abject than the
next. One would think that, for a nurse-practitioner such as Betty,
the sight of all those eye patches, slings, plaster casts, neck braces,
portable oxygen tanks, electric wheelchairs, and rolling IV stands, all
those frail people weeping and falling to the ground, would make
viewing the show a sort of busman's holiday, and yet she'd surrendered to the salmon-colored couch, setting a box of Kleenex on her
lap in case a miracle moved her to tears. When I told her I was going
to take my father upstairs for an afternoon nap, she told me to yell
down if I needed help. Try as she might to turn her head, she
couldn't wrench her eyes from the set, where Hinn was frantically
snapping his fingers near the ear of a blinking deaf-mute who may
or may not have heard the audience break into applause.

At first my father refused assistance, poking the tip of his crutch
at the lowest step as if testing its strength. Then he glanced toward
the top of the stairs—Kilimanjaro capped in white shag—and
handed me the crutches.

With his arm slung over my shoulder and mine around his waist, my father and I made halting progress. He had to pause every few steps and wait for the pain in his foot to pass, sucking air through gritted teeth. This gave him ample opportunity to assess aloud each nuanced throb: *What a doozy. Coulda been worse. Like a toothache in my toe.* Meanwhile, the sound of the TV—the chords of an electric organ punctuated by yelps of praise—grew fainter and more terrestrial the higher we climbed.

No sooner had we entered the bedroom than I noticed that not only was his side of the bed unmade, but also the side that had been my mother's. The bed had been my parents' refuge in sickness and in health, and as far as I was concerned, they hadn't merely slept on, but possessed, their respective sides. They'd purchased the bed, with its high mahogany headboard and king-size mattress, before I was born. This was the bed in which I'd been conceived (to the extent that any parents can conceive of the child they actually end up with). What upset me wasn't the idea of my father sleeping with another woman—it had been a decade since my mother's death—or the idea of him sleeping with another woman in that particular bed. What upset me was the sight of my mother's side abandoned; the bedspread had been thrown back to reveal a swath of linen as pale as a shroud, the impression of a head indenting the pillow. It was as if my mother's resting place in life had suddenly merged with her resting place in death, and I felt, as strongly as ever, the intractable fact of her absence.

"With all this hopping around," said my father, winded from the stairs, "my good foot hurts as bad as the bad foot." I propped the crutches against the wall, and before I could turn around, he'd plummeted into a sitting position atop the bedspread. He paid no attention to the disarray on the other side, perhaps thinking that if he ignored it, I would, too.

I debated whether to say anything. Two years earlier, when I'd told my father that Brian (who he referred to as "your mental-doctor friend") was more than just my friend, Dad knitted his brows and stared into the distance. With his other sons dead and his youngest gay, his lineage would end with me, the genealogical road-block. At least that's what I worried he was thinking, and I scruti-nized his face for signs of disappointment. Finally he took a breath and blurted, "Love is no one's business," which sounded like a depressing generalization without the addition of "but your own," though I knew what he meant and gave him a hug, hoping my dis-closure might help make our future relationship more frank and even-keeled and agreeable.

But now, taken aback by the state of his bed, I found myself unable to offer him the same quick, unstinting acceptance he'd offered me. Surely the people who ran the home-care service would object to these sleeping arrangements. Such intimate proximity might not only jeopardize Betty's job, but compromise the way she cared for my father, in both the medical and personal sense. If the two of them are just going to throw the rules of decorum out the window, I thought unironically, at least they could have waited a decent amount of time. Coincidentally, Brian and I had just talked to a friend whose affair with her boss had come to an unpleasant end, and the three of us agreed that, with its potential entanglements, romance at the work-place was usually a bad idea. Imagine how much more complicated it would be if the workplace was someone's bedroom and the only thing keeping employer from employee was the figurative partition of self-restraint. It's one thing to be bedridden in the presence of a nurse, and it's quite another to be bedridden with her.

"I take it Betty sleeps with you?"

"What do you mean, sleeps?"

"Oh, Dad."

"Don't *Oh, Dad* me. There's sleeps and then there's *sleeps.*"

"I mean *sleeps.*"

"Okay. She sleeps with me."

"As in *falls* asleep?"

"Eventually, yes."

We were like two men racing each other on stationary bicycles.

"You know," I told him, "I'd never object to your having com-panionship . . ."

"That's very big of you."

". . . but I wonder if these are the best circumstances."

"For what?"

"A girlfriend."

"She's not my girlfriend for God's sake!"

"Does she usually share a bed with the people she's taking care of?"

"Where else is she supposed to sleep?" he asked. "On the floor?"

Saying, *No, Betty shouldn't sleep on the floor,* would have been the same as saying, *Yes, Betty should sleep in your bed.* As often happened when my father and I reached a rhetorical impasse, I began, against my better judgment, to consider things from his point of view: if half a perfectly good mattress is just sitting there empty, why waste the space? The bed is so big he probably can't even see her without putting on his glasses, and how enticing is a blurry nurse? It's as if they're sleeping in twin beds, really, except the beds touch.

"Well?" he asked.

"You should elevate your leg."

My father lay back and, without protest, allowed me to lift his foot by the heel and set it on a stack of pillows. A long *Oy* escaped him like steam. The swollen toe, even covered by a sock, was painful to see.

Betty could have stayed in my old room down the hall, or she could have slept in a foldout bed provided by the home-care service, but by the time these suggestions occurred to me, silence seemed like the best advice. Besides, I had to admit that my father's irrepressible interest in sex was the genetic trait I most hoped to inherit, a legacy I could share with Brian for the rest of our lives, or at least until one of us was no longer ambulatory. Still, the business with the bed worried me. Asking me whether Betty should sleep on the floor wasn't so far-fetched. Someone *had* once slept on the floor of his bedroom, and that someone, as it happened, was Dad.

In 1983, a sordid story about a divorce proceeding appeared in the pages of the *Herald Examiner,* which by then had featured both *The*

*Case of the Baking Newlywed* and *The Case of the Captive Bride.*
Reporters from the paper routinely visited the Los Angeles County
Courthouse, where they combed through divorce petitions in search
of claims sensational enough to merit a few inches of print. One day
a reporter stumbled upon an ideal tale of failed love, of good behavior devolving into bad, the claimant leveling such scandalous accusations at his spouse that matrimony and acrimony were one and the
same. The article contained my father's name, but unlike his earlier
appearances in print, he was the plaintiff in the case instead of the
attorney.

The defendant was his second wife, Anna Hill. Their marriage
had lasted four months, during which he disappeared from my life
and also, it seemed, from his own. I'd first heard about Anna when
he phoned to tell me he'd met a woman in line at the bank who he
planned to marry the following week at her Episcopal church.
Shock made my congratulations sound a little shrill and helium-
filled, and therefore indistinguishable from delight. Don't get me
wrong; I was happy for him, but in order to reach that happiness, I
had to jump over a few hurdles:

*Wife. A week. Episcopal church.*

"I should warn you," he said. "Anna's younger than me. You'll
agree I'm no spring chicken."

"If you say so."

"I'm saying so. But I'm not dead yet, either. I have needs and she
meets them. She's a wonderful woman."

"As long as you love each other."

"How'd you like to join us for dinner tomorrow night?"

"I'd love to, Dad."

"Do me a favor, though, and don't call her 'Mother.'"

"It never occurred to me to call her 'Mother.'"

"Of course it wouldn't have occurred to you; I just now told you
about her. The point is, your mother will always be your mother.
She was your mother when she was alive and she's still your mother
when she's . . . not alive."

"Absolutely. One mother."

"Anna might not be comfortable calling you 'Son.'"

"First of all, I'll be her *step*son, and besides, what we call each other doesn't matter. The important thing is that you found someone."

"It does matter," he said, "and I'm telling you not to."

"Okay," I said. "I'll call her 'Mommy.'"

My father made a disgruntled puffing: antilaughter. "I don't appreciate your making fun."

Jokes about marriage usually made my father howl. "Take my wife," said Henny Youngman on *The Ed Sullivan Show.* "Please." How often my father repeated that gag, relishing the pause before the punch line. Cuckolds, floozies, louses, shrews—these were matrimony's cast of stock characters, and if anyone required proof that this was true, they need only have switched on the television or leafed through the pages of the *Herald Examiner.* Wherever there were couples there was strife, public or private, mild or grinding. I'm sure my parents took one look at the world in which they lived and consoled themselves with the thought that their marital unhappiness was the symptom of a general condition.

"I'm sorry," I said.

"Just call her Anna. Is that too much to ask?" His voice quavered. "Will you come to the wedding?"

"Of course! Can I bring Brian?"

"This is a family affair."

"Brian is family."

"Not by blood."

I could hear myself breathing into the receiver.

"I have to draw the line somewhere," he protested.

"You're only inviting blood relations?"

"I'm only inviting the two of you."

"You mean, me and Brian?"

"Who the hell do you think I mean?"

"You just said . . ."

"Do you want to come or don't you?"

"Yes," I said. "I—we—want to come to your wedding."

"Anna's inviting her daughter and her uncle. That's it for the guest list. When you get to be my age, you don't want to do the whole schmear."

"I'm going to have a stepsister?"

"She's not going to live at the house with us like she was my kid or anything. Anna owns a few rental properties in South Central, and Pam—that's her daughter—is going to manage the duplex or the triplex or . . . one of Anna's plexes. She's seventeen, and I need a teenager hanging around the house like I need a hole in the head."

"So you're keeping the house?"

"I'm sitting on a gold mine. I'd be crazy to sell."

As my father's only heir, I'd counted on inheriting my boyhood home. Leasing it out—I was too attached to the place to sell it—might bring me enough money to pitch in on some of the bills Brian had been paying while I crawled toward that mirage called tenure. Would Anna, a woman who apparently possessed a knack for amassing real estate, now stand to inherit the house?

"We'll see you at the Brass Pan?" he asked. "Around six-thirty?"

"It's a date," I said. I'd almost replaced the phone on its cradle when I heard the faint cry of my father's voice. "Come back!"

"What's wrong?"

"Nothing's wrong with it."

"With what?"

"She's black."

"I thought you said . . ."

"I did. She's black. Do I have to say it again?"

His defensiveness suggested that the few people he'd already told hadn't exactly shook his hand and proposed a toast. All but the most liberal among his cronies probably greeted the news with scant congratulations, reacting to the mention of Anna's age and race and religion with shades of dismay. But my father needn't have worried about so much as an iota of shock or objection on my part. I positively writhed with approval. I took it upon myself to single-handedly compensate for the prejudice he may have encountered up to that point, and while I was at it, to compensate for the prejudice he might encounter from that point forward. He certainly didn't have to justify his decision to me. Love now obliged us both to defy convention, and I saw this as a fresh source of father-son solidarity.

"I'm so proud of you!" I gushed, a statement I've only recently come to realize can be a backhanded compliment, insinuating that the person you're proud of has had to overcome some character flaw to do whatever they've done to make you proud, so what you're really saying is not that you're proud, but that you're *surprised* the person has made you proud. At any rate, I commended his progressiveness and told him he was paving the way for other couples—black and white, young and old, gay and straight—to follow their hearts. A patently romantic assumption, since I'd never met Anna and for all I knew their relationship was based on mutual cruelty or shared delusions.

Even while singing his praises, I was nagged by retroactive doubt. Now that he'd told me his fiancée was black, his insistence that I not call her "Mother" seemed less about giving credit to his departed wife for having been the one and only woman to gestate and raise me, and more about his fear that it might make me uncomfortable to call a black woman "Mother" in public. Or, more likely, make *him* uncomfortable. As long as he believed he was protecting me from embarrassment, he could protect himself from the knowledge that it was *he* who would be embarrassed. By addressing Anna as "Mother," I'd essentially broadcast to all the sedate, mostly Caucasian diners at the Brass Pan, with its red leather booths and flattering candlelight, that my father and this young black woman were sleeping together, and also quite possibly *sleeping* together. I couldn't think of a polite way to tell him that unless he and Anna whispered and giggled and fed each other food, no one would necessarily assume—and so what if someone did?—that they were a couple.

After we hung up, I thought about how my father, like many Jews of his generation, referred to African-Americans as *schvartzes*. When I once complained that *schvartze* was a derogatory term, and that the Jews, of all people, should abhor bigotry, he argued that it was merely descriptive. "It means 'black' in Yiddish," he said, "and I'd never say it in front of a *schvartze*." "Because it's derogatory," I persisted, to which he said, "I can't even open my mouth before you jump down my throat!"

During my boyhood it had been difficult for my father and me to converse, let alone argue, and as a teenager I found myself being contrary just to make up for lost time. I'd spar as though he were an insufferably conservative warmongering Republican instead of a sentimental Democratic who'd hung a portrait of John F. Kennedy in his downtown office and, later, in the utility room at home, where he'd stored the remains of that office: a rickety swivel chair, boxes of onionskin stationery and dog-eared legal briefs. In his own way, my father had been a crusader for civil rights, like the right of a San Bernardino housewife to charge people admission to take a peek at her living chicken dinner, or the right of parents to keep their underage daughter locked in her bedroom, hidden from the suitor who bellowed verse into the darkness of the barrio. Perhaps not matters significant enough to make it to the Supreme Court, but it's the small irregular rights, let us not forget, that add up to this great free-for-all we call democracy.

Late that night, with Brian sound asleep beside me, I remembered visiting my father's office as a boy and listening to his conversations with the Continental Building's black elevator operator. As Jimmy finessed the lever and we rose slowly toward the sixth floor, he and my father would grouse about a corrupt politician or a deceptive ballot measure, shaking their heads in consternation, two men united beyond the dictates of mere politeness—until the elevator bobbed to a stop and they went their separate ways.

Then there was the Samoan high talking chief, Pele-Pele, for whom my father won a divorce from the one Los Angelena among his dozen wives, a victory Dad celebrated by taking the chief and my mother and me to Disneyland, where visitors gawked at the sight of a corpulent brown foreigner dressed in his traditional lavalava. ("Pele-Pele, lavalava—is there an echo in here?" joked my father.) When park employees dressed as Mickey and Minnie scurried toward the chief for a snapshot, he fearfully exclaimed, "Big man-and-wife mice!"

My father frequently relied on Mr. Gutierrez, manager of the Pico Union hot sauce company, for business tips. Against my mother's wishes, Dad had sunk a large portion of their savings into a line of Kosher burritos, a culinary area in which he was perhaps the first and last venture capitalist. When supply, not surprisingly, outweighed demand (the burritos were stuffed with corned beef and dill pickles), it was Mr. Gutierrez who urged my father to cut his losses before he lost his shirt.

The Democrat in my father bristled against the prescribed limits imposed on friendships between men of different races, but perhaps these very limits also allowed him to express toward Jimmy and Chief Pele-Pele and Mr. Gutierrez a warmth and trust he rarely felt in the company of white men, who, advancing in the business world with a minimum of friction, could at any moment exceed him in reputation or net worth, a possibility that kept him on guard around his supposed peers.

"The conundrum of color is the inheritance of every American, be he/she legally or actually Black or White," wrote James Baldwin, whose essay about the death of his father, *Notes of a Native Son,* was a staple of my syllabus. It was one thing to unpuzzle my father's relationships with men of other races; add sex and gender in the person of Anna, and the question became erotically charged and exponentially more perplexing. In less than twenty-four hours and counting, I'd be introduced to my father's new wife. Numbers glowed on the bedside clock. Conclusions grew more elusive by the minute.

My father and Anna huddled side by side in a red leather booth at the far end of the restaurant. A constellation of brass pans hung on the wall behind them and glinted in the dim light. He leaned against her shoulder with an affection detectable from across the room, and when he noticed me squinting past the maître d's podium, he lifted his hand in vague gesture of recognition, like a man who couldn't quite rouse himself from a deep, voluptuous sleep. To my surprise, he didn't pull away from Anna and sit upright as I walked toward them and slid into my side of the booth. Neither Anna nor I over-stayed our handshake, opting for caution over headlong warmth. "Well," said Dad, "here we are." And indeed we were. Seated in a fancy restaurant, no less, a setting lush with bouquets of carnations and filled with the odor of roasting meat. He managed to catch the attention of a harried waiter and ordered a celebratory round of drinks, all the while keeping his shoulder pressed against Anna's. He showed no sign of the embarrassment I'd expected from our phone conversation. The tilt of his body against hers spoke of his longing with a candor he'd never allow himself to express in words.

When my father had warned me about Anna's youth, I hadn't taken the relativity of his perspective into account, and now it took some getting used to the fact that his fiancée was a handsome, almost matronly woman whose skin had slackened into middle age, faint lines radiating from the outer edges of her tired brown eyes. This revelation was not without its pang of disappointment, for I would have achieved a certain cachet among my friends were I to intro-duce them to a young, dashiki-clad stepmother with a pneumatic Afro. Anna, however, wore a tailored navy blue dress and a gold brooch, the kind of tasteful outfit that calls attention to the wearer, but not too much, since a bid for attention even one jot more obvi-ous might be viewed by others as vain or ostentatious. I respected her sartorial restraint because Brian dressed for work with a similar humility, eschewing loud ties and busy shirts and any other apparel that might trigger disquieting associations in his clients. For the suc-cess of therapy in general and transference in particular, he became a blank slate onto which people could project whoever it was they most needed him to be. All of which led me, I suppose, to project Brian onto Anna so that she might seem, in this awkward situation, more knowable than not.

"Isn't she bee-yoo-tee-full?" Dad asked. This was the highest tribute he could offer, praise divided into syllables, each one stressed and savored in its turn.

"Your father," said Anna, shaking her head with embarrassed pleasure.

How I wished she could have finished that sentence. "Yes," I said, "he's really something."

My tone was jovial, but I suddenly fought a surge of fury on my mother's behalf. Never, once, had I heard my father flatter her. Not so much as a crumb of praise from the loaf he'd been hoarding for Anna. "Never" is not an exaggeration. I thoroughly searched the archives of my memory, with its twisting halls and hidden rooms and admittedly disorganized filing cabinets. I wasn't looking only for lavish examples of flattery, but also for equivocal compliments such as, "That dress is nice every time you wear it," or, "You look okay for a change." Forget full sentences; I would have settled for a grunt of interest, a lascivious whistle, a "wow" as blunt and helpless as a belch. Certainly, if I concentrated hard enough, I could recollect a pet name he'd whispered to my mother: *Something Lips* or *Yummy Something*. I hunted, in other words, for any and all vocalizations that fell within the range of human hearing and might, by some stretch of the imagination, be interpreted as your garden variety regard. And still I came up empty-handed.

Maybe when my brothers were young (it's too late to ask them) my parents were free with their compliments and reached for each other with eager hands. But by the time I came along, my mother watched the love scenes on soap operas with an expression I can only describe as a wistful grimace, and my father referred to any couple who weren't wringing each other's necks as "lovebirds," so sweet was the absence of antagonism that it seemed to him commensurate with love. The parents I knew were like two feuding neighbors who tried to drown each other out by playing, louder and louder, the broken record of their discontentment, and if that didn't work, by shouting insults over the fence: *idiot, lunatic, bastard, bitch*. Years before my mother died of a stroke in her sleep, she'd been confined to the house with heart problems, and only then did the ferocity and volume of their arguments subside. Neither my mother's voice, muffled by medication, or my father's poor hearing could account for that final, saturating quiet. There's a term in Brian's profession for the attentive nods and steadfast eye contact meant to prod a client toward disclosure—*active listening.* My parents, in contrast, practiced *active disregard,* the silence between them impervious to demands or entreaties, to threats or curses or tender words.

My father beamed at me and said, "I've told Anna all about you."

"Oh?"

He turned to Anna. "And Bernard knows all about me." I swallowed what felt like a solid ball of vodka. To call this an overstatement would be an understatement, but I let it ride for the sake of politeness. "So, honey," he said, "let's tell him all about yourself."

The *let's,* I assumed, was a verbal stitch meant to knit them together. It soon became clear that my father took it upon himself to draw Anna out during lapses in the conversation. Whenever he spoke, Anna fixed him in her melancholy gaze, fingers settling heavily on the stem of her wineglass. He, in turn, would prod her beyond her reticence, insisting she tell me more about an eccentric tenant, say, or a galling property tax. She didn't bring herself to speak so much as let herself be brought, remaining provocatively laconic and soft-spoken, a woman pleased, if not quite eager, to have her say. Only by asking direct questions did I find out more about her— she'd once worked as an elementary school substitute teacher, advocated brisk walks, and read paperback thrillers in her spare time—but with each generic bit of information, I felt I knew her less. Her elusiveness, her tendency to retreat, went a long way in explaining why my father hovered by her side, his voice solicitous, tact unflagging. I'd seen my father buy and barter and scheme for things, seen him pull out his wallet and fan his cash, seen him wave his checkbook and MasterCard at clerks. But I'd never seen him want anything, want anyone, this much.

I could almost hear how my mother would mock him if—God forbid—she'd sat at the table and witnessed dinner. *Mr. Sweep the Lady off Her Feet. Mr. Prince Among Men. Mr. Pitch the Woo.* But no sooner had I imagined these sarcasms than they turned into haunting compliments, accurate observations of the smitten man before me. My father hadn't lost so much that he'd also lost hope; for better or worse (as he soon would vow) there were vestiges left.

What should I have done, Mother? Begrudge him love?


Even fewer people attended the wedding than the four who'd been invited. Anna's daughter, Pam, had been visiting friends on the East Coast and her plane was delayed in a snowstorm. Brian stayed at home with the flu. This made Anna's stately, gray-haired uncle Reggie and me the only guests. We introduced ourselves and wondered aloud if we were now stepuncle and stepnephew or just abruptly related strangers. We each complimented the other on his suit, then opened our jackets and compared the linings, as close to personal disclosure as we were likely to get. At some point during our conversation, Reggie and I arrived at a tacit understanding that it was up to us to impersonate a crowd and make the occasion as festive as two people who barely knew each other could. Before the ceremony began, we claimed one pew apiece on either side of the aisle, sprawling nonchalantly in order to take up the maximum amount of space. My father and Anna were sequestered offstage, and although they'd known for hours that only two of the four people they'd invited would be able to attend, I couldn't help but anticipate the sight of their crestfallen faces when they saw the dearth of guests firsthand. I swiveled around every few seconds, hoping to see the miraculous advent of a crowd: Sunday-school children streaming through the doors (it was Thursday) or last-minute parishioners taking their seats for the evening prayer service (it was two in the afternoon). No live or prerecorded music played—a good thing, considering that even a three-piece ensemble would have outnumbered the guests, the notes of Papas Hayden and Bach echoing through the empty chapel.

While fidgeting in the pew, I thought about the years of isolation my father must have experienced while living alone in that large house, and before I knew it, my sense of his particular loneliness had expanded into one of those universal emotions the Germans probably have a compound word for, something like *collective-singularity*

or *wish-to-escape-the-self-cage*. I was beginning, in other words, to
understand why people cry at weddings. Which was odd, considering that up until that day, my reaction to the weddings I'd attended
had been one of anthropological detachment, as if I were watching
a PBS program about aboriginal courtship rites. The grinning imp
who strews rose petals for the wedding procession to mash underfoot; the bride and groom force-feeding each other wedges of
frosted cake; the best man's drunken tribute to the newlyweds, peppered with references to their former sexual escapades; the bride's
backward bouquet toss and the subsequent stampede of single
females. It's strange, ritualistic stuff, and watching people I loved get
married had never made it less so. The financial and legal advantages
of marriage are one thing, and I fully support them for homosexual
as well as heterosexual couples, but Brian and I would no more have
a big fancy marriage ceremony than we would throw a party where
we sat on thrones and wore paper crowns and made people listen to
royal proclamations about how much we enjoyed French-kissing and
taking long walks on the beach, for which shared proclivities the
guests would present us with expensive gifts. I knew exactly what my
father meant when he'd told me that he and Anna didn't want to "do
the whole schmear." Still, I secretly believed that they secretly
believed that the more people who witnessed their wedding, the
more irrevocable wedlock would be.

Prompted by a cue I must have missed, my father and Anna
emerged from one end of the stage and walked toward a suntanned
priest at the other. Dressed in black vestments, the priest solemnly
watched them approach. He squared his shoulders, cleared his
throat, and opened the Bible he held at his chest. Rays of sunlight
slanted through the clerestory window. Reggie and I sat absolutely
still. Not a cough or creaking pew. Standing side by side, my father
and his new bride were almost the same height, and for lack of other
signs to go on, I told myself this boded well. Once they'd turned to
face the priest, their expressions had to be guessed at from behind.
There was the coiffed blossom of Anna's hair. Light rippled through
her silk skirt as she shifted her weight (excitedly? impatiently?) from

foot to foot. The plump flesh of my father's neck bulged over the starched collar of a dress shirt he hadn't worn in years. A blush colored his bald head when he (timidly? calmly?) spoke his vows. The voices were theirs, but because I wasn't able to see their expressions, and given the empty, reverberating church, their "I do's" could have come from anywhere. Out of thin air. After the priest nodded his permission, the newlyweds merged for a consummating kiss, their eyes wide open, as if in surprise.

I found out about their divorce as abruptly as I'd found out about their marriage. I was sitting in a molded plastic chair at Launderland, watching my clothes swoop around with Brian's in an industrial-sized dryer and thinking about the first line of a poem by James Merrill:

> *Again last night I dreamed the dream called Laundry.*

I loved the rolling-overness of that line, its rhythm an exact match for tumbling clothes. It took a while before I noticed a copy of the *Herald Examiner* lying on the empty chair beside me. One headline read: *Who's Been Sleeping in My Bed?* I may not have given the article a second look had my father's name not leaped from the text.

Attorney Edward S. Cooper's wife didn't take kindly to his decision to retire for the night in her bedroom, according to a $25,000 lawsuit Cooper filed yesterday. In fact, Cooper said his wife, Anna Hill Cooper, brandished a twelve-inch knife, punched him repeatedly, and smashed his eyeglasses while demanding that he get out. As a result, Cooper's suit contends, the attorney suffered "severe shock . . . severe pain in his right ear . . . is in fear of becoming totally deaf, thereby losing his right to earn his livelihood from his profession." He also suffered a groin injury and a cut under his left eye. According to the Superior Court action, the assault took place on July 9, when Mrs. Cooper found her husband sleeping in the master bedroom of their Hollywood home. The Coopers had occupied separate bedrooms since May 30, the suit said.

The newspaper, limp from moisture in the air, felt as soft as cloth when I picked it up. My father had been married to Anna for only a few months. Toward the end of their honeymoon in Greece, I'd received a postcard of the Parthenon. On the back he'd written, "This is where it all began." He meant Western civilization, though in light of their divorce, the message struck a Sibylline note, as if the seed of their marital undoing had been planted in that parched and foreign soil.

He'd been hard to get hold of ever since their return, and unusually slow to return my calls. On the few occasions we spoke, he didn't report anything out of the ordinary. They were busy doing "this and that." Pressed to elaborate, he'd say, "Eating. Sleeping. What people do." His reticence wasn't unusual and, considering that he and Anna hadn't known each other for long, I figured their marriage would begin with a phase of daily, hourly adaptations. My father and his bride had a private life to relish and protect, and so I didn't pry.

It was difficult to reconcile the couple I remembered from the Brass Pan with the article's pugilistic wife and her slumbering husband. My father had been exceptionally deferential toward Anna that night at dinner, but no campaign of adoration or self-sacrifice would have compelled him, ever, to give up the comforts of his own bed. Lynn and her feminist friends would have said that terms like *king-size mattress* and *master bedroom* were coined to flatter the sovereignty of men, and my father was no exception. It may well have taken a sneak attack to boot him from that room. If that's what really happened.

Despite his age, my father could rally a bullish strength whenever he felt threatened, his poor hearing and eyesight making him even quicker to react than he had been in the days when his senses were dependable. I'm certain he would have thrashed back with enough force to injure an assailant, especially if startled from sleep. And yet, judging from his story, or its omissions, Anna came through the row unscathed. I balked at the "twelve-inch" knife, the kind of meticulously specific detail one often finds in exaggerations. The "groin injury," whether true or trumped up to win him sympathy, may have been a bruise or a strained muscle, but because it was followed by the mention of "a cut under his left eye," the wound became a jewel of allusion, implying that my father, peaceful and prone and defenselessly dreaming, had barely escaped a castrator's knife with his manhood intact.

It was hard for me not to admire his use of writerly devices, however debatable their literary merit or vengeful their intent. The repetition of the word "severe" to emphasize his shock and pain, the phrase "right to earn his livelihood," as if he'd been denied a constitutional guarantee—Dad had crafted a malediction. What troubled me, though, was that he claimed to earn a livelihood from his profession when he had, in fact, been retired for years. Preposterous allegations may have been his stock in trade, but it seemed unwise to put in writing, and file in court, an assertion so easily disproved. This worried me not just because it was an outright lie, but because it was the kind of lie my father had once been sharp enough to catch before it damaged a client's credibility and called their other claims into question.

I glanced up from the *Herald*. The air was humid, dense with the lemon scent of detergent. How did the rest of the poem go?

> . . . *the sheets and towels of a life we were going to share*
> *The milk-stiff bibs, the shroud, each rag to be ever*
> *Trampled or soiled, bled on or groped for blindly.* . . .

Customers absently fed dollar bills into the change machine or folded garments still warm from the dryer. Sleeves and pants legs clung to each other, crackling with static when peeled apart.

I showed the article to Brian the moment he got home. He shook his head as he read it and said he wasn't surprised.

"Not surprised! I think it's incredible."

"Oh, it's incredible," he said. "I'm just not surprised."

"Why not?"

"Because past behavior is the best predictor of future behavior."

"If he's never been divorced before, how is this predictable?"

"He's no stranger to divorce. Or to marital conflict."

"Don't you think people can change?"

"Not very quickly and not very much."

"That's sort of pessimistic for a shrink."

"No. It's optimistic. That way, I'm not disappointed by the rate at which people change." His tie softly rasped as he tugged it through his collar. "Psychology is based on the idea that human behavior is made up of repeating patterns."

"What about aberrations in human behavior?"

"They're part of the pattern."

I followed Brian into the bedroom and dove onto the bed, sighing the sigh I had learned from my father—a melancholy too immense to vent in one breath. "Do you think I should I ask him about it?"

"If your father wanted to talk to you about it, wouldn't he have brought it up already?"

"What's he going to say, 'Oh, by the way, Anna came at me with a twelve-inch knife'?"

"Allegedly came at him." He unbuttoned his shirt. "Would you want your father to know if I attacked you with a knife?"

"You'd never."

"Supposing."

I pictured Brian lunging toward me, a blade glinting in his upraised hand, his pretty blue eyes as homicidal as I had the imagination to make them. "No," I said. "I wouldn't want to worry him. Besides, I'd be ashamed I'd had the poor judgment to trust you."

"There's your answer," he said. He stepped out of a pair of polished but innocuous brown shoes, then walked into the closet to hang up his pants.

I shucked off my clothes, tossed them onto the floor, and pulled the covers up to my chin. The sheets smelled like Launderland.

My father may have balked at inviting Brian to the wedding because he thought it would be harder to go though the ceremony in front of someone who'd been trained to detect trace amounts of doubt and self-deception. Little did he know how willingly my "mental-doctor friend" left his occupation at the office. Once Brian changed out of the tabula rasa of his work clothes, he allowed himself to be as mystified by human behavior as everyone else. Which meant, at the rate he was undressing, I had only a few more seconds to ask for his professional advice.

"If the headline says, *'Who's Been Sleeping in My Bed?'* is my father Goldilocks, or one of the three bears?"

Hangers clanged. "He's Goldilocks."

"Because?"

Brian reappeared in the nude. "Because the bear finds him in her bed."

"But it's his bed, technically, so wouldn't *he* be the bear?"

Brian switched off the light and pounced onto the mattress. Before my eyes had adjusted to the dark, I felt his hands gripping my shoulders, his breath against my neck. "Everyone," he whispered, "wants to be the bear."


The next morning I phoned my father, having resolved not to mention his divorce unless he mentioned it first. Keeping mum allowed me to conduct an experiment of sorts. Now that I knew the truth, but he didn't know I knew, I could observe his methods of dissembling, could see how far he was willing to go to hide what had happened and spare himself disgrace. A purely imaginary disgrace, since the person to whom he'd make his admission (me) wouldn't think of him as disgraced so much as entangled, as all of us are, in a boundless net of human failings, which is history itself. But my father harbored a superstitious belief that truth floated in a misty limbo, dormant until it was spoken aloud. To say a thing was to make it true.

I let the phone ring at least a dozen times in case he was puttering around the house without his hearing aid, though once he'd taken it out, all the clanging bells in the world couldn't get his attention. I was just about to hang up when he answered, or rather, when someone picked up the telephone without saying a word. The silence was willful as silences go, a silence with heft and dimension. Whoever lifted the receiver meant to challenge the caller, to throw them off guard. And so I was certain I'd dialed the right number. He must have been expecting Anna. I was about to say hello when something stopped me. I'd always been at odds with my father's silence, and now, grasping the undeclared rules of the game, I found myself compelled to play along, even though he thought his opponent was someone other than me. We held our breath, kept absolutely still. I hadn't shaved that morning and I had to make sure the mouthpiece didn't grate against the bristles of my beard and make a sound like amplified sandpaper. Gripping the receiver too tightly might make it creak, but easing my grip might make it creak, too. There were strategies to master, advantages to gain. Not speaking demanded stamina. The silence from his end said, *I dare you not to talk.* The silence from mine said, *Try me.* No unretractable slips of the tongue. No oscillations of temper and regret. All that my father would never tell me about himself, and all that I would never tell him, fit snuggly into our speechlessness like a ring into a velvet box. Only a few seconds had passed, but who knows how long we could have gone on if his hearing aid hadn't squealed and broken my concentration.

"Hello?" I said.

"Oh. It's you."

"What was that all about?"

"What was what all about?"

"You didn't say hello."

"*You* did. It doesn't matter who says it first."

"Well, actually, the person who picks up the—"

"You called to tell me how to talk on the phone?"

"No, I called to see how you are."

He may not have heard me.

"How are you, Dad?"

"How should I be?"

"You should be—I don't know—telling me how you are."

"My back is sore, for starters."

"Did you pull a muscle?"

"I've been sleeping on the floor."

"Oh, come on."

"*You* come on. You asked why my back hurts and I'm telling you."

"Why on earth would you sleep on the floor?"

"I toss and turn and it bothers Anna."

I noted his use of the present tense. "What if you slept in another bed?" I'd almost used the *Herald*'s phrase: *What if you "occupied separate bedrooms"?*

"I can't fall asleep if I'm not in my room. You get used to things and then, if they get taken away, you can't get used to them."

"Couldn't Anna sleep in another bed?"

"You try telling her."

"I just can't picture you sleeping on the floor."

"Why would I make something like that up? *I* don't write books."

I let that one pass. "Is there something you can do to make your back better?"

"Yes," he said. "Sleep in my own goddamn bed. But Anna won't have it."

Why hadn't he mentioned this in his deposition? It was at least as damning a charge as attempted castration. Of course, he'd fought off that indignity while he'd submitted to this one like a dog who'd been banished from its mistress's bed, a humiliation my father would never make public, however dramatically it vilified Anna or illustrated the untenable conditions of their marriage. There was no way to tell this story without revealing its pitiful gist: the night may be cold and the mistress hardhearted, but the poor mongrel has no choice but to slink off the bed and curl around itself for comfort; the floor is its place in the scheme of things.

Had he actually camped out on the shag, or was this a fabrication meant to turn me against Anna so that when he finally told me she was gone, I'd be glad to see her go? Other sons may have been better at sorting fiction from fact, but in defense of what may sound like extreme credulity on my part, let me say that my father tended to nod off in circumstances that could keep a narcoleptic awake. While he watched wrestling matches on TV, for example, with the volume full-blast, his lids drooped and his head tilted back, his nap undisturbed by the bellowing crowd or thunderclaps of colliding flesh. The sight of two wrestlers in a headlock was as soporific to my father as the sight of my father napping on the couch would have been to them. No matter how awake he seemed, how pointedly impatient, at any moment the chasm of a yawn might open and expose his gold molars.

As for his sleeping on the floor, I'm not saying it's possible, I'm saying it's not *im*possible. I feel compelled to phrase it this way because I've heard several friends fondly reminisce about how, when they were children, their fathers told them, "Anything is possible," a fatherly promise that opened a door to the wondrous world as opposed to the lid of a Pandora's box from which leaped a headless chicken, or a bride who baked pies so her husband wouldn't touch her. For me, the words "Anything is possible" haven't served as a bolstering of hope as much as a warning to run for cover. The one hope I have when I hear that phrase is the hope that whatever happens next won't demolish the laws of cause and effect.

"The carpet has a thick underpad," said my father.

"What difference does that . . . ?"

"Some people sleep on wooden boards because they say its good for the spine."

"You're saying you *want* to sleep on the floor?"

"I'm not saying want."

"Because you're certainly entitled to sleep in your own bed."

He cleared his throat. "I'm glad you think so. I sometimes wonder."

A rare admission of fragility. "Dad," I said, "everyone's entitled to sleep in their own bed."

"That's ridiculous!" he snapped. "What the hell did you call for, anyway? Did you call to tell me something important, or to spout some meshuggener philosophy about who's entitled to what?"

Then I understood my mistake. The first remark—"You're entitled"—elevated him above others. The second—"Everyone's entitled"—lumped him with the hoi polloi. If everyone was entitled to what my father was entitled to, then everyone was entitled to sleep in his bed. Which meant that Anna was also entitled. And if—bear with me—Anna slept in my father's bed, then my father would be forced to sleep on the floor. There hadn't been a note of ridicule in my voice, not a half note or a demiquaver, but after the sounds issued from my mouth, traveling the distance from my phone to his, they still had to spiral into his ear and reach the receptors of his hearing aid, which transmitted vibrations to his cochlea, which started a synaptic chain-reaction until he grasped my words verbatim. Then turned them into the mocking comment he (wrongly) suspected I'd been thinking all along: *Sleep on the floor for all I care. That's where you belong!*

"Hello?" said my father.

"I'm listening," I said.

"That's funny," he grumbled, "'cause I haven't been talking."


How did he finally tell me they'd divorced? He never did. Anna, he said, was visiting her daughter. Substitute teaching. Showing a house. Indisposed. It was up to me to add up the long column of her absences until I realized she was gone for good. Then never mention the woman again. Having read about their divorce in the newspaper allowed me to play along without getting lost in a maze of ambiguity. The facts were "written in print," as my father would have said, and as long as I didn't depend on him for facts, I could nod at his improvisations, responding with a calm "I see." Instead of resisting his attempts to steer the conversation away from Anna, I'd swerve to an entirely different subject with such disarming agility and speed, my non sequiturs rivaled the master's. My refusal to probe

at first relieved, then pleased my father, as if by swallowing false-
hoods whole, I'd at last done something to make him proud. The
greater his appreciation, the more I excelled at complicity. He wasn't
deceiving me, I began to believe, so much as obliquely hinting at the
truth.

He never pursued litigation against Anna. His petition for divorce
ended up among thousands of accounts of marital discord housed
in the County Hall of Records—an enormous vault of a building
not far from his old Spring Street office—never to be read again.

She left behind several possessions. Blueprints for a Mar Vista
subdivision were stored in a drawer. The spines of paperback thrillers
announced their titillating, sideways titles from a shelf in the upstairs
hall. A few of her dresses still hung in a closet, running the gamut
from gray to navy blue.

These abandoned belongings remained exactly where she left
them, and one could reasonably argue that, by failing to either return
or discard them, my father was the one who'd left them behind.
When I first came to visit him after their divorce, the sight of Anna's
things reminded me how capricious and fleeting people's allegiances
can be. Eventually, however, her possessions became a common
sight, blending into the rest of the house. By keeping her belongings out in the open and subjecting them to his diligent neglect, my
father was making them disappear without so much as having to
touch them.

One possession of Anna's convinced me that there had been a
mitigating circumstance in the demise of their marriage. The medicine cabinet in the master bathroom contained a bottle of Tofranil
with Anna's maiden name printed on the label. I'd discovered it one
day when my father asked me to bring him one of his blood pressure pills. The word Tofranil sounded familiar; I'd overhead Brian
talking with his colleagues often enough to associate the suffix *nil*
with the power of drugs (or at least with the promise of drug companies) to nullify depression. Brian would later confirm that Tofranil
was among a class of antidepressants known as tricyclics. In fact, he
was able to close his eyes and recite the drug's side effects from

memory, the way he could a Joyce Kilmer poem he'd learned in grade school—*I think that I shall never see / A poem lovely as a tree*— though this recitation, with its grim rhythm and incessant symptomology, was closer in spirit to Sylvia Plath: dry mouth, difficulty swallowing, decreased libido, tremors, fatigue, neuropathy, hallucinations, nightmares.

As I held the bottle of Tofranil, the memory of dinner with my father and Anna underwent a swift revision. She still sat across from me in a red leather booth, but her weariness, a weariness I'd attributed to middle age, deepened into a resignation that age alone couldn't explain. Her eyes were slower in meeting mine. Her handshake was leaden in retrospect. How could I not have noticed the gravity and drag of depression?

From there, I extrapolated days and nights of Anna's inertia, and my father pulling out all the stops to lighten her mood. If I've portrayed Edward Cooper as a humorless man, allow me to correct that impression. He knew his mischief forward and back. The tension that usually churned in his stomach, knotting muscles and causing heartburn, was sometimes funneled into kibitzing, which, as any kibitzer knows, is an art much harder to master than it looks. You have to walk a line between antics and madness. You have to let your hair down, if you have any left. You have to march in a one-man band, harmonica firmly clenched between your teeth. While flooring the Cadillac on the freeway, captain of all that humming tonnage, my father was likely to burst into song. "Clang, clang, clang, went the trolley," he sang, and "Mares eat oats and does eat oats and little lambs eat ivy." He bellowed every note for effect, conducting an invisible orchestra with hands that should have been gripping the wheel. And when the Chevron attendant filled the tank, Dad would clutch his stomach and groan, "I'm getting gas!"

The problem was, he expected you to play the role of tireless sidekick. You had to humor him for humoring you. It was tit for tat. Itch my back and I'll itch yours. At first he'd succeed in cracking you up, but gales of laughter are hard to sustain. Your cheeks begin to ache. Your guffaws grow hollow. My father watched closely and measured your reaction, and anything less than a robust chuckle raised a red flag. "What's the matter?" he'd ask midjoke, the punch line hanging in the air like a boulder.

It was one thing for me to egg him on; this jaunty father intent on my reaction was a wish fulfilled. But Anna may have seen herself as hopelessly stony compared to her husband, neither pleased nor piqued by his nonstop vaudeville. I can see her smiling wanly at his gags, sorry to be such a "stick in the mud," as my father tended to call nonlaughers. (Unless it was he who wasn't laughing, in which case the joker was "a pain in the ass.") The further Anna sank into the doldrums, the more zealously my father would prod, trotting out puns and knock-knock jokes, refusing to lose his wife to despair, to botch a second chance at marriage, no better than the lovelorn schmucks he'd fought for in court. It was Anna who swallowed the Tofranil, but the drug etched pathways in both their brains, altering their futures one neuron at a time.

I liked to visit my father during this fictitious phase of his marriage. Once a week, after my three o'clock class, I'd maneuver my sputtering Fiat up the driveway, and before I came to a full stop, he'd appear at the front door, his jumpsuited figure sunstruck against the dark interior of the house. Even if his hearing aid had been turned up all the way, the sound of the engine couldn't have alerted him to my arrival, so it wasn't completely far-fetched of me to believe that he may have been waiting at the living room window, the brick-and-mortar curtain parted, his breath clouding a pane of glass as he scanned the length of Ambrose Avenue searching for my car. As soon as I walked through the door, he'd open a can of salted peanuts and we'd sink into the living room couch just in time to watch *Wheel of Fortune*. I think I speak for both of us when I say that we were pleasantly surprised to find that we could yell out answers to the word puzzles without our usual displays of competitiveness and poor sportsmanship.

When it came to words, my father believed I possessed an

unfair advantage. I'd intuited the rules of grammar at a young age. Idioms and figures of speech stuck in my head as stubbornly as TV jingles. Yet I wasn't able to explain to my father (or to myself) that language helped me navigate a world of half-truths and lawyerly rationalizations.

For all his impassioned eloquence in court, my father still made verbal slips, such as, *You want I should check the time?* or, *The guy don't know what he's talking about.* And when he did, his eyes widened at the realization, and he'd bluster with fancy, ready-made phrases: *Be that as it may . . . In light of the fact . . . Contrary to popular opinion . . . By the same token.* Still, vestiges of the scrambled syntax he'd inherited from his Russian immigrant parents, along with the "dem" and "doze" of an adolescence spent on the streets of Philadelphia, seeped into his patterns of speech. It wasn't uncommon for high and low diction to collide midsentence: *Be that as it may, the guy don't know what he's talking about.*

To this day I know almost nothing about my grandparents (had he spent his fund of stories on my brothers?) except for this: Abe and Ruth Cooper—an Anglicized surname given to my grandfather, a barrel maker, at Ellis Island—parted company with friends by calling out in unison, "See you yesterday," instead of, "See you tomorrow." My father laughed when recounting the story, but it caused him to blush with an ancient shame. What embarrassed him, it's taken me decades to realize, wasn't just his parents' grammar, but their "yesterday" in the larger sense: the backwardness of greenhorns slow to adapt.

His parents spoke broken English. My parents spoke broken Yiddish, but only in the presence of other Jews or when they wanted to talk in code around their children. They shifted into Yiddish with the relief of people removing a pair of tight shoes, their conversation suddenly peppered with exclamations such as *Pish!* and *Feh!* Liberated by Yiddish, my father shrugged theatrically, batted at the air, and cast imploring glances toward God. Should he stare into the distance, his sighs prolonged, I'd wonder if he was telling stories about his childhood in Atlantic City or his adolescence in Philadelphia. Perhaps such stories were diluted by English, vibrant only when told in the language of his past.

My longing to return with him to the scenes and people of his youth (if the past, in fact, was what he'd been discussing) amounted to a shared nostalgia, each of us, in his different way, succumbing to the gravitational tug of a lost world. When I could no longer contain myself and ventured a question, he seemed pleased, but instead of answering, he'd turn toward whomever he'd been addressing and make, in Yiddish, what I supposed was a comment about my curiosity. It was disconcerting to see him inspired to such expressiveness by a language meant to exclude me, his mother tongue providing a kind of exuberant background music as I went about my chores.

Nothing infuriated my father as much as having his grammar corrected, especially by a precocious kid. In the rare instance I dared to correct him—"The guy *doesn't* know what he's talking about"— he'd glare at me, his body rigid, the tell-tale vein protruding at his temple. He wanted to defend himself, but once he'd been admonished, he couldn't fire back. I hadn't simply pointed out a grammatical error, I'd declared myself American—more American than he—and lumped him in the league of greenhorns. His only recourse was to leave the room before he proved me right with a flustered rebuttal or a wordless blow.

Perhaps it's poetic justice that I eventually came to share my father's dread of self-betrayal, came to know firsthand his fear that he risked ridicule and ostracism merely by opening his mouth to speak. Throughout my adolescence I worried that if I didn't watch every word I said, my sibilant *s*'s and flamboyant gestures were sure to articulate, all too clearly, who and what I was.

After Anna left him, however, my father and I found ourselves able to communicate with unusual ease. He finally seemed convinced that teaching three classes a week constituted a legitimate workload. I learned to defer to his opinions and to tread lightly around conversational powder kegs. "God bless you!" he'd blurt whenever I used a word that sounded to him like a bunch of noisy syllables. *Chanteuse.* "God bless you!" *Phlegmatic.* "God bless you!"

In order to keep up the appearance of normalcy—that is, in order to perpetuate the myth of his marriage—I kept thinking I should inquire about Anna, but every time I thought of asking where she was, I heard his answer echo in my head: *What do I look like, the FBI? She'll be back when she's back, and until she is, she's somewhere else.* That he'd edited a wife out of existence didn't strike me as a portent for the future of our own relationship. Or perhaps I chose to ignore it. In those days we'd come as close to courtship as a father and son can come.

While watching contestants spin the wheel of fortune, its prizes and penalties blurring together, we passed the can of peanuts back and forth. Light dimmed beyond the picture window. We were too mesmerized by Vanna White turning blanks into letters to wrench ourselves from the sofa and switch on a nearby lamp. As darkness enlarged the living room, our guesses at the unsolved puzzles—"The something you something may be your something!" "Never something today what you can something tomorrow!"—rang truer than any adages I knew.

My father sprawled on the king-size mattress, his crutches propped against the bedroom wall as if they were holding it up. Woozy from anti-inflammatories and winded from our trip up the stairs, his eyes slowly closed. I stood at the foot of the bed and watched him sleep, just as he may have long ago stood at the foot of my bed and watched me. His eyes darted beneath the lids, mouth twitching with sentiments that were anybody's guess. In the throes of a dream, he flung out his arm and it came to rest on the empty side of the mattress. My mother's side. Anna's side. Now Betty's, I supposed. On the nightstand lay her white leather Bible, a crimson ribbon saving her place.

Distant voices from *This Is Your Day* drifted upstairs. Benny Hinn and his congregation were speaking in tongues. Vowels reverberated. Consonants clicked. I made a mental note to use the word *glossolalia* when explaining onomatopoeia to my class. A kind of murmuring

religious fervor charged the air, and I couldn't help but wonder if
Betty lay beside my father at night and read Bible passages aloud,
promising an afterlife in return for placing his faith in Jesus. Given
his gout, she had a captive audience, and if they were in fact *sleeping*
together, I wouldn't be surprised if my father listened to excerpts
from the New Testament in the hope that his attentiveness might
lead to sex, though how he'd manage to have sex while his toe was
swollen was something I no more wanted to think about than he'd
want to think about me having sex with my mental-doctor friend.
Having sex with Brian, however, was something I not only wanted
to think about, but found myself thinking about whether I wanted
to or not. My father and I were allied in our attitude toward physical gratification; we considered ourselves lucky that we were driven
to distraction by sex instead of by some monotonous hobby like
stamp collecting. The only difference was that I wanted to have sex
with a doctor and he with a nurse. This may explain why he'd
greeted the news of my relationship with Brian with equanimity,
and why I had written about his extramarital affairs with what I
hoped was a similar equanimity, though it was hard for me to appreciate our mutual equanimity while knowing he'd explode if he ever
found out that the essay had been published in a literary review, and
was about to appear in my first book, a collection of essays from a
university press.

Now I had to keep the news of my publication secret from the
one person I most wanted to impress with the fact that all those
years I'd spent hunched over my desk, typing with two index fingers, had, at the age of thirty-eight, finally led to the publication of
a book. Of course, I'd brought this problem upon myself by writing
about him, but Dad never expressed interest in my work, and I
couldn't ignore a subject that took hold of my imagination with
such insistence.

It's not that writing had been my way to understand him; his life
was larger and more surprising than my capacity to understand it.
Understanding my father was as unsustainable a state of mind as
euphoria or patience. Maybe I understood him for a few minutes at

a time, and maybe, for a few minutes at a time, I understood him better than anyone else understood him, but if I said my understanding was definitive, I'd be saying that the man was static, a done deal, a wrapped package, never slipping out of character or spilling over with contradictions, never driven by affinities and fears that even he himself couldn't fathom. By delving into the riddle of him, I hoped to know his mystery by finer degrees. Through language could I inhabit him as much as he had inhabited me. Through language I could dream that dream called Father.

When I bent close to make sure his foot was securely elevated on the stack of pillows, he winced in his sleep, as if his swollen toe was so tender he could feel the pressure of my passing shadow. He lifted his head, aimed his gaze in my general direction. His mouth was dry from diuretics, his voice weak and garbled from sleep, as if he were one of the distant multitudes talking in tongues. He said (I'm guessing), "You're just going to stand there?" Then his head fell back and he started to snore.

# The Shortest Distance
# Between Two Points

After leaving my father to his afternoon nap, I remembered something on the drive back home that I hadn't thought about in a long
time: my father and I both possessed identical moles on the bot-
toms of our right feet, smack in the center. Neither my brothers
nor my mother could boast such a mole, and so this shared trait,
which he'd brought to my attention when I was a boy, suggested
that no matter how distant we were from each other, a line drawn
between those two points would always unite us in a filial connect-
the-dots.

As I waited for a traffic light to change, I wondered if the mole
had in fact been a childish fantasy, a willful elaboration on a freckle
or a speck of dirt, marks I'd imagined in order to link myself more
closely to a father whom I suspected, even back then, of being
remote and unknowable. Just as I was about to reach down and pry
off my shoe so I could check and see if the mole was still there, the
light turned green, and the driver behind me began to honk, and
since I needed that foot to press the accelerator, I was forced to wait
till I got home.

Brian was reading *Modes of Psychotherapy* when I rushed through the front door. I plunged into the nearest chair and yanked at my laces. He looked up from his book and asked, "Is there something in your shoe?"

"I think so," I said. "At least there used to be." I tossed the shoe to the floor, shucked off my sock, and there it was, as concise and final as a period, as indelible and dark as ever.

# One Art

"Your father's in serious arrears," said the man from the phone company.

"Serious arrears?"

"It's been six months since he's paid his bill. Our Collection Department sent him the usual overdue notices, of course, and then the matter was turned over to me. I'm Mike Delaney, regional supervisor. I've contacted him several times to answer his questions and help arrange a payment plan, but I'm afraid that courtesy hasn't worked."

According to Mr. Delaney, my father denied having made the calls he'd been charged for, refused to pay for them "come hell or high water," and finally threatened to sue Pacific Bell for harassment. On the one hand, this threat had been peppered with enough legal jargon to make it plausible. On the other, it was fantastic enough to qualify my father as a crackpot, though the supervisor used a more tactful term. After being warned that his phone would be disconnected, my father said he'd be happy to rip it out of the wall himself if it meant that Delaney couldn't bother him again. When told that his account would be turned over to an independent collection agency whose tactics would make Pac Bell's look like a walk in the park, he'd calmly replied, "Let them get me."

As a last-ditch effort to reason with my father, or to find a third party who could, Mr. Delaney searched through company records to find out who Dad had named as the person to notify in case of an emergency. So often had my father been sardonic about my "sit-around-and-daydream" writer's life, so often had he told me I'd forget my head if it wasn't screwed on, that it surprised me to learn, by way of this phone call, that the name he wrote in the blank was mine. Perhaps he'd wanted to provide the name of another relative, but there'd been fewer and fewer with whom he'd kept in touch since my mother's death. Naming a former colleague was out of the question since he no longer socialized with anyone from the Continental Building. He couldn't have named a next door neighbor due to his long-standing feud with the neighbors on the right, because their sprinklers made the lawn soggy on his side of the property line, and with the neighbors on the left, because he was sure their automatic garage door opener vibrated powerfully enough to cause hairline cracks in our living room walls. Even if he'd arrived at my name after excluding half the population of Los Angeles, I felt chosen, honored, exonerated.

"I'm a patient man," Mr. Delaney assured me. "I've worked at the phone company for fifteen years and I'd like to think I know a thing or two about human nature and how to get around it." He'd considered himself, for a while at least, my father's ally, giving him several chances to redress his debt. The supervisor seemed to be asking me why his ordinarily successful methods of persuasion had failed. I heard strains of my own exasperation in his voice and wanted to do what I could to help remedy the situation without taking sides.

As much as I empathized with Mr. Delaney, it had always been a relief when my father directed his wrath toward someone other than me. Hearing about Dad's transgressions also stirred an unexpected pride. Wasn't his belligerence a form of self-defense, a martial art? Whatever "guff" was, it was something he wouldn't take from anyone. By standing up against the phone company, my father remained triumphantly guffless.

"He can be difficult," I told the supervisor.

"May I ask if this is typical behavior?"

"He's always been erratic. Although, if someone is always erratic, I guess they're consistent."

Mr. Delaney cleared his throat. He may have thought that my father and I were peas in a pod. There I stood, tethered to my kitchen wall by a curling phone cord, speculating with some muckety-muck from the phone company about my father's refusal to pay his bill, all the while knowing that, given my income, if asked to send a check in Dad's stead, I'd soon be refusing to pay the bill, too. Were my father's circumstances contagious? If they were, I was about to find myself in serious arrears.

"According to our records, your father was born in nineteen-oh-six?"

"*Aught*-six."

"Pardon?"

"*Aught* is what he was taught to call zero. Way back when."

"Then it's safe to say he's getting on in years?"

"Safe to say to me, maybe. Not to him."

He chuckled dismally. "You're right on that score. I made the mistake of telling him he was one of our oldest customers."

"He's eccentric, if that's what you're getting at, but I don't think he's senile." Over the years, Dad's personality had been distilled into a set of essential peculiarities—but whose hadn't?—and I wasn't sure if this indicated a slide toward senility or if it was an inevitable process whereby time pared each of us down to some fundamental self who, after all the *mishigas* we've been through, can't help but be a little muddled.

The supervisor's questions were putting me on the defensive. The expectation that I could provide information regarding my father only reminded me how little I knew him. I worried that the more questions a stranger asked—*Why had your father gone into law? How did he get along with his parents?*—the faster I'd run out of answers. My father and I were not only foreign to each other, but foreign to what sometimes seemed like a worldwide confederacy of well-adjusted fathers and sons whose grasp of each other was a given, encoded in their DNA. If I couldn't explain my father to myself, how could I explain him to a stranger?

Delaney must have sensed my unease. He said, "I'm not here to cast aspersions."

You're not here at all, I wanted to remind him.

What if I *could* afford to be magnanimous? What if I squared away the debt without breathing a word to my father? One day he'd notice that the "nut" from Pacific Bell had stopped badgering him. One day he'd open his bill to discover that aught was due.

"How much does he owe?" I asked.

Rustle of paperwork. Rapid tapping on a calculator.

Outside my kitchen window, a cloudless blue covered the L.A. basin. If property owners also owned the air above their lots, then a parcel of sky belonged to my father.

"One thousand seventy-four dollars," said the supervisor, "and forty-eight cents."

I inhaled sharply. "Were the calls long distance?"

"Recently, yes. To Irving, Texas."

"Irving, Texas?"

"Would your father have reason to contact the Benny Hinn Ministries?"

"That faith healer on TV?"

"Our records don't specify the nature of Mr. Hinn's ministry."

"First of all, my father's Jewish . . ."

"That may be true, Mr. Cooper, but—"

"I think his girlfriend—I mean his nurse—made those calls."

"Do either of them have access to his phone?"

"They're the same person. She's lived with him for about two months."

"It's not just the calls to Texas your father claims he didn't make. He denies having made local calls, too. He says he hardly uses his phone. He says I'm the only person who calls him."

"That's absolutely untrue! He has gout and I've been calling him a lot! Going over to visit him, too. He didn't even know he had gout until I told him about . . ." I was going to mention Sylvia Plath, then thought better of it. "I'm his only son, you know."

"Actually, I didn't. Not until I found your number. Your father told me that all of his boys had passed away."

"He did?" Then I heard it perfectly. *I lost all my sons. Who the hell am I gonna call?* It stung to imagine my father summarily dispatching me to the afterlife, but it would have stung more had I not been familiar with his all-or-nothing logic. Claiming he had no sons left to lose would fill him with bitter exhilaration. His excuse curtailed future grief—how could I die if I wasn't alive?—and financial obligation to Pacific Bell.

"Any suggestions?" asked the supervisor.

One thousand seventy-four dollars and forty-eight cents. If my brothers and I could have divided our father's debt four ways, we'd each have to pay . . . I had trouble making the calculation. It involved long division in the temporal sense, winnowing and continuous. My brothers had been good at math. My brothers were gone.


Instead of going to college after he graduated from high school, my eldest brother, Bob, signed up for a state-approved home-study course on becoming a licensed private investigator. I was in fifth grade at the time, and there seemed to be a link between his choice of career and the Hardy Boys books he'd collected when he'd been my age. A row of enticing, telegraphic titles—*The Hidden Harbor Mystery, The Disappearing Floor*—still lined a shelf in his bedroom. The course included lessons on how to do background checks, trace missing persons, pursue suspects on foot and in vehicles, and make arrests—what amateur sleuths Frank and Joe Hardy generally referred to as "foul play" and "shady characters." At the beginning of every month, when our postman delivered a new tutorial sealed in a bulky envelope, Bob thundered downstairs, tore it open, and began reading on the way back to his room.

"What did I tell you?" my father said when Bob marveled at

how well the lessons were going. "Investigation is nothing more than horse sense."

"He has an *aptitude*," corrected mother.

I asked what horse sense meant.

My father turned to my mother. "Open your ears, Lillian. That's what I just said."

"It's the kind of smarts," Bob explained, "that even a dumb animal has."

The three of us looked at my father.

"Why are you looking at me like that?" he asked.

Bob had to complete two years of fieldwork before receiving his credentials, and so, after passing the oral and written exams, he moved into an apartment in Glendale and began his life as my father's salaried employee. The job took him to far-flung parts of town—Montebello, El Camino, names as exotic to me then as Shangri-La—where he served subpoenas, located men who were delinquent on alimony or child support payments, and surveilled, through the tinted windows of his Pontiac, husbands and wives suspected of what my mother called "assignations." She used the euphemism for my sake, unaware that after I'd spent hours poring over my father's scrapbook, it was too late to shield me from the meaning of *infidelity*. I'd come across the word in several clippings, then found it in my dictionary between *inferno* and *infirmary,* which seemed to explain why my father's chain-smoking, foot-jiggling clientele were nervous people.

It was difficult to know whether Bob possessed a talent for surreptitiousness before he studied private investigation or whether he developed it on the job. Laconic and watchful, he moved with agile silence despite his husky six-foot frame. People were often surprised to find that he'd entered or left a room unnoticed. He listened closely to conversations he gave the appearance of ignoring, able to repeat long afterward who said what to whom. Bob worked best— that is, most inconspicuously—at night, his dark car camouflaged as he idled curbside and noted the comings and goings of his "mark." His brown eyes were capable of a disconcerting fixity, and large enough to suggest—at least to a boy eager for signs of his brother's superhuman prowess—nocturnal vision. Whenever he came home to visit, I could have sworn that his black hair and gabardine suits gave off the scent of night itself, the way other men returned from work with the smell of tobacco embedded in their clothes.

Bob kept a Smith & Wesson .38 wedged into the shoulder holster beneath his jacket. Or so I was told. No matter how much I begged to see it, even a glimpse of the gun was strictly forbidden, a condition imposed by my parents and one Bob upheld with a gravity befitting the eldest son. To "get me off his case," he one day opened his wallet and unfolded the license that entitled him to carry a concealed weapon. A wrinkled piece of paper was a poor substitute for the silvery thrill of a gun, but I forgot my disappointment when I studied the intricate whorls of his thumbprint, like a tiny map of concentric streets.

Back then I didn't see him as the shy young man I later came to understand he was, but as a scout who'd traveled into adulthood before me. If he was the most remote among my brothers, I figured it was because he was nearly twenty years older than I, had prowled the Pacific aboard a submarine during the Korean War, and lived beyond the walls of our house. His boxy stucco apartment building was improbably called the Emerald Arms, a name that made his independence all the more exotic.

Three years younger than Bob, Ron had to channel his ambition toward the practice of law by giving up what he called, with unconvincing dismissiveness, his hobby. Ron's bedroom was always pungent with the smell of linseed oil and turpentine. An easel stood beside his bed, ready (or so I thought) should he jump up inspired in the middle of the night. His oval palette, encrusted with every conceivable color, was a messy, epic artwork in itself. If I opened the door while he stood at his easel, my ordinarily friendly brother would freeze, brush in hand, his narrowed eyes a warning to back off. His privacy was as palpable as a wall. From my point of view— no further than the portal—Ron's works in progress were always of a single subject: a stretched canvas glimpsed from behind.

It never ceased to surprise me that Ron's allotment of solitude yielded actual paintings: still lifes in which the apples and grapes our mother bought at the A&P would stay edible forever, in which the birds-of-paradise clipped from our yard lifted their slender necks from a vase, the blooms a tropical, avian orange my brother had captured exactly. Ron painted the view from his second-story bedroom window in different seasons and at various times of day: streets and cars and terra-cotta roofs sprawling beneath the neighborhood's congregation of ancient palms, their mangy fronds tossed by the wind or drooping and darkly varnished after rain. He once hung this series of paintings along the wall so I could see them all at once—a row of windows opening onto a world that refused to stand still, time and light spooling through them like a reel of film through our father's Bell & Howell. Ron was quick to acknowledge his errors in perspective and proportion, pointing out details blurred by haste or clumsy brushwork. Instead of causing him frustration, one painting's deficiencies drove him to begin another. The only chance to rectify his craft was to start anew, to fail again.

Left to his own devices, Ron would have become a painter. He had about him the apologetic air of a person who feels himself tugged, despite every compelling reason against it, toward a life about which our suburbs and schools and television shows remained essentially silent, unless you counted the paint-by-number kits sold at Thrifty or the tale of Vincent van Gogh lopping off his own ear. Ron was the only person I knew who took painting seriously. The scarcity of other people who shared his interest only strengthened my impression that artists, along with eccentrics of any stripe, were banished to a place called Bohemia in much the same way that bad Catholics were banished to purgatory, except that Bohemia was closer to New York.

Our father looked upon Ron's artistic ambition, and later on mine, with the silent disapproval of a man whose child is drawn to a world he will never comprehend or be a part of, an exclusion that must have been particularly exasperating for someone who'd shed his own history so that he could become an indivisible citizen of the nation into which his children were born. But our father's scoffing wouldn't have been enough to deter Ron if he hadn't harbored reservations of his own. He was a practical young man—punctual, organized, judicious in his opinions despite a flaring temper my mother attributed to the firebrand of his red hair—as much as he was a young man dizzied by the possibility that everything he saw in three dimensions could be rendered in two. Ron's decision to pursue a conventional profession didn't result from a failure of nerve; giving up art was the greater risk, and his life as a lawyer, like every life, was perilous, experimental.

That Richard, the youngest of my brothers, was closest to my age only accentuated the fifteen-year gulf between us. Like Ron and Bob, he was an altogether different species from me, a giant whose footsteps shook the floor. He could juggle three oranges at a time, which, from my grade school point of view, was a crucial rite of passage into manhood. While I inhabited the family's sidelines, Richard counted himself among a shoving triumvirate of brothers who jockeyed for a spot before the bathroom mirror, each dousing his hair with Vitalis and sculpting it into the "fenders" and "flattops" he'd primp throughout the day. Nothing, absolutely nothing would muss it up except maybe the wind of a hurtling convertible or a woman running her fingers through his hair—or so they'd boast to one another as they wiped swaths of steam off the mirror, young men grooming themselves for a shared daydream of speed and release.

Richard "took to water," as my mother liked to say. (High praise from a woman whose own swimming feat I'll get to later.) During the summer, he worked as a lifeguard at a public pool near Griffith Park. Perched in the crow's nest of a canvas chair, he peered through a pair of regulation sunglasses at the splashing pandemonium of swimmers doing laps and cannonballs while screaming kids in water wings bobbed across the chop.

By his freshman year in college, my brother had grown ruddy and muscular, sharp planes emerging from the baby fat of his face, the masculine angularity softened by long eyelashes. Wherever we went, I saw women giving him second looks, or pretending not to. Because I first became aware of the ripple effect of adult desire in Richard's company, his body seemed to possess an elemental power that affected everything around it, like weather and light.

One summer, instead of working at the public pool, Richard placed an ad in the *Bel Air News* offering his services as a swimming instructor for children as young as three. My brother's middle name was Gary, and in a brilliant stroke of self-promotion, he billed himself as the Gary Cooper Swim School. The gangly, handsome actor of the same name had recently been nominated for an Academy Award for his role as a Quaker patriarch in the film *Friendly Persuasion*. My parents said that celebrities like Tony Curtis and Paul Newman contacted Richard under the assumption that the swimming school was sanctioned by the star, and when a tanned and enterprising young man arrived for an interview and instantly set the record straight, showing them his Red Cross water-safety certificate and a letter of recommendation from the Hollywood Department of Parks and Recreation, they introduced him to their sons and daughters and hired him anyway.

Everyone in the family began calling him Gary. My mother relished telling people her son had become the "swimming instructor to the stars." Technically, he was the swimming instructor to the *children* of the stars, but I wasn't about to point this out and spoil her pleasure. I spent my Saturdays roaming over famous names engraved in the pink terrazzo of Hollywood Boulevard, and *stars* meant something entirely different to me than to my mother. Stars meant a walkable constellation strewn with crushed cigarette butts and wads of chewing gum. Stars were stepping-stones that led to the novelty shops where I spent my allowance on puddles of rubber vomit and sticks of trick gum that blackened the chewer's tongue and teeth. Stars decorated the pavement onto which lushes staggered from the Frolic Room, rumpled men and women disgusted by the sunlight. But if I took my mother to mean the lights pulsing in the night sky, if I convinced myself for even a second that my brother had instructed *those* stars to swim across the cosmos, then I understood how splendid a claim she was able to make, and why she made it as often as she did.

In no time, Gary had earned enough money for a down payment on a Thunderbird convertible, shiny and green as a cocktail olive. The car made me and my other brothers jealous, and even our mother, who didn't drive, dreamily ran her hand along the dash. It took a lot to stir our father to a state of awe, but that summer, whenever he asked Gary, "How's Tony Curtis doing?" his voice betrayed such wonderment that he might as well have been asking if we'd landed on Mars. Mother never failed to add that Curtis's real name had been Bernie Schwartz—"changed by those movie moguls, just like at Ellis Island."

"Was *our* name ever changed?" I asked.

"Of course," said my father. "We're Americans, aren't we?"

And then he switched to another subject before I could ask him what the name had been. History moved forward in our house, rarely back, and making a point about Bernie Schwartz's origin didn't acknowledge a shared past so much as a shared future: Jews could be admired, Jews could be famous, Jews could be a force.

The few times Gary took me with him to Bel Air have blended together to form a single memory. I can plumb that memory for the faces and handshakes of the famous, but what is salient, what remains, is the narrow, winding hillside roads, the flawless box hedges and empyrean rows of cypress behind which stood houses whose grandeur, though hidden, was everywhere apparent. Sweet with the scent of jasmine, wind blew through our hair as the speeding T-Bird, low to the ground, took hairpin turns as easily as straightaways. Almost close enough to touch, the road glittered with bits of quartz as we sprinted from one address to the next. I was certain I'd entered the daydream my brothers had talked about when standing before the foggy bathroom mirror, but the sky above us was clear, the sky was glassy and factual. "I've made lots of important connections," Gary shouted over the rushing air, "and after I graduate law school, I'm going to join Dad's practice. I've already got the clients, right?" What I said back is lost to me now, but this much I know: the flattery of being taken into his confidence, of being a peer in his sleek two-seater, overshadowed any answer I gave. The drive couldn't have lasted long, yet we seemed to shoot through endless striations of sun and shade, sun and shade, every now and then the city flashing through a break in the foliage, a vista reaching beyond the Santa Monica shoreline and out to the curving rim of the Pacific before it was suddenly shuttered from view, lying in wait at another turn.

What satisfaction it must have given my father to know that he'd raised a commingler, savvy and charismatic. A born go-getter, Gary went and got. Gary was able to make the acquaintance of the famous with little of the self-consciousness about class and religion that haunted our father. My brother's self-assurance wasn't simply a matter of temperament, but a birthright of the indigenous: *I am here and always have been.*

If our father had undertaken a mission to recruit any of us into the legal profession in general, or into his practice in particular, this mission was unspoken. I never got the impression he cared one way or another what I did for a living; just about any profession was fine except for the pipe dreams of painting or writing. As far as I know, each of my brothers arrived at the decision to join the firm without being coaxed or pressured to do so. Our father wasn't the kind of man who easily expressed, or even recognized, his need for approval (need equaled weakness, and weakness undermined a man's author-ity), but he was pleased by his sons' wish to emulate him, and his pleasure, though fleeting, fed their devotion and encouraged them further. Because my brothers' desire to work alongside him predated me, I assumed the inclination was innate, a genetic tendency I didn't share. That is, I didn't share their calling to law, yet each of us was captivated by our father's mercurial moods and fluctuating sense of justice, and together we shared the apprehension that our future was somehow bound to his.

By 1961, all three of my brothers worked at the Spring Street office. The *Herald Examiner*'s coverage of my father's cases had been a boon to his practice, and the waiting room teemed with people. Gary, then twenty-four, and Ron, twenty-six, had graduated from law school at the University of Southern California and, seemingly

overnight, took occupancy of two small offices in my father's newly
renovated suite. Those offices may have looked small only because
they were furnished with identical desks (graduation gifts from our
father) massive enough to take up half the space and confer instant
status on whoever sat behind them.

The roster stenciled on the office door—

Cooper, Cooper & Cooper, Attorneys at Law
& Cooper, Private Investigator

—announced a troop of Coopers who specialized in untying nup-
tial knots as fast as the marriage bureau could tie them. So quickly,
in fact, that marriage seemed like a rocky prelude to the stable, enduring state of divorce. The 1960s would be the last decade in which
the California legal system required attorneys to present evidence of
marital misconduct, and with Dad as their guide, Ron and Gary were
inducted into a fellowship of faultfinders as old as jurisprudence itself.

Despite Gary's social graces and Ron's meticulousness with
detail, our father assumed they'd joined the practice not to contribute their skills, but solely for the benefit of his mentorship, a condition that went into effect the moment they sat at their desks. That
the desks were too big for the rooms was a reminder of our father's
expectations, the foremost being that his every expectation would be
met. Having three grown sons as partners in his law firm served as an
advertisement for his personal magnetism, a public endorsement for
the Solomon-like wisdom with which he settled disputes, that is,
with which he fought to divvy up community property and win vis-
itation rights. As the senior partner and biological top brass, my
father felt free—obliged, in fact—to admonish Ron and Gary for any
strategic weakness they displayed in court, even when the cases were
decided in their favor. This was especially true, Ron once grumbled,
when there were other attorneys within earshot, my father stentorian
while his peers were watching, then mute and brooding when the
audience had gone. Ron and Gary were thought of, and began to
think of themselves, as boys with briefcases, unable to voice an objec-

tion unless they were prepared to suffer through a cold spell of our father's disfavor.

My brothers quietly complained to each other that, because they were thought of as novices, our father assigned them cases where little was at stake. They listened to the myopic squabbling of couples who didn't have "a pot to piss in," as my father described certain clients' financial circumstances, and wasted days on claims so small that the spouses who made them seemed trivial too, misers dividing grains of sand.

The tensions of apprenticeship might have come with any new job, but there was more. No matter how scrupulously they tried to avoid the specifics while talking in my presence, I picked up hints that our father was guilty of some deceit, and that my brothers' revised vision of him threatened to obscure, perhaps forever, the man they thought they knew. Years later I'd learn that, one afternoon, Gary had walked in on our father just as one of the firm's ever-changing array of secretaries, who'd been kneeling between his legs, quickly drew back from his lap and ducked beneath his desk, thinking she hadn't been seen. This alone would have been awkward, but my father quickly rolled his chair to the desk's edge in a halfhearted effort to conceal her. He continued to talk with Gary as if nothing happened, his hands calmly folded atop an ink blotter. "Should I come back at a better time?" Gary stammered. "Now," said my father, "is a better time," meaning that successful indiscretion has neither a before nor after. The whole thing might have been comical had my father not locked Gary in an icy stare, daring him. Meanwhile, the temp huddling beneath the desk was afraid to breathe and give herself away, unaware that a split-second pact had been established and it hardly mattered now if she sneezed or giggled or typed a letter; her presence was not only known but forgotten.

My brothers joked about a number of such incidents with a bravado born of discomfort. *Dictation, pro bono* . . . one double entendre followed another. But humor couldn't ease the responsibility that came with the knowledge of our father's affairs and the pressure to keep them secret from my mother and me. Dad was drawn to womankind, and also to a game of brinksmanship. He flashed his women like stolen jewels. He wanted his sons to be dazzled. He wanted to leave them speechless.

At the time, all three of my brothers were dating women they were crazy about, and it would have been in their best interest not to tell them about our father's infidelities, which might have caused their girlfriends to wonder if straying was a tendency passed from father to son. Had my brothers or their love interests been anything like the hippies who gathered on weekends at nearby Griffith Park to play guitars and dance half naked, infidelity wouldn't have been an issue; they'd have looked upon monogamy as a middle-class hang-up that kept my parents from . . . well, from doing pretty much what they already did: dad practicing "free love" with a kind of communal exuberance, mom transcending her helplessness through a strenuous meditation on housework, the immaculate bathrooms reeking of bleach, the bedsheets spitefully bright. As it was, my brothers and the women they were courting wanted a marriage similar to that of my parents', minus the problems, which wouldn't have left much but the license itself.

The nights my brothers brought girlfriends home to have dinner and meet the family were as nerve-wracking as test flights or dress rehearsals. The clatter of iron skillets and Pyrex casserole dishes, thudding oven and cupboard doors, announced the approaching hour. Judging from the sound alone, my mother could have been remodeling the room instead of cooking dinner in it. She believed that the success of the evening, and therefore the marriages of her sons to their prospective brides, and therefore the happiness of her nonexistent grandkids, hinged entirely on the tenderness of her beef brisket or the firmness of her Jell-O mold. Better to labor under the illusion that it was she who was responsible for the evening's repercussions than to acknowledge that the outcome lay mostly in my father's hands. Not that he made any special effort in the way of preparation—his primary role was to turn on the porch light so the date didn't "break her neck on the steps and slap me with a lawsuit"—but even after knowing how important a certain girl was to one of my brothers, Dad's reaction could go either way.

Despite the number of times he'd heard judges instruct jurors to base their verdict solely on the evidence presented, my father's judgment of the girlfriend in question snapped shut like a bear trap the second they met. When he'd made up his mind to dislike a girl, which happened all too often, given the pressure put on him to like her, he'd welcome her inside and then greet her every remark with a repertoire of gestures that were relatively benign to the uninitiated but signaled, to those in the know, impending rejection:

Rapid blinking = disbelief
Sustained smile = waning patience
Cleaning his nails with the tines of a fork = outright hostility
Napkin origami = boredom
Latinate discussions of the law = disregard

As the evening wore on, he might decide to weigh the evidence—her manner, figure, intelligence, wit—then interpret each aspect of her character according to the opinion he'd formed when she'd first stepped through the door. In this way our father foresaw the future, then brought about the future he foresaw.

However eagerly the rest of us had waited to lay eyes on the girl we'd been hearing so much about, to discover if she matched or contradicted the pictures in our minds, when the doorbell rang we'd dash into the entry hall and turn toward my father as he opened the door, holding our collective breath and assessing him as if *he* were the stranger who'd come to pay a call. How odd it must have been for the nervous girl standing outside, whose back was perhaps being stroked for reassurance by the brother who'd brought her, to look upon the photogenic cluster of us casting sidelong glances at Dad, unable to tear our eyes away till the last brassy notes of the doorbell faded. Of course we welcomed the girl, soaked her up, but all the while we noted every twitch and furrow, every shade of appraisal on Father's face.

Gary's girlfriend, Sharleen, attended UCLA and came preap-
proved with what my father considered a stellar pedigree: her father
directed movies starring the Three Stooges. Since Sharleen had
grown up around movie folk, my father decided to show her his
suave side. He poured her a glass of boysenberry Manischewitz
(thick as pancake syrup) at just the right angle to let the full bouquet
escape, all the while proclaiming her lovely and commending his
son's good taste, for which he was quick to take credit: "Where
could my boy have got it from?" With her glossy blond hair, her
green eyes outlined like Cleopatra's, Sharleen was game for my
father's compliments and quick to return his banter. Versed in flirta-
tion, leggy and bold in her miniskirt, she knew the precise amount
of surprise with which to register his suggestive remarks—"They
didn't make young women like you in *my* day. It was probably
against the law!"—both playful enough to scold him and stern
enough to draw the line. In the meantime, Gary, knowing what he
did about the goings-on at the office, must have detested every
mock-coy minute, yet I saw him brighten and start to enjoy himself
the moment dad had said "my boy." The encounter with Sharleen
left our father happily flushed, as if she'd raced him a couple of
laps—and let him win.

You can't imagine our relief once those evenings got off to a
good start. There existed a mysterious aspect of my father's charm
that was difficult for those affected by it to explain, for unlike charm
in its common incarnations, my father's didn't promise you fondness
so much as it promised to spare you from the trouble he'd cause if
you dared to give him grief. He used his charm to protect you from
himself, which was, in the end, an act of kindness.

I'm sure Ron's girlfriend, Nancy, was nervous on her first visit to
our house, yet she seemed to take the evening in stride, relaxed while
walking the get-to-know-you gauntlet. She assessed us while we
assessed her. Nancy, it gradually became clear, could be quick with
her laughter and opinions, but more often than not she listened
intently and her face went still. She followed conversations without
a lot of nods or "uh-huh's," those signposts that let the speaker know

he's in the lead and being agreed with. Her reserve bothered my father, and instead of taking it as patience, he took it as her groundless resistance to his hospitality. He liked ingratiation in his women, and it was clear that his usual means of making an impression—the dapper flirt, the attorney whose cases were covered in the *Herald*— were not about to work with Nancy. The last straw was her failure to sustain appreciative laughter at the jokes he told during dinner, and though she threw her head back and smiled, mere bemusement didn't make the grade. Nancy possessed a student's seriousness and curiosity; she was earning a degree in Jewish education. Her fluency in Hebrew and familiarity with Talmudic scholarship was a reminder of the Jewishness my father held on to with one hand and batted away with the other. This, along with her jet-black hair, her dark eyes gleaming with thoughts held back, must have intensified his impression of her supposed antipathy. Certain from the start that she'd judged him harshly, he never cared to draw her out.

Bob had been dating a woman named Grace, whose fleshy arms and loose dresses made her seem as soft as bread. Her hair was tied back in a limp ponytail. She wore no makeup and smelled of soap. When Bob offered her a drink, she settled for a glass of water instead of wine. Her name and modest appearance led me to believe that she'd rejected worldly things for the sake of some religious principal. Bob treated Grace with care verging on caution, gallantly assisting her when she sat or stood, refilling her glass before she had to ask. She moved with a sleepy tranquillity that made me want to whisper in her presence and protect her contentment.

Regardless of Grace's almost contagious calm, her visit to our house agitated my mother, who boiled an unusually perfunctory meal of chicken and potatoes and initiated several long pauses during dinner while joylessly chewing her food. Every bland bite was a lesson to us all. My father also seemed to hold a grudge. He hardly bothered with the standard rush to judgment. He let Mother do the disparaging. He sat back in his chair, a passenger.

"Why don't you like her?" I asked my mother later that night. "I think she's nice."

"Yes," said my mother, drowning a stack of dishes in the sink, "she's very maternal, isn't she? Naturally a child would be drawn to her." I was so insulted by being called a child that it didn't occur to me that my mother was telling me—which is to say, telling me without telling me—that Grace was pregnant. Family rumor had it that my father, believing the child wasn't Bob's, paid Grace a handsome sum to stay away. True or not, she stopped seeing my brother abruptly and never gave him a reason why. Bob must have been mystified to think that love and not animosity had brought his loneliness about, as if the two emotions were interchangeable, different routes to the same sorry state.

When first Gary, and then Ron, hinted at the possibility of leaving the firm, our father suspected Sharleen and Nancy of conspiring to incite mutiny. The idea that his sons were manipulated by their wives was easier to take than the possibility that they'd arrived at the decision on their own. It was easier to blame the supposed machinations of ambitious women than it was to admit how much he didn't want his sons to go. Then Bob considered leaving, too. Never one to grovel, Dad aimed for groveling's opposite: the pretense that he couldn't have cared less. He said there were plenty of young men fresh out of law school who'd give an arm and a leg to have what his boys were throwing away. "Go ahead and leave," he told them. "See how long you last."

The brief history of my brothers' apprenticeship at the Spring Street office is best summed up in the changes that took place on the frosted glass door, the gold letters stenciled on and then scraped away by the Continental Building's maintenance man:

Cooper
Cooper & Cooper
Cooper, Cooper & Cooper
Cooper, Cooper, Cooper & Cooper
Cooper, Cooper & Cooper
Cooper & Cooper
Cooper

I came to consider this a poem of sorts, an elegy entitled "Cooper & Sons." It may not have rivaled the couplets my father composed for *The Case of the Captive Bride,* but it carried as direct a message, and he was just as much its author.

My father came home later and later, less and less. Every morning he left my mother's allowance on the kitchen counter. How else, but by letting herself be placated, was she to have money? She didn't drive, didn't possess the skills to earn an income. Her dependence— she knew it pressed upon her husband, that it nagged him as much as it did her—was a weapon as surely as Bob's Smith & Wesson.

When Bob had lived at home, he never would have believed that those mornings he'd spent grooming himself in front of the bathroom mirror with Ron and Gary would one day be replaced by the fear of his own reflection. Fear was there before he awoke in his bed at the Emerald Arms. He could hardly bring himself to leave the warm sheets, sheets that preserved him like a leaf between the pages of a book. He could hardly bring himself to walk across the cold floor when he knew what he'd see in his bathroom mirror: bruises from blows so soft and common he couldn't recall what caused them. Knocking on a door, bumping his knee on a table—these were enough to change him, to discolor his skin with the purples and yellows of rotting fruit. Blood seeped from his gums for hours after he brushed his teeth. It tinted the water and sluiced through pipes, washing out to sea. The sea became clouds. The clouds became rain. The rain, inescapable, pelted his roof.

My parents didn't tell me he'd been diagnosed with Hodgkin's disease until the day his Pontiac, loaded with his possessions, pulled into our driveway. The sight of it stung, but I didn't ask questions; by then I knew my parents' tactics: mother believed it was best to wait until the last minute to break bad news, postponing the shock, whereas father believed that by never breaking news of any kind, shock was prevented altogether. Ron and Gary had moved away from home, and since Bob had been the first to strike out on his own, his return was especially portentous, as if forces were at work to draw matter backward, and the work had just begun.

Bob reclaimed his old room. Placed books and blankets exactly where they'd been. Took the same seat at the dining table. Made his furtive entrances and exits. Yet he went about life at an eerie remove, as if he'd recalled his habits but not their motivations.

Round after round of radiation hollowed him out, left him stunned by his cells' rebellion. During his decline, gravity exerted a stronger pull inside our house than out. As a countermeasure, my parents discussed, in buoyant voices loud enough for Bob to over-hear, rumors about miraculous remissions, experimental treatments in clinics across the Mexican border, a promising new drug made from ground apricot pits (an early version of Laetrile) that would be available any day now, any day. Bob would have none of it. He was done with hope long before the rest of us. Always a quiet boy, his silences widened, a gulf empty of everything, even disbelief. The animal peering out from his eyes knew only a dull and faithful wait-ing. His uncommon stealth, his gift for moving unseen through city streets, dwindled into mere invisibility. He kept to his bedroom. Sleep, a great labor, was accomplished in fits and starts, unrelated to the earth's rotations and beyond the logic of clocks. His black hair grew sparse, exposing the shiny pallor of his scalp. Papery from radi-ation, particles of dry skin drifted to the floor when he scratched his arms and legs. I'd sit cross-legged on the white carpet, answering his questions about what had happened that day at my elementary school or in the neighborhood, and he'd prop his head on the pil-low, listening with a dim but wistful interest.

"Maybe it's better," he once said out of the blue, "that Grace isn't around to see me like this."

"Like what?" I said, knowing perfectly well.

"Do you know why she broke up with me?"

"No. Why?"

"I don't know either. I've gone over it a hundred times. There's too many pieces missing, too much that won't add up. I'm a detec-tive and I should be able to figure out this kind of thing in my sleep. I was ready to . . . I would have done anything for her. Now, every time I think about her I hate her more. I hope bad things happen to her. Not like this," he said, looking down at his body beneath the blanket, "but bad."

That's when I got it in my head that Bob was dying of love, and that this phrase, which I'd heard on the soap operas my mother watched, wasn't the dramatic exaggeration I'd thought but a diagnosis as dire as Hodgkin's.

In the end, the stories I reported to Bob during those afternoons in his room, the adolescent pranks, the feuds and flirtations among our neighbors, concerned people who were privileged with good health, people free to yearn for, or dread, or simply expect consequences. Telling my brother about a single day had the unintended effect of suggesting that days would eventually pass in his absence, one after another, until no story, however rich with incident or filigreed with gossip, could do justice to their sum. If talk reached too far into the future, Bob would swiftly yield to fatigue—a privilege of the sick—and close his eyes to convince us both he'd fallen asleep. Rising from the floor to leave, I'd sometimes find shed bits of his skin clinging to my palms, as pale and weightless as flecks of ash. I began to examine my hands again and again to see if I held him without knowing it, if some measure of his flesh was mine. I'd brace myself and watch my fists unfurl. A fortune foretold. A prognosis. Afraid of contagion, I avoided touching the carpet with my bare hands, even decades later when I watched my father search through it for a key.

The rift between my parents widened with Bob's illness. I recall them engaging in only one civil discussion during that period. A truce had been called long enough for them to slump on opposite ends of the couch like two weary travelers waiting for a train, exhaustion all they had in common. They didn't look at each other as they spoke but stared into the middle distance, considering what to rename their son. Changing a person's name, according to Yiddish lore, is a way to change that person's fate. They were seeking a name as different from Robert as language would allow. Nor could they choose the name of someone they knew or had ever known. It had to be a fresh appellation, stripped of both good and bad associations. My parents didn't put much stock in superstitions held over from the Old World, but neither were they so removed from the Old World that they could ignore a chance to waylay fate. They tested names aloud, as though for a newborn—Benjamin, Paul, Andrew, Carl—to hear how the sound of it fared in the world. Hadn't this tactic worked for Gary? For Tony Curtis?

Any name would have been too late. One day, blood began seeping from the corner of Bob's mouth. My parents called an ambulance and went with him to the hospital, thinking it best to leave me behind. When the double doors slammed shut, I could see my mother and father and the attending paramedic through the small rear window as the ambulance sped away.

Gary phoned me at home later that day—he'd joined my parents at the hospital—to tell me Bob was dead, explaining that our mother and father were too distraught to tell me themselves. His voice was steely to the point of dispassion. And yet, once we hung up, what reverberated wasn't only what he'd said, but the keening he'd swallowed in order to speak.

A decade later, the same steeliness braced Gary's voice when he told me he'd been diagnosed with colon cancer. He had just turned thirty-four, and the luck that lasted since the day he went by another name had started to change. Illness didn't fit the life that he and Sharleen had made for themselves. Didn't fit his new law firm, the glass house in Encino, the walk-in closet full of Nehru suits and op-art dresses, the heated swimming pool that steamed like a bowl of blue soup when the valley nights were cool.

By the time Gary received a second medical opinion, which confirmed the first, I felt myself giving in to numbness, which brought with it a perverse sort of conviction, a sustenance very close to hope. Bob's death had left me suspicious of remission—a promise that never materialized—and yet I somehow convinced myself that this steeliness of Gary's would be the very thing that spared him, that he would defy cancer not by recovering from it, but by continuing to outlive the disease until his diagnosis was false, a rumor time would disprove. I'd witnessed Bob's decline in close quarters, seeing

his body surrender and rally with dispiriting regularity, and the geographical distance between Gary and me—even one drivable by
freeway—made his illness easier to disbelieve. Except when I went
to visit.

One afternoon toward the end of summer, Gary and I were sitting together at the edge of his pool, dangling our legs in the water.
He wore a loose T-shirt and shorts, and I saw that the once-robust
muscles of his thighs had grown thin. Beneath the water, his skin
turned blue-white, and as he lazily stirred his legs, bands of tendon
shifted along the length of his calves. Each hair and pore, each clinging bubble of trapped air, was magnified by the water and articulated
with a terrible clarity. Gary also seemed to be looking at his legs, but
he bent forward, reached out, and, as I'd seen him do many times
before, dipped his hand into the pool and scooped a flailing bee from
the surface, water dripping through the sieve of his fingers. He pivoted to one side and tipped his hand so the insect would tumble off
his palm and onto the flagstone, where it could dry off and, if it
revived, fly away. He used to do this to keep the children to whom
he gave swimming lessons from accidentally getting stung, and it had
become an unthinking mercy as well as a sport whose challenge was
to save the insect from drowning and himself from pain. Watching
him do it always made my stomach drop because it was hard to tell
if the bee was dead or merely stunned, whether it had spent its
stinger in the struggle to escape from the heavy, clinging surface of
the pool or was so agitated that it would sting at the least provoca-
tion. In a mock-mystical tone, Gary would always tell me, as he held
the bee aloft and treaded through waist-high water toward the pool's
edge, that he could think a bee into submission by aiming a ray of
his psychic power. This time though, the usual remark about mind
over matter wasn't forthcoming, and the bee in his palm began to
stir. But that's not what caused me to catch my breath. When Gary
had leaned to the side, his T-shirt rode a few inches above the waistband of his shorts, revealing a plastic pouch, a small pillowy reser-
voir the likes of which I'd never seen before and whose purpose I
couldn't place. A tube entered a hole in my brother's body that sur-

gical tape and gauze hadn't entirely covered, a tear so raw and red and unexpected that, instead of having been implanted, the tube could have pierced his flesh just then. No sooner had I seen this than he let out a yelp as loud and helpless as any I'd ever heard from him—pain emanating, I thought, from this fresh wound. All at once blood banged in my ears and stars blazed and skidded through my field of vision until he lurched back, swearing and clutching his hand, and the laws of cause and effect resumed.

The sliding glass door behind us rumbled open and Sharleen peered out to see what had happened, wary, I was sure, that one more intolerable surprise awaited her, one more degradation of the body she made no mystery of desiring, once confiding in me that Gary was the sexiest man she'd ever known, adding how good it felt to want someone that much, and how lucky I was to have that hunger in store for me. Now, standing behind the screen door, she appeared more fragile than the last time I'd seen her. Every failed treatment took its toll on her as well as Gary, as if she too had undergone invasive tests and experimental therapies, which in a sense she had.

Gary must have seen the shock on my face, because after that day we began having uncharacteristically long conversations, the topic of which was often our father. That's when he told me about walking in on Dad and his secretary, and how our father believed that Grace would ruin Bob's life unless he took drastic measures. "Ruin his life," Gary repeated, too tired for irony. "You can forgive Dad all you want, but after a while, you realize he respects you more when you hold things against him. He wants a sparring partner."

When Gary died, I prodded everyone for details, especially Sharleen, hoping not to appear morbid, but driven to risk rudeness just the same. The moment of Bob's death had never been discussed, and so it was a blur in my imagination, the missing passage of a text. I couldn't have articulated this at the time, but I was asking for a story whose particulars could continue to be lived through.

Gary and Sharleen had been watching the late-night news, and after remarking on the stupidity of a used car commercial, my brother gave the finger to their TV, downed a couple of pills, and kissed his wife. He found, after a few labored adjustments, a position comfortable enough to carry him through the night. Sometime toward morning, Sharleen dreaming beside him, he stepped beyond the threshold of sleep and entered the boundless end of sensation.

However brief, however reconstructed or secondhand, I was glad to have a story in which Gary was present till the very end; the story withstood what happened next. Less than a month after Gary's funeral, my father showed up unexpectedly at the house in Encino, asking if he could visit. Sharleen offered him a chair in the living room and went into the kitchen to get them something to eat, but he wasn't sitting there when she returned. She assumed he was in the bathroom, and so she set down the tray and waited. My father wasn't the type to show up unannounced and Sharleen was certain that grief had brought him there on a sentimental impulse. He was a difficult man, she thought—all the lingering ill will about Gary leaving the practice—but that was a while back, and what was the point to grief unless patience or concern or some other human virtue could occupy the emptiness? She never thought she'd be a young widow sitting alone in her living room wondering such things, and she felt the unstoppable welling up that came upon her in those days at the drop of a hat. She wiped her eyes on a napkin, glad my father hadn't walked in when her eyes were wet, afraid the sight of her crying might have set him off, too. She remembered him afflicted by violent sobs at the funeral, the storm of it silencing those who, until they heard him wail, only mistook themselves for mourners. Sharleen began to worry when she realized he'd been gone for a long time. She got up and walked down the hall toward the bedroom. The closer she came, the more clearly she heard a dull tapping through the walls, as urgent and otherworldly as a table knocking at a seance. The sound grew louder as she entered the bedroom.

The door to their walk-in closet was open, and inside, with his back to Sharleen, stood my father. He briefly inspected one of Gary's shirts before sweeping it aside. The wooden hanger tapped against the wall in an almost code. One shirt, another. His brisk efficiency suggested that he had a plan. He checked each tag for the shirt size, sometimes thrusting his arm into the garment as if to wrench it inside out. Unable to move, Sharleen watched him go for her coats and search inside the pockets.

She heard herself say, "Stop it."

He neither turned around nor stopped.

She tried again. "What are you looking for?"

"You know what I'm looking for."

"I wish I did," she said. "You're scaring me."

"I'm looking for the new man in your life."

"What?"

"I know you've been seeing another man."

"Ed. That's crazy."

"I'm not crazy."

"Stop this or I'm calling the police."

"By the time they come, I'll have proof."

"So what? What if I *was* seeing a man?"

My father turned. His hands were shaking. "It's too soon."

"I'm lonely." She said this not as an admission, but because the truth of it hit her just then, stark and remarkable.

She stepped back as my father barreled past her. "I'm lonely," he echoed, and she couldn't be sure whether this was blurted in mockery or commiseration. He raced out of the house, left the front door open. She watched to make sure he'd driven away, then shut the door and locked it.

Ron and I must have talked about our father's surprise visit to Encino a dozen times since Sharleen told us about it. Each time, Dad became less culpable because we considered his grief—now as incendiary as his temper—a mitigating circumstance. We weren't necessarily dutiful sons, at least not by our father's standards, but we were saddened by what was happening to our family and hesitant to add more reasons for mistrust than we absolutely had to. If we knew anything, Ron and I, we knew that our father's losses had started to deform him; we felt its deforming pressure in ourselves. Dad began to settle ever more deeply into silence, a silence breached infrequently, and only by explosion. Over the next several years, Ron and I were allied first and foremost by the puzzle of how to love such a man.

Sometimes, when contemplating the possibility of my father's death, I'd ask Brian if he thought, when the time came, I'd be inundated by all the unresolved emotions my father and I had accumulated over the years. He'd think for a moment and say, "No. Not necessarily. It might be a relief." Then, when I asked him if he thought my father's death might be a relief from all the unresolved emotions we'd accumulated over the years, he'd say, "No. Not necessarily. It might dredge them up." And so, the night Brian and I returned home to a message from Nancy on our answering machine, asking me, in a small anguished voice, to call her the moment I got back, I told Brian I was sure my father had died, and whatever was coming was going to be hard.

It fell to me to tell my father, but not before contacting my father's doctor, who warned me that high blood pressure made Dad's health precarious enough that he should be told of Ron's death while under sedation. And so, on the implausible pretext (I was too distraught to think of anything better) that the doctor, unable to reach my father by phone, had contacted me and insisted I bring him in for a checkup, I drove by the old house in Hollywood and picked him up. During our drive to the medical center, I couldn't stop wondering what it must have been like for Nancy to find Ron wide-eyed and lifeless at the top of the stairs, or whether my brother felt the last bright fragment of consciousness dislodge as his heart seized and he plunged toward the floor. It was all I could do to keep my mind on the road and my grief hidden behind a scrim of small talk. That my father failed to notice my distress or question our mission was a testament either to my acting ability or to what had become for him, at the age of eighty-three, an obliviousness both self-protective and involuntary.

The doctor met us in the waiting room before we'd had a chance to sit down. If initially gladdened by the special attention, Dad was a little surprised when we breezed right past the receptionist and the people looking up from their magazines. We were ushered into an examination room, where, without so much as having to be asked, he clambered onto the padded table, an unwrinkled length of fresh paper crackling beneath him. He blithely offered his arm for the stethoscope and the blood pressure cuff—"Whaddaya hear, Doc? Is there an echo?"—and then for a hypodermic, which the doctor sank, with practiced alacrity, deep into the waiting vein. Not until the plunger had been fully depressed did my father ask what drug he'd been given or what all the fuss was about. Instead of answering, the doctor dabbed at the ruby bead of blood and instructed his patient to hold the cotton ball firmly in place. Then he spun on his heel, giving me a solemn nod as he left the room. My father finally registered a fateful irregularity in the normal course of things. Fear seized his expression for a few seconds before it let go. His shoulders slowly lowered, the gauze of Valium softening his eyes, his pupils opening their black apertures to the point where I thought I could see myself inside them, speaking in the dark. "What!" he yelped, when I told him the news. "What the hell are you saying?" He drew back his arm tried to strike me. The punch missed by inches. He overshot his center of gravity, his fist continuing to sail past my cheek, my ear, the momentum almost causing him to topple over. I had to steady him atop the table, but he bristled meekly, wouldn't let himself be righted without a fight. He wanted, I think, to look at me, to look *into* me, and gauge the truth of what I'd said, but the sedative made it hard for him to focus, and so his rage was strangely familiar: feral, diffuse, alarming, useless.

I took down Mr. Delaney's number and told him I'd see what I could do about my father's overdue phone bill. After we hung up, I got to thinking how, late in the course of family life, the child is often called upon to assume the role of parent, and the parent, due to age or illness, often reverts to the role of child. So common is this reversal, I figured, that even a man as stubborn as my father, as proudly self-sufficient, would open his hands when hardship befell him and accept what his son was able to offer. He didn't have to accept it happily or with gratitude. What mattered was that he'd stay out of debt.

The time had come for me to father my father. The aphoristic chug of this phrase—father my father—gathered steam. I'd simply call Dad up and tell him, as nonchalantly as possible, that I'd pay the bill myself, and that way his phone wouldn't be disconnected. Getting him to go along with the idea might, I realized, require a little coaxing, but sooner or later he'd hand me the baton of responsibility. Never mind that I had plenty of evidence to suggest that he'd hang on to that baton for dear life—*A son doesn't help his father up*—I was intent on repaying a kindness to the man who'd inspired me (in the Greek sense of *breathed life into*) to write about him. Over the years, I've checked and rechecked my motives for coming to his rescue, searching for any traces of self-righteousness on my part, and you'll just have to take my word for it when I say that my motives were absolutely pure. Except, perhaps, for a smudge of martyrdom. A tiny speck of ascendancy. A trapped bubble of unacknowledged guilt. In any case, my sense of parental duty was magnified by the fact that I didn't have children and was frankly pleased with myself for being a person who knows he isn't inclined toward parenthood and therefore doesn't have kids, as opposed to being a person who knows he isn't inclined toward parenthood and propagates anyway. Fathering my father was propagation enough.

"Dad?"

"Hello there!"

"Am I disturbing you?"

"Not at all. I had to get up to answer the phone."

"Very funny."

"It's laugh or cry, boychick."

Thankfully, I'd caught him in a good humor. "There's something we should talk about."

"It's your dime."

"The regional supervisor from the phone company called me today and—"

"What!"

"Some guy from the phone company called me today and—"

"What the hell business is it of yours?"

"Calm down. He called *me*."

"What'd you tell that SOB?"

"I didn't tell him anything. I listened."

"You think *I* didn't listen? I listened plenty. It's a good thing I'm not allergic to bullshit; if I was, he'd of killed me."

"Well, how about if I just go ahead and pay for—"

"Pay for calls I didn't make? Don't be an idiot."

"Technically, the calls were made from your phone, so—"

"Let me ask you something. If you borrowed my Caddy and wrecked it, who should pay the damages, you or me?"

"That example isn't—"

"You?" he shouted. "Or me?"

"This is a totally different situation."

"You should have to pay, is who!"

"I'm trying to help you!"

"If I want your help, I'll ask for it."

"I'm not so sure you would. That's why I'm volunteering."

My father fell silent, proving you can't volunteer in a vacuum.

I took a breath and began again. I'd help him whether he liked it or not. Come hell or high water. "I'm pretty sure Betty made the calls to Texas. One day when I was over at the house she was watching a faith healer from Texas on TV."

"She's a very religious person. I've met plenty of pious people in my time and they may seem like nuts to the rest of us but they're not *shysters*. It goes against her religion to lie and steal." It gave me a start when I heard a woman's voice in the background, but it must have been the television; he wouldn't implicate Betty if she was standing right there.

"Did you ask her about the calls to Texas?"

"I don't have to ask her nothing. It's my phone and she's free to use it whenever she wants. She's not a prisoner. She's here of her own free will."

"I'm glad she's there. I'm glad she's doing whatever it is she does for you. But you're late on your phone bill."

"What's that supposed to mean?"

"It means you haven't paid on time."

"I know what *late* means, for Christ's sake. That thing you said before. *Do whatever she does for me.*"

"Cook. Shop. Make sure you take your medications. Help you up the stairs."

"What's wrong with her helping me up the stairs?" The stairs led to the bedroom, which led to the bed, on which was heaped insinuation.

"Nothing's wrong with it. She's your nurse. I'm glad she's your nurse."

"Is that sarcasm?"

"I don't . . . I didn't . . ." Here's where logic began to bend. Anything was possible. "Did it sound like sarcasm?"

"If you have to ask, it's sarcasm."

Spoken in my father's voice, any random statement, any empty maxim—*A frozen steak never fed the hungry; good is the bird who stifles its chirp*—could bear down on me with the weight of unassailable truth.

"I didn't mean to be sarcastic."

"About what?" The voice belonged to Betty. My father had put her on the phone. Probably thrust it into her hand. Years of disinformation when it came to his women, and now this.

"Betty! Hello!"

"Yelling is bad for your father's blood pressure."

"Yes. I wish he'd calm—"

"Try not to yell at him. He's a good man, your dad. Not the best patient in the world," she said loudly enough for him to hear, "but you'll be glad to know I'm doing all I can to watch out for him. In this life and after."

"That's very above and beyond the call of duty of you to do. His 'after,' though, isn't what needs watching out for so much as his, you know, toe." I grew even more flustered when I heard myself speak.

I wanted to make sure Betty wasn't proselytizing my father by acting as his travel agent for the afterlife, yet I also wanted her to like
me, especially if I was destined to wake up one morning and discover that she was my stepmother.

"Don't you worry," she assured me. "I make him stay put. He's
been resting his feet and doing some serious thinking. That'll happen to a man when he's incapacitated. Each of us has only so much
time to get right with the Lord."

"I respect your religious beliefs," I said uncertainly. "But you
believe in medicine, too, don't you?"

"Of course I believe in medicine," she said. "I wouldn't wear
these awful white shoes unless I had to!" Her laughter was brief but
tonic, and I understood how my father would take pleasure in its
sound, would hope to provoke it. "I'm one step ahead of Dr. Graham when it comes to your father's welfare. Just last week I asked
the doctor why Ed—I mean, your father—wasn't getting any better. After all, I watch him like a hawk. Got him to throw away the
saltshaker and go with low-fat foods. He's lost twelve pounds."

"Water weight," my father shouted in the background.

"Thanks to me, he's been drinking eight glasses a day for—
what's it been?—two months? Three? I feel so comfortable here I've
lost track of time. But the uric acid should have been flushed out of
his system by now. Your father relieves himself ten times a day."

"Twenty!" Dad corrected.

"So I said to doctor Graham, 'Could you cross-check Mr.
Cooper's medicines? Something isn't right.' You can't be too careful, Bernard. I don't need to tell who gets blamed when the patient
under a nurse's care doesn't jump right up like Lazarus."

I pictured the chicken.

"That kind of healing is done by a greater power than me or any
other medical professional and it's plain vanity to think any different. You'd be surprised how many doctors take credit for successful
treatments, but if the treatment isn't doing what it's supposed to, they
pin it on the nearest nurse, or on some poor orderly, or worse, on
the patient. So I get Dr. Graham to look up the side effects of

hydrochlorothiazide in his *Physicians' Desk Reference* and he gets this funny look on his face and excuses himself to consult with another doctor in the office. He was gone an awfully long time. Left your father sitting on the examination table in a paper gown."

"That was no gown," said my father. "That was a goddamn napkin."

"Well, Dr. Graham comes back and tells us that medicines with *zide* at the end of them *raise* the levels of uric acid! Not lower, raise! The medication forces the pancreas to produce uric acid even when the Indomethacin works to get rid of it. Your father's pancreas has been fighting itself this whole time! God knows, I made him take his pills, for all the good it did him. But the acid was turning to crystals in his bloodstream. Can you imagine having sharp little crystals in you?"

"Hurt like hell is what it felt like!"

"The blood wasn't cleansed and, oh, did your dad ever suffer." She was talking on the wall phone in my father's kitchen and her voice resounded off the tile walls. Betty had adopted Benny Hinn's calmly oracular manner; her voice never sped up or ascended to a higher register, yet it teetered on the edge of revelation. "Lord knows we're all flawed merchandise, stubborn and wrongheaded down to a man. Here's where mercy enters the picture. Why waste a single one of us, is how I believe He thinks. If He brings us low He has His reasons. Now, I'm not supposing I know exactly what's on His mind, but it's my personal belief that your father came down with gout so the two of us could meet."

"Is he off the hydro-whatever?"

"I got him off it right away. Of course, they've had to put him on several other meds to cancel out the meds they put him on before. Don't get me wrong, I've had to care for too many sick Christian Scientists in my time to be antimedication, but you can't just throw pills at an illness. Your poor father didn't fully appreciate his toe until he couldn't take a single step or stand up on his own without agony. Multiply that agony by a couple of months and I think you'll agree that he has every reason to sue."

"Sue?" I leaned against the wall. "But he's getting better, right?"

"No thanks to Dr. Graham."

"Maybe it's not Dr. Graham's fault. Maybe—I don't know—the side effects weren't listed on the bottle."

She repeated this to my father.

"I'll sue the pill people too."

"Betty, is this the right time for my father to alienate his physician? He's been Dr. Graham's patient for ages. Even if Dr. Graham misjudged the prescription, it's going to be difficult if not impossible to prove negligence. Does my father have the energy for a long, involved lawsuit?" Wait a minute, I said to myself, suing *gives* him energy.

"Don't worry," said Betty. "I won't let him do anything that isn't in his own interest."

Let him? Interest? Were my father and Betty hatching a plan to make some extra income from his gout, drawing each other into a ruinous lawsuit? Or were they simply two litigants in love, corroborating an allegation, traveling hand in hand down the road to restitution? In either case, Dad considered this woman—nurse or lover, it didn't matter—a worthy accomplice. Like my father, Betty possessed a certain elasticity in her outlook, which stretched from science to prophecy, from bald self-interest to round-the-clock care. When it came to contradictions, the two of them were as limber as gymnasts.

"You honor your father, don't you?"

I didn't like the sound of that question. Get ready, I said to myself, he's going to sue the universe. "It depends on what you mean by *honor.*"

"What'd he say?" asked my father.

"He said, 'It depends.'"

"Betty, please! I'm telling you these things in confidence. You have no idea what my father and I have been through. Our relationship is complicated. I love him in my own way, and vice versa."

"He loves you, he says, and vice versa."

My father shouted, "What's the vice versa?" He sounded hurt. Shocked on top of it. His hearing aid squealed.

"Put him on the phone, Betty."

"What's the vice versa?" he asked again.

"It's that I love you in *my* own way and you love me in *your* own way."

"Oh. I thought it was . . ." His voice trailed off.

"You thought it was what?"

"Hate." He expelled the word like a cough.

"Dad! I don't hate you."

"You never know," he said. "Worse things have happened."

"Worse things have, but I don't."

"You get checkups?"

I was taken aback. "Yes."

"And you don't have the AIDS?"

I'd taken the test a year ago and waited an endless week for the results, frightened for myself and for Brian, for the friends I'd lost and might lose still. I was about to tell my father I'd tested negative when I heard a clatter on the other end of the line. Then Betty said, "I guess he went to take a nap. Ed?" she called after him. "Ed?" Then into the mouthpiece, "I should probably go. I don't want him climbing those stairs by himself."

My father had sobbed for each of my brothers, sobbed raggedly, a cataract, his face clenched as tightly as a fist. Beyond shame or consolation, he wailed into the empty air, *It should have been me,* until weeping had siphoned the life from his eyes, the dazed figure sagging in a chair as close as a man had ever come to perishing in place of his son. And now, finding myself on the phone with Betty, beyond shame or consolation myself, I envied my brothers their unenviable deaths—a final sibling rivalry—for death would have been the only way to solicit an emotion from my father as abiding as his grief.

Then again, with three sons dead, what was left within him to solicit? What reserves of emotion remained? That he'd had to hand the phone to Betty, that he'd had to walk away without a word, was a measure not of callousness but love—brusque and evasive, too difficult for him to bear for long, but love nonetheless. He'd rather his question go unanswered than be met with bad news.

"Don't hang up yet," I said to Betty, trying to compose myself. "I wanted to ask you about some phone calls."

"Oh Lord," she sighed. "You know about them. Why on earth would Anna call and ask for her things back after all this time?"

"Anna?"

"Your father told me to tell her that possession is nine-tenths of the law. She didn't like that one bit! Another time I told her to let bygones be bygones. Did you know she threatened your father with a knife?"

"I read it in the . . . yes. But it's not Anna's calls I'm talking about, Betty. I'm talking about calls to Texas. To the Benny Hinn Ministries."

Betty brightened. "Your father calls the prayer line every morning."

"No. Uh-uh. I don't care if he's saying Hail Marys . . ."

"That's Catholic."

"Betty, my father may not go to temple or wear a yarmulke, he may not even be religious, but he's Jewish to the core, and no ministry is going to change that. Believe me, if he's calling a prayer line, he's only doing it to please you."

"How sweet!"

"Yes," I said. "He's a sweet old Jew."

"Well, I think it's wonderful that he's so open-minded at his age. It can't hurt him to learn about Jesus. Jesus the man, I mean. It's an interesting part of history. An inspiring way to start the day."

"It's costing, though, Betty, and he hasn't been paying his phone bill. I had a long talk with a man named Delaney from Pacific Bell, and they're not going to let it slide forever. They're going to disconnect his phone."

She mulled this over. "I'm surprised to hear that because your father just gave me a generous raise."

I steeled myself, about to ask if she would have a talk with him about the bills. "Maybe you could . . ."

"I will," she said resolutely. "And you pray too."

*Our Father of non sequiturs, of reductio ad absurdum and quid pro quo. Our Father for eternity, ipso facto.*

And then Betty told me she'd pay for the calls to Texas with the money from her raise—"It's almost like filling Reverend Benny's coffers"—and have a talk with my father. My gratitude was lavish; I not only wanted to thank her in the present but recruit her for my future thanks.

"Oh, now," she said, happily abashed.

Betty was keeping my father in check, not helping him plot a frivolous lawsuit. I was sorry for having doubted her. All this time I'd been blind to the auspicious possibility that Betty might love and nurse him both. Far be it from me to limit the definition of love. Or of round-the-clock care. How little faith I sometimes had in people, in their adaptable, inventive connections. Betty, I was coming to believe, had enough faith for all three of us. She was ready and willing to pick up our theological slack. What difference did it make if his prayers were vicarious, or directed toward the goyims' God? They'd been answered with companionship and improving health. Come to think of it, my prayers had been answered, too; the matter of the bill had been resolved. I'd done a good deed, or at least instigated it, without having to spend (though I would have if I'd had to) one red cent.

"Soon," Betty assured me, "he'll walk without crutches. Things are about to change," she said. "Just wait and see."

I had to wait only ten minutes. "Listen," hissed my father when I answered the phone. I'd been filling my briefcase with books and notes for an afternoon lecture on the poet Elizabeth Bishop. "My bills are my business. Not Betty's. Not yours. I'll pay when I'm good and ready. You can't seem to grasp the fact that I have reasons for doing things the way I do them. It's not your place to understand or not understand. It's not your place to question me." His voice rushed like wind through a cavern. "No one can make me do what I refuse to do. No one can twist my arm. That's the point I've been trying to make to you your whole life, but you don't hear so good, I guess.

"Who should an old man like me depend on? You? With the money you make? You live in a dream world. You may be a teacher, but you're still in school, is the way I see it. Betty? Everything to her is God's will, good or bad. I'm not ready to give my will away; I might need it someday, and I don't think God's going to care if I keep it. All's I do is sit there and listen to the prayer line while she makes me breakfast. What else do I have to occupy my mornings? I'm getting saved all right—saved from having to think of things to talk to her about. We don't have much in common, in case you haven't guessed. But that's fine by me 'cause I don't need to have things in common with people. Not like I used to. What I need is a little peace. A little peace is all I'm after. If I wasn't listening to 'the Lord sayeth this and the Lord sayeth that,' I'd be walking around the house wondering, What if? What if now's when I fall down the stairs? What if the numbness in my arm isn't nothing? What if these pills are killing me? I'm supposed to rely on a doctor who makes me his lab rat, pumps me so full of drugs I don't know whether I'm coming or going? Graham's sixty if he's a day, and putting my life in the hands of another old man doesn't exactly—how do you call it?—inspire confidence. Me, myself, and I, that's who a person can depend on in the end. Someday you'll understand what I'm saying. You'll look around and shout, 'Hello?' and your own voice will echo back. The sooner you get that through your head, the better."

"How crazy is my father?" I asked Brian. I'd wanted to ask if he thought my father was crazy, period, but that phrasing begged an either/or answer, and after all those phone calls and a long day at school, I could only cope with gradations of crazy. Brian looked surprised by my question because the two of us had an ongoing disagreement about diagnostic evaluations. As a psychotherapist, he thought terms like *manic-depressive* and *narcissistic* helped define human nature. As a writer, I thought they simplified human nature by forcing it into preexisting categories. He thought that categories were illuminating; I was inspired by the uncategorizable. He was washing the dishes; I was drying them.

"Did something happen?" he asked.

I told him about Mr. Delaney.

"The telephone company is trying to triangulate."

"Triangulating bastards," I grumbled, only half joking.

Brian's eyebrows lifted when I told him about my father putting Betty on the phone. After years in private practice, he'd perfected a nonjudgmental expression with which to greet even the most shocking revelations, so this slight change in his face was the equivalent to someone else's jaw dropping. He sponged a plate and handed it over. "On what grounds is he refusing to pay?"

"Grounds?"

"Of course." He smiled. "What was I thinking?"

"Betty offered to pay for the long-distance calls and have a talk with him."

"Good."

"The way you say 'good' makes it sound bad."

"Well," he said, "whether she takes care of it or not remains to be seen."

"I can't afford to mistrust her at the moment."

"Then don't."

"Don't? Okay. Poof! Everything's fine."

"Let's not continue this conversation if you're going to act like that."

"*Don't* isn't just some button I can punch."

"Too bad," he said. "I'd like to punch it right now."

I laughed. "Good one."

"Insults come easily when I'm with you."

I leaned over and kissed him.

"Well," said Brian, "want to hear my diagnosis?"

"Yes, Doctor." I couldn't resist calling him Doctor in situations that gave his credentials an illicit charge; I was doing the dishes with my doctor, for which procedure my doctor had stripped off his shirt, his sinewy forearms glistening with water, pectorals flexing as he rinsed a plate.

"The diagnosis will have to pertain to you, not your father, if you want it to be useful."

"Go ahead. I'm ready." I must not have been, though, since I handed him back the plate I'd just dried.

"Drainer," he said.

"What?"

He looked at the plate in my outstretched hand.

"Oh. I thought that was the diagnosis." I set the plate in the drainer and leaned against the sink.

Only one other time had I asked Brian to diagnose me—goaded him into it, really. It happened about a month after our first date (which wasn't a first date so much as a bout of energetic sex not twenty minutes after we met). We were sharing mounds of Thai food at a local restaurant when I pointed to the tablecloth and mentioned that a stain made by the black bean sauce resembled a Rorschach blot. This naturally led to a discussion of diagnostics. Brian described the Thematic Apperception Test, for which the subject is asked to supply the story behind an emotionally loaded image of, say, a boy holding a broken violin, the shadowy figure of a woman peering in at him from a doorway. But there was another test, called the Minnesota Multiphasic Personality Index, that he considered an even more revealing diagnostic tool. He shook his head sternly when I asked if he would administer it after dinner. He warned me, gallantly I thought, that taking the MMPI might not be an appropriate way to spend time together at this early stage of our dating, since dating was a personality test in itself. I argued that the test would determine how well our relationship withstood tests in general. If we passed—that is, if we were still speaking to each other by the end of the evening—then this whole dating process, which ever-so-slowly doled out clues regarding our compatibility, would be expedited by leaps and bounds.

And so we found ourselves back in Brian's tiny apartment above a two-car garage in the Silver Lake foothills. His living room overlooked a stand of towering trees. Where the foliage thinned, distant city lights shone through the branches like luminous fruit. I'd been cavalier about the test in the restaurant, but it became clear that my psyche was being prepped for dissection when I saw Brian thumbing through the instructions on how to accurately interpret the test, then sorting dozens of clear plastic overlays printed with cryptic, zigzagging graphs for measuring the results. The spiral-bound test booklet looked formidable. Still, it would have been cowardly to back out now. Brian sharpened a pencil, set the booklet on his dinette table, and fine-tuned the dimmer switch till the overhead light was bright enough to read by but not so bright as to suggest interrogation or dentistry.

"Remember," he said, "this was your idea."

The MMPI is a true-or-false test, but the testee is advised to think of his responses to the statements—here Brian read from the manual—"As either TRUE or MOSTLY TRUE, or as FALSE or NOT USUALLY TRUE," a distinction for which I needed several refresher explanations.

I vacillated for a long time on the first statement: "I have met problems so full of possibilities that I have been unable to make up my mind about them." Some statements appeared more than once but in a slightly rephrased form, giving the testee several opportunities to reveal either his consistency or hypocrisy. Taken as a whole, the unrelated statements gave my deepest concerns a narrative clarity they lacked in the rush and befuddlement of daily life:

My father is a good man.

I have had very peculiar and strange experiences.

I sometimes have trouble sleeping.

A minister can cure disease by praying and putting his hand on your head.

I like poetry.

Most of the time I would rather daydream than do anything else.

I used to like hopscotch.

Once in a while I laugh at a dirty joke.

There seems to be a fullness in my head most of the time.

I like dramatics.

My family does not like the work I have chosen.

I certainly feel useless at times.

I love my father.

My hardest battles are with myself.

At times my thoughts race ahead faster than I can think them.

Taking the test, it turned out, *did* hasten the knowledge we'd hoped to gain by dating; I knew I loved Brian when he stood beside my chair, speaking softly but not condescendingly, unsure about the wisdom of administering the test, but not so responsible that he wouldn't use the tools of his profession to probe his date's personality and, once it had been indexed, get him into bed. Unaware that I'd considered backing out of the test, he thought I either had nothing to hide or trusted him with whatever I might be hiding. I was the kind of guy who'd argue with the results as ardently as I'd begged to take the test, a guy too neurotic, paradoxically, to play the role of client to his shrink, which was fine by him.

Brian tossed the sponge into the sinkful of dirty dishes and turned to face me. I considered asking him to put on a shirt so I could concentrate on what he was about to say.

"You're on a variable ratio, variable interval reinforcement schedule."

"I am? At least I'm on a schedule. What is it?"

"You don't get love from your father every time you try to get it, and every time you do get love from your father, you don't get a lot. So you keep coming back again and again."

"You're saying its the kind of situation where a person is stuck wanting something he almost, but won't really, get?"

"Close enough," said Brian. He swiped the dishrag from my hand. "Let me dry for a while."

\*   \*   \*

Reading Elizabeth Bishop's poem "One Art" to my class that after-noon, I'd tried to inflect the refrain—"The art of losing isn't hard to master"—with the poet's diminishing conviction. I wanted the students to hear how, each time Bishop repeats that phrase, she grows less and less certain about her ability to master loss until she must finally exhort herself to "*Write* it!" By the poem's end, she suspects her claim is little more than false solace, a solace she must neverthe-less force herself to believe in, and commit to paper, if she is to go on, unbowed by grief. This is the opposite of mastery, which isn't defeat so much as the admission that one is whistling in the dark, saying to oneself whatever must be said to ward off the apprehen-sion that losses will come "harder and faster" no matter what we do to protect ourselves against them, and that even the small, bearable losses—lost keys, forgotten names—are a harbinger of larger losses: homes and cities left behind, loved ones gone forever.

Generally speaking, the inevitability of loss is not a topic a room-ful of restless freshman, some of whom haven't even lost their vir-ginity, want to contemplate. And who can blame them? When I was twenty I would have squirmed in my seat and thought that the teacher was grasping at the straw of this sad lady's poem as a way to justify his pessimistic view of the future. Oh, I would have felt sorry for the guy, but I would have considered him an exception to the rule that no matter how much loss a person endures, they'll grow ever more contented and wise until they're old and, hopefully, famous. I would have glanced at the classroom clock and wished I'd signed up for a different elective.

That night in bed I replayed my lecture, deleting its infelicities and adding passages designed to make even the most disinterested student see how Bishop captures, in six short stanzas, the friction of ambivalence. All the while, Brian lay sound asleep beside me. He'd once joked that the reason he could fall asleep at the drop of a hat and I couldn't was that *he* had a clear conscience. He may have been teasing, but one look at his placid face, the easy rise and fall of his chest, and my conscience seemed murky and clogged by contrast. Sure, there were nights when Brian twitched and whimpered, but far more often he laughed in his sleep. If you haven't been awake at dawn, feeling every tremor of regret while your slumbering lover lies there and laughs, then you haven't had insomnia.

I turned on my right side, my left. I began to wonder whether cumulative loss defies the laws of simple addition, its effect exponential. Could this be the one art of the poem's title? *One* because loss is ongoing, *art* because one must make, and make again, a life despite who and what is missing? Faint gray light began to seep beneath the bedroom curtains and I remembered, with the unwelcome clarity that's visited upon the sleep-deprived, those rare moments when my father's features were freed from the grip of rage or suspicion or nervous mirth. His face didn't relax so much as settle toward emotional bedrock. The expression that remained wasn't simply one of sorrow, but that of a man stunned by sorrow, by its indifference and ubiquity, by its power over his waking moments, and though he didn't know it, over mine.

# Winner Take Nothing

When I received word informing me that my first book had been chosen for the PEN Ernest Hemingway Award, I held the letter in trembling hands while the following thoughts, in precisely this order, shot through my head:

1. I won the Ernest Hemingway Award!
2. I don't deserve it.
3. My father's heard of Ernest Hemingway!

I ran a couple of laps around the house, elated not just because of the letter, but because I remembered seeing a hardback volume of *The Snows of Kilimanjaro and Other Stories* on the shelves in my father's upstairs hall. Perhaps the book had belonged to one of my brothers, or was left behind by Anna. In any case, a book by the award's namesake was shelved right there in Dad's very own home library, which would, as far as he was concerned, lend credence to the whole affair.

I had to admit that my father had managed perfectly well without literature for the past eighty-six years, and I had no illusions that writing, especially mine, could enrich his life. He sometimes read *Consumer Reports,* but largely, I think, to sustain through retirement the image he had of himself as a citizen with buying power. His primary reading material was *TV Guide,* a map by which he and Betty navigated nights in front of the Sony console, watching *Wheel of Fortune,* followed by the healings of Reverend Benny Hinn. In the few instances I told him I'd had something published in a magazine or literary review, the first question he asked was, "How much they pay you?" I suppose he thought "they" were a faceless jury, twelve arbiters of taste. Imagine telling a man who keeps his cash in a gold money clip shaped like a dollar sign that, after working on a piece of writing for months, you've been compensated with a complimentary copy of the publication. "You're kidding," he'd say, shaking his head as if I'd been duped in a shell game.

Over time, I'd cultivated a certain temperance when sharing literary news with my father. I'd come to consider it unfortunate, but not devastating, that he was unable to recognize the arc—or was it the bump?—of my career. Still, I ached to have him slap me on the back, wanted to hear his unstinting praise, and in it the honeyed pronouncement: son.

Toward this end, I'd once given him something of mine to read. I chose a brief reminiscence about my mother, who had once dreamed of writing a book into which she'd pack every anecdote she could recall, starting with her immigration from Russia to the United States. *Immigration* isn't quite the right word; what she told me was that she and her parents swam across the Atlantic Ocean to the shores of North America when she was two. I was young enough at the time to believe such a feat was possible, and my credulity inspired her to add that if the "authorities" ever discovered she'd entered the country illegally, they'd knock on our door and deport her, and *that's* why she never applied for a driver's license. Needless to say, my gratitude for having a mother grew instantly acute. I thought my father would find the tone of this reminiscence unmistakably fond. And so I handed him the pages one day, neatly stapled. Before I let go of the manuscript (feeling him tug it from the other side was the closest I'd come to his tangible enthusiasm), I told him I hoped he'd enjoy reading it and assured him he was under no obligation to offer comments.

Days went by. Weeks. Months. In all the times we saw each other or spoke on the phone, he never mentioned reading it, and pride prevented me from coming right out and asking. If it hadn't been for a chokingly potent vodka tonic I drank when we met for dinner one night at the Brass Pan, I may not have asked him to this day.

"Hey, Dad. You've never mentioned the essay I wrote about Mom." He peered at me over his bifocals. In the dim light of the restaurant, he looked anything but adversarial. "Well," he sighed, "what can I tell you? You wrote down your opinion."

I stirred the booze with a swizzle stick and took another swig.

My father wasn't the first person I called about the award (I reached Brian during his break between clients, and then made short work of my address book), but when I dialed Dad's number and told him him the news, his "Oh" was as round and buoyant as a bubble.

In my excitement, however, I'd overlooked one crucial hitch: now that it had been deemed worthy by a panel of judges, my father might decide to read the book—specifically the passage where I mentioned his affairs while married to my mother. If only I'd used a pseudonym or the putty nose of fiction, but the man was unmistakable, the ink completely dry.

Sure enough, once my father learned of the award, he phoned several local bookstores and, to my relief, was told that my book, which had been in print for several months, had sold out. Little did he know that the bookstores had ordered only a couple of copies in the first place, one or both of which had been bought by my friends. I wasn't about to disabuse him of the idea that my fame was a wave that swept through the city, washing my work from the shelves. I told him the publisher was planning another print run that would be available *after* the PEN ceremony in New York. By lying, I'd bought myself more time to plan the least upsetting way to let him know he appeared in the book. Should he react badly, at least I wouldn't arrive at the ceremony feeling defeated. No, defeat would have to wait until after I received the award.

A few days later my father and I were talking on the phone about my plan to buy a suit for the big night, and though it usually made

me bristle when he gave unsolicited advice, I listened with pleasure
to his description of the dress code that prevailed in the courtroom,
and to his suggestion that I try a men's store downtown I was sure
had long ago gone out of business. "Listen," he said, "we'll fly to
New York together, share a room, and take in some Broadway
shows. Betty will take care of things while I'm gone. To tell you the
truth, I could use a break from her, and probably so could she from
me." I was stunned by his offer, and more than a little touched. Since
he had no compunction about expressing bemusement at my small
successes, it never occurred to me that he might need to take an
active part in my large ones.

I didn't know what to say. Without Betty there to monitor his
diet and medications, the responsibility for his well-being would fall
to me, and I didn't want to be encumbered. Not on this trip.
Besides, Brian had booked our flights and hotel room weeks ago.

"Nothing could make me happier than knowing you're proud of
me," I told him, "but I'm only going to be in New York for three
days." I explained that I'd made plans to see a couple of old friends
and had promised to read for a creative writing class. As terrific as a
trip with him sounded, I wouldn't have time to go to Broadway
shows or give him the attention he deserved. Although his gout was
finally under control, he still walked slowly and tired easily, and I
suggested that Manhattan might not be the best city for him to visit
until he had less trouble getting around. "Tell you what," I said. "Let
me take you and Betty to the Brass Pan just as soon as we get back.
That way the four of us can relax and celebrate properly."

After I stopped talking, I gave my little speech high marks; it had
been a good mixture of respect and autonomy. But the longer he
remained silent, the more aware I became of the telephone's static,
a sound growing vast, oceanic. "Dad?"

"Fine," he said. "If that's what you want."


Brian gave me his window seat as soon as we reached cruising alti-
tude. I thought that looking out the window might make me less

claustrophobic, but no matter where I sat, the plane seemed to stay aloft solely because of my death grip on the armrests. When panic finally gave way to the Valium I'd taken twenty minutes before take-off, my hands and feet grew rubbery, the view of earth abstract.

Once we were inside the terminal at JFK, it finally dawned on me that I'd survived the flight to receive an award. Luggage spilled onto a carousel. Sunlight burned through a bank of windows and warmed the glaring terrazzo floor. Outside, people swarmed toward a fleet of cabs and were whisked away to meetings and reunions. Possibility charged the air, dense, electric. In my happiness I turned to Brian and faced my father.

At first I thought I might be drugged or dreaming, though by then, only the mildest trace of Valium remained in my system. I looked at him and couldn't speak. The entire busy terminal contracted to a point the size of his face. Was he omnipresent like Santa Claus or God? Dad looked back and blithely smiled.

"Surprise," he said.

"How . . . ?" I sputtered.

"Your plane. I went first class."

Suddenly I understood that all the questions he'd asked about the details of my trip—time of departure, name of the airline—questions I'd interpreted as paternal concern, were part of a perfectly executed plan.

Brian, who at first had been as stunned as I, rushed in to fill the conspicuous silence. He shook my father's hand. "Are you staying at our hotel?" he asked.

I recalled with a start that Brian had booked rooms at a gay bed-and-breakfast.

"I'm at the Warwick," said my father. "Quite a fancy place, according to the automobile club." Two familiar carryalls were making aimless circles in the periphery of my vision, and before I knew what I was doing, I yanked them off the carousel and threw one over each shoulder. "We're going," I announced, a decision I'd regret within minutes. I marched toward the taxi stand.

"Bernard!" shouted Brian, dashing after me.

"Share a ride?" my father shouted.

I didn't look back.

The cab rattled like an earthquake, the driver barely missing other vehicles as he swerved from lane to lane. *If this Caddy had another coat of paint,* my father liked to say after a close call, *we would have been in an accident!* He could be funny, my father, which made me a heel for leaving him at the airport. But he'd gone ahead and followed me to New York. If he and I weren't going to sleep in adjacent beds and take in the town like sailors on shore leave, we were going to arrive on the same flight, split a cab, and share who knew what other adventures. It wasn't that he was "eccentric," as the jacket copy of my book (a book whose publication I was in no mood to celebrate) claimed; he was unpredictable, capable of acts that were unimaginable until they happened. I'd spent much of my life having to appease or second-guess him, and look where a stab at independence had gotten me: grinding my teeth in the back of a cab, vacillating between guilt and fury while Manhattan slipped past the windows, unseen.

Once we settled into our hotel room, with the faux hominess of its antique furniture and antimacassars, I took a shower and tried to gather my thoughts. Pelted by hot water, I returned to what was left of my senses and began to worry that I'd acted rashly. Had I been a different person, I might have poked my father in the ribs and teased him for being a stubborn coot. But in order to be a different person I'd have to have been raised by a different dad. The one I had was an old Jewish genie who materialized wherever he willed and granted any wish—as long as it was his.

After changing into fresh clothes, I called the Warwick. My father answered on the second ring. Allowing himself to sound upset would have presumed he'd done something wrong, and so it was to his advantage to act as if nothing unusual had happened. "Hey there," he said.

"We'd better have a talk, Dad."

"It's your dime."

"I thought you understood that I wanted to do this on my own."

"Fine. I'll pack up my goddamn bags and go home."

"No. I *want* you to stay now that you're here. I'm just trying to explain why I reacted the way I did at the airport."

"So now you explained it. Is that what you wanted to talk about?"

There had to be more. In the shower, I'd rehearsed ways to tell him that his surprise was an intrusion disguised as kindness, a success usurped. But now, I couldn't recall what I'd wanted to say, or why each of us always found it so important to win the other's capitulation. After all was said and done, my father had come here because he was proud of me.

"We'll have lunch tomorrow," he said.


The dining room at the Warwick, with its ambient chimes of silverware and ice, offered a quiet retreat from the city. My father looked small and harmless as he sat waiting for us at a table. He peered nearsightedly around the spacious room, hands folded before him in a boyish pose, almost contrite. As Brian and I walked toward the table, it struck me that he was not at all the giant of the nursery I was prone to imagine; when I didn't have the actual man before me, he ballooned into myth. There arose a somewhat leery conviviality as we seated ourselves at the table. Brian had had experience with couples counseling, but of course, expecting him to mediate the situation between my father and me would have burdened him with a professional responsibility while he was on vacation. It would also mean that the couple to be counseled was you know who.

"So, Mr. Cooper," asked Brian, "what have you been doing?"

My father toyed with the silverware. "Nothing much. I watched a little TV."

"What did you watch, Dad?"

My father cocked his head and thought. "They got this channel where they show you all about the hotel, where the lobby is, and the fire exits, et cetera."

Brian and I looked at each other.

"Have you gone anywhere, Mr. Cooper? I hear there are some wonderful restaurants in the area."

"I had breakfast at a deli across the street. Haven't had corned beef hash in so long, I'm telling you I got tears in my eyes! Don't tell Betty, though. If it was up to her, I'd be eating air."

"Is there anybody you know in New York who you could go to dinner with tonight?" Please, I prayed.

"We'll find the name of a great place," offered Brian. "And make your reservations."

"I got relatives in Jersey. Or used to twenty years ago. I should look them up next time I'm here." His hearing aid squealed with feedback and he fiddled with its tiny dial.

"The thing is, Dad, we can't go to dinner with you tonight."

"I know," he said curtly. "You're *very* busy."

The maître d' brought us huge glossy menus, the covers printed to look like marble. I opened mine, expecting an engraving of the Ten Commandments: *Thou shalt honor thy father, who gazeth at the entrées.* Without lifting his eyes from the menu, he waved his hand in a gesture of largesse. "Get whatever you want," he said. "Sky's the limit."


The morning of the ceremony, I added an additional paragraph to my acceptance speech. In it, I thanked my father for reading me stories as a child. His rapt voice had transported me, I wrote, and his enthusiasm for telling tales had introduced me to the power of language. I wasn't certain whether my father had, in fact, read me stories as a child, but he wouldn't contradict the sentimental notion, and our collusion would be a kind of bond.

That evening, when the elevator doors opened on the tenth floor of the Time-Life Building, my nerves lit up like a chandelier. The representative of PEN introduced himself and pointed to a table where the books by the various winners and nominees were on display. My father had stationed himself beside it, staring down at a small stack of my books. I waited to see if he'd pick one up to

peek at a page or turn it over to scan the jacket copy, but his hands
stayed clasped behind his back.

Half a dozen awards were handed out during the ceremony.
Almost every author who received one had written a speech identical to mine, a sort of apologia in which they expressed surprise at
having won and either implied, or insisted, they were undeserving.
The motif of modesty had been exhausted by the time I walked up
to the podium, but I'd already revised my speech that morning and
was far too nervous to change it again. When I came to the part
about my father, I looked up from the wrinkled sheet of paper, eager
to find him among the crowd and make eye contact, but I had to
look back quickly for fear of losing my place. The paragraph I'd
added struck me as a little schmaltzy, and I worried that my apparent sentimentality would discourage people in the audience from
buying my book. In the end, it didn't really matter; my homage was
meant for Dad's ears alone, and reading it aloud righted the night.

Or so I thought. Immediately after the ceremony I found my
father milling in the crowd and raced up to ask him how he'd liked
my speech. "Couldn't hear a damn thing," he said, chuckling at his
rotten luck. His hearing aid, unable to distinguish between fore-
ground and background noises, had amplified both. From the rear
of the auditorium, my father saw me reading in the distance, but he
heard ubiquitous coughs and whispers, a battle of creaking leather
coats, the rubbery acoustics of someone chewing gum.

That trip to New York completely changed my life. In three days I'd
charged so much money to my credit card that I had to teach two
additional classes when I returned. Along with teaching, I began to
publish in a few well-paying magazines. My combined income was
still meager by any standard except my own, but at last I could speak
my father's language, a lexicon of hard cold cash.

By that time, however, my father reacted to news of my solvency
with a foggy acknowledgment. At the mention of money he'd look
at me wistfully, nod his head, then look away. My father was going

broke from lawsuits. Although Betty, true to her word, had paid the phone bill, Dad filed a harassment suit against Mr. Delaney. A judge dismissed the case before he heard it, admonishing my father to pay his phone bill on time and scolding him for clogging an overtaxed judicial system with a frivolous complaint.

Next, he took Dr. Graham to court, and this time a judge not only dismissed his case, but ordered him to pay the doctor's attorney fees. He filed a claim against the neighbor whose sprinklers turned his lawn into "a swamp," and also against the neighbor whose rumbling garage door opener purportedly cracked his plaster walls. Most ominous of all, he began to prepare proceedings against Gary's wife, Sharleen, and Ron's wife, Nancy, claiming they had promised to repay him money he'd long ago loaned to my brothers.

"I'm entitled by law," he'd say when I tried to convince him to drop the suits, "to take action against a party eight times before they can even *think* of claiming malicious prosecution. Believe me, I know what I'm doing. I didn't just fall off the boat, you know." He represented himself in court and lost each case. The judges were corrupt, he'd claim, his witnesses inarticulate. Defeat never seemed to give him pause or lessen his zeal for prosecution. He was in the throes of a lawyerly tantrum; if the world refused to yield to his will, he'd force it to yield to the letter of the law.

I protested his plans to sue my sisters-in-law, though to stay in his good graces, my objections were tempered. In the convoluted scheme of things, I found it flattering to be, along with Betty, one of two people in his life exempt from litigation. My worth as a son was verified daily by the absence of a summons to appear in court. Betty must have been as backhandedly flattered as I. As a nurse, her bedside manner was stern, but off duty, so to speak, she flirtatiously teased my father about his bullheadedness, charmed by the very trait that made him a difficult patient, not to mention a tenacious legal foe.

Every now and then, my father and I met for dinner at the Brass Pan. Some nights, when the waitress asked for his order, he'd tell her a story based on his choice of entrée, so that filet of sole, for example, segued into a fishing trip with my brothers. At first I thought his brevity—a boat, an ocean, three rambunctious seasick boys—was in deference to the busy waitress. Then I'd see that he was stranded in the shallows of a thought, unable to remember more. On other nights, he'd stiffen and eye the waitress with suspicion, tense as a man being cross-examined. She'd hover above him, pencil poised, till he blinked and finally lifted his hand, pointing to a dish on the menu.

Eventually, he grew too distracted by his legal battles to return my phone calls. On the rare occasions when we spoke, he said he was too busy to meet me for dinner. More often than not, the answering machine picked up after several rings and played its refrain: *I am not at home at this present time.*

After months of an elusiveness he couldn't be coaxed out of, I drove over to my father's house one afternoon to ask why he'd been unwilling to see me, why he hadn't returned my calls. Such phases of estrangement were nothing new; for as long as I can remember, our relationship had been punctuated by weeks of his withdrawal followed by fits of generous attention. But there I was, hoping, I suppose, to make the reinforcement schedule a little less variable.

Dad answered the door of his Spanish house, preoccupied but glad to see me. Time had taken a belated toll, as though weariness had waited till now to irrevocably claim his face; his eyes were puzzled, hair unkempt, chin bristling with patches of stubble the razor had missed. His polyester jumpsuit, after years of looking supernaturally pressed, was finally worse for wear.

Betty rushed in soundlessly from the kitchen. She'd recently left the home care agency, taking short-term jobs that didn't require her to drive too far from Hollywood, and she was dressed in her uniform and silent white shoes. "I'm going to say hello and good-bye," she announced, slinging her purse over her shoulder. As she had on the day of her interview, Betty stood squarely, the very picture of dependability, and yet she had about her a breathlessness, an air of agitation I hadn't noticed before. Even this slight change in her seemingly limitless composure—it had to be limitless, I thought, if she maintained a peaceful relationship with my father—forced me to recognize just how much I depended on her to take care of him. "Your dinner's in the refrigerator," she shouted at my father. "Give it five minutes in the micro."

She looked at me and whispered, "Remind him. Five."

"What?" said my father.

"I left Mrs. Travisi's number near the phone," she shouted. And then she was gone.

My father and I sat down at the dining room table. Yellow legal tablets and manila folders were scattered across it, scraps of paper saving his place in law books that rose in precarious stacks. He lowered himself into a chair with a troubled gust of breath. Age had robbed my father of the prowess he believed a triumph in court could restore.

"Are you sure you're not angry at me about something?" I asked. "Because, if you are . . ."

My father fiddled with his hearing aid. "What makes you think I'm angry?"

"You're so . . . unavailable these days."

"How many times do I have to tell you? I'm busy. Swamped. Do you need me to spell it out for you?" He rose to his feet, and I thought he might begin to sound out the letters. "You have no idea. No goddamn concept."

I stood, too, trying to rise above the childlike vantage point that came with being seated. "All I'm saying is that you have to eat dinner anyway, and we might as well . . ."

"Who says?"

"What?"

"Who says I have to eat dinner? Where is it written? Is it written here?" He hefted a law book and let it slam back onto the table. Stray papers jumped and fluttered. I made a move to calm him down, but he began to prowl around the table, stirring up motes of sunlit dust. "Don't you ever tell me what to do!"

"Having dinner is not something to do! I mean, it *is* something to do, but I'm not *telling* you to do it." At a loss for logic, I was barking back.

"Don't you raise your voice at me!" He rushed up and grabbed the back of my shirt, a hank of fabric twisted in his grip. "I'm eighty-six years old," he shouted. "I can do whatever the hell I want whenever the hell I want to do it." He pushed me toward the door, breathing hard, his face red and alien with effort.

"Dad?"

"That's right," he said. When he opened the door, the daylight was blinding. "Don't ever forget that I'm your father. Now get the hell out and don't come back."

Since high school, I've been both taller and stronger than my father, but just as we reached the threshold of the door it occurred to me that I might flatter him into relenting if, instead of resisting or fighting back, I let my body be heaved outside as though from an admirable, manly force.

Acquiescence didn't help. Before the door slammed shut behind me, I turned and glimpsed his indignant figure sinking inside my childhood house. The door hit the jamb with a deafening bang, the birds falling silent for half a second before they went back to their usual racket.

On a daily basis I relived the particulars: the shirt taut across my chest, the heat of his breath on the back of my neck, the flood of light as the door swung wide. As with so much that's transpired between us, the sheer abruptness and implausibility of what had happened made me wonder if I'd perhaps misperceived it. Had I said something thoughtless or cruel to set him off?

In lieu of an explanation, I started making changes in the story. Suppose I hadn't mentioned dinner? Suppose I hadn't raised my voice? Suppose we'd stood instead of sitting? Say the day had been cooler, the hour later, the dust motes churning in another direction? Would the outcome of my visit have been any different? Who knew what crucial shifts of fate had hinged on the tiny details?

Several nights a week, I had to drive past his house on the way home from teaching, and the closer I came, the greater its magnetic pull. More than once, I turned the steering wheel at the last minute, aiming my car through a tunnel of trees and parking across the street from his house. *So this is what it was like,* I thought, *for my brother Bob:* parked and watchful for hours on end. My behavior pained me, yet the urge to spy on my father was nameless, as deep and murky as the darkness it required.

There was little to learn from my nights of surveillance. Light would suddenly burn in a window, but I couldn't see anyone move through the rooms. Even if I had, what would a glimpse of his silhouette tell me? A walkway led toward the large front door, the stepping-stones flat and blank in the moonlight. Betty's yellow station wagon was parked in the driveway on the nights she wasn't working, but my father's Cadillac always sat there, gleaming, impassive, white as an iceberg. Despite my vigilance, nothing happened, except that every now and then I'd glance at my phosphorescent watch, its ghostly hands advancing.

During the first year of our estrangement, my entreaties and apologies and furious demands for contact were recited into his answering machine. On a few occasions he picked up the phone, then slammed it down at the sound of my voice.

By the second year, resignation took hold. I'd lost the desire to drive by his house or reach him by phone. I recalled that afternoon less often, and when I did, I refused to probe the memory for meaning.

By the third year, his absence settled inside me like a stone.


"I realize my phone call must come as an unpleasant surprise," the social worker told me. "But I believe your father's deterioration is significant enough to make legal guardianship a necessary step. We routinely ask the nearest relative before resorting to a court-appointed guardian, since it's in the client's best interest to place their finances in the hands of someone they know."

Mr. Gomez assured me that I didn't have to make up my mind right away; it would be several months before the case came before a judge. An anonymous caller had phoned Adult Protective Services to say my father needed help. If I assumed legal responsibility, my father's Social Security checks would be placed in a trust, and he'd need my permission for every expenditure: medicine, groceries, clothes.

"Careful monetary management is especially crucial in your father's case," said Mr. Gomez. "As you may know, the bank has begun foreclosure on the house."

I couldn't bring myself to tell Mr. Gomez that I hadn't known a thing about it. I certainly couldn't explain that even if Dad and I *had* been on speaking terms, he might not have bothered to mention foreclosure till a moving van pulled up to the curb.

"Hello?" said Mr. Gomez.

If the city was a compass, my childhood house was magnetic north, and always would be no matter where I moved.

I promised Mr. Gomez that I'd give our discussion serious thought, and said good-bye. I'd become so guarded against any emotion having to do with my father that the prospect of seeing him again roused only a dull ambivalence. After three years, I'd finally decided it was *I* who didn't want contact with *him,* a decision that redefined circumstance and made my banishment bearable. And now, out of the blue, a social worker urged a reunion.

If I did take responsibility for my father's finances, wouldn't receiving an allowance from his son—an *allowance!*—cause him to resent my authority, just as I once resented his? How well would he be able to understand that I hadn't wanted or asked for this role?

Had I been in my father's position, I'm the last person to whom I'd give fiscal responsibility. I can barely balance my checkbook, let alone manage someone else's finances. Ask me about money, and instead of thinking *stocks and bonds and dividends,* I remember a trick my father showed me when I was six. He rolled up his sleeves, waved his empty hands in the air. "See," he said, "there's nothing there." With a little flourish, he reached out and plucked a quarter from my ear—were there more coins, I wondered, hidden in my head?— leaving me, as only he could, slack-jawed with astonishment.

*   *   *

I'd been writing when the telephone rang. Though I don't usually answer the phone when I'm working, I was expecting a call from Mr. Gomez.

"Bernard?"

"Dad?" Saying the word made my mouth go dry.

"I sold the house and the people who bought it want to move in pretty soon, so I've been cleaning out closets and I came across all sorts of drawings and photos of yours. You wanna come get them? Is four-thirty good?"

"Four-thirty's good." I wasn't sure I was ready to see him, but assent was automatic.

"Okay. See you later."

"Wait," I blurted. "How have you been?"

"Fine. And you?"

Three years. "I'm fine, too."

"Good," he said, "as long as you're fine." His harried voice softened. "Well," he said, "I'm really swamped."

Only after I hung up the phone did I realize he hadn't said hello.


I approached the house with apprehension; who knew in what condition I'd find him? Since I'd last spied on the house, the first-floor windows had been covered with bars. The front door stood behind a wrought iron grate, and no matter how decorative its design, it made the house look so aloof it might as well have been surrounded by a moat.

No sooner had I rung the doorbell than my father appeared behind the bars, pale and slow, jangling keys like a castle keep. All the while he burbled greetings. My hands were jammed in my pockets; I couldn't act as if things had been normal without damaging a sense of reality that, especially in my father's presence, could flounder like a little boy's. "Come on in," he said, unlocking the grate. I found his hospitality suspicious, and as much as I wanted to make amends, I also wanted to run the other way. I'd come to think of my boyhood house as a place I'd never visit again, and now that I stood on the verge of return, I practically had to astral project and give myself a push from behind.

The house was even more crammed with memorabilia than I remembered. He must have strewn souvenirs about the rooms as he cleaned out the closets, a last-minute effort to make his mark on the home he had to forfeit. The breakfront doors yawned open, his scrapbook packed in a cardboard box. The portrait of JFK leaned against the wall, as did still-lifes and landscapes by my brother Ron. Spread across the coffee table, in the careful, printed letters of my childhood, were compositions I'd written about the sun's brightness and my love of dogs; they called back the distant, mesmerizing triumph of being able to describe the world and contain it on a piece of paper. Pictures from a photo booth showed a mugging ten-year-old who bore as much resemblance to me now as I to my father; I wanted to warn that oblivious boy of what was to come. I couldn't look at the stuff for long, and I gathered it up, ready to go.

"Sit," said my father.

I did as he asked.

"What's new?"

"Lots."

"Written any more books of yours?"

"Trying to. Yes."

"I see," he said. "Tell me what else has been going on." He leaned forward in the chair, cocked his good ear in my direction.

"Look, I appreciate your willingness to get together, but I'd think you'd be glad that you raised a son who cares enough to want to know why his father hasn't spoken to him in three years."

His brows furrowed.

"Why haven't you talked to me?" I shouted.

"Look. You live, things happen, you go on. That's the way it works."

"That's not the way it works for me."

"Well, the truth of the matter is that you were getting irritated with me about my hearing aid. You were always screaming, 'What? What? I can't hear you! Turn up your damn ear!'"

"First of all, Dad, you're the one who shouts, 'What? I can't hear you.' Second, I'd never scold you because you're hard of hearing."

"I'm telling you, that's what happened."

"It didn't."

"Did."

"Okay," I said. "Suppose you're right. Is that any reason not to speak to me for three years?"

My father sat back, stared into space. He gave the question due consideration. "Yes," he said, lurching forward. "Yes, it is."

"You see, this is why I can't just 'go on.' Unless we can talk to each other like two mature adults, I worry that some misunderstanding might set you off again."

"All right," he said. "All right already." He looked at his feet, then back at me. "I've lived in this house for fifty years. Do you remember when we moved in?"

"I wasn't born yet."

"Do you remember what day it was?"

"I wasn't . . ." It seemed pointless to repeat myself. "Tuesday?" I guessed.

"No," he said. "It was your mother's birthday. Did you know that she never knew her real birth date?"

"Her birthday was the fourth of July."

"Ach," sputtered my father, waving his hand. "That's the birthday they gave to lots of greenhorns at Ellis Island, people who didn't know or couldn't say in English the year they were born."

"Dad," I asked, "what's our original family name?"

"I sold the place to two very nice guys. By the way, how's that friend of yours, what's his name?"

"Brian's fine, he . . ."

"What do I need all these rooms for, anyway? It was either sell the house or get kicked out on the street."

I shook my head in commiseration, pretending to know nothing about the foreclosure.

"Some meshuggener social worker wanted to have someone else do the real estate negotiations. Said I couldn't handle the sale myself.

I showed him. Closed escrow on my own, then told Hernandez to take a hike."

I stopped myself from blurting, *Gomez.*

"The kicker," he continued, picking lint from his jumpsuit, "is that I got Betty to report me to the guy in the first place."

"What!"

"See," said my father. "You *do* shout, 'What!'" He bristled a moment, shifted in his seat. "It was the only way to save myself. If she said I was, you know, soft in the head, the bank couldn't foreclose."

Betty walked into the living room and sat beside my father, her hair dyed a metallic shade of blond. She'd gained weight since I last saw her and it took her a couple of labored adjustments to settle into the valley of the couch. "Non compos mentis," she said, shaking her head at the whole mess. "That's what the social worker called it."

I must have been wide-eyed because my father added, "Don't look like that! She didn't tell them I was crazy out of the kindness of her heart. She gets something out of it too."

Betty glanced at him sharply. "I was protecting us both."

My father nodded, but I don't think he heard her.

"Did you know that Gomez called me?" I asked.

My father sighed. "I figured he might. I got a pretty penny for the place, but I owe a lot too. There are liens and things. A second mortgage. I'm looking at a mobile home in Oxnard. Not the best place in the world, but it looks just like a regular house, and it's what I can afford."

"We," said Betty. "What *we* can afford."

"Betty's from Oxnard. She knows some people up there, so its not exactly like starting from scratch. You'll come up and visit." He cleared his throat. "You sure have grown since the last time I saw you."

"Dad, I've been this tall since high school."

"Taller than me?"

"For years," I said.

My father shrugged. "Then I guess I'm shrinking."

\*   \*   \*

After loading mementos into my car, I came back inside the house to say good-bye. Betty nudged my father and this reanimated his grave face. He slapped his palm against his forehead. "Almost forgot your present," he said. I followed them into the kitchen. Dad stationed himself in front of the counter, then beamed at me and stepped aside.

A pink bakery box yawned open to reveal a cake, its circumference studded with strawberries of an uncanny size and ripeness. The fruit was glazed, and beneath the kitchen's fluorescent lights, it looked succulent, moist, aggressively tempting. Slivered almonds, toasted gold, had been evenly pressed into a mortar of thick white frosting, every spare surface dotted with florets.

What I noticed next made me catch my breath. Written in the center, in goopy blue script, was *Papa Loves Bernard*. For a second I thought there'd been some mistake. I'd never called my father Papa. Dad, yes. Pop, perhaps. The nickname belonged to another parent, didn't mesh with the life I knew.

I looked at Betty. For the moment her attention was elsewhere. Probably in Oxnard.

My father began yanking open drawers and kitchen cabinets, offering me anything that might not fit into his new trailer, which was just about most of what he owned. A punch bowl set, napkin rings, two-pronged forks for spearing hors d'oeuvres—artifacts from his life with my mother, a life of friends and fancy repasts. His barrage of offers was frenzied, desperate. All the while I politely declined. "This is more than enough," I said, gazing at the cake. As hungry as the sight of it made me, I knew a slice would be sickening, dense with sugar, rich with shortening, every bite a spongy glut. Yet it looked so delectable sitting in his kitchen, Betty Crocker's Sunday bonnet. If years of my father's silence had an inverse, that clamorous cake was it. Within it lay every grain of sweetness I'd ever declined or been denied. While my father jettisoned old possessions, I swiped my finger across the frosting and debated whether to taste it.

# D-L-R-O-W

Along with the cake and a box full of childhood memorabilia, I left my father's house with a scrap of paper on which he'd written his new address and telephone number. As I drove down Ambrose Avenue, I watched the Spanish house my family had lived in grow smaller and smaller in my rearview mirror, like a stucco galleon drifting out to sea. The neighborhood hadn't changed much since the days I barreled down that same street on a pair of roller skates, vibrations from the pavement shooting up my skinny legs and rattling my teeth. Driving past the grab bag of architectural styles was like visiting Montana ranch land, the British Isles, and the French countryside in a few seconds flat. It wouldn't have seemed odd if the residents watered their lawns in costume: *Bonjour! Howdy! Jolly good day!* Hollywood had been an ideal setting for someone as tight-lipped about his past as my father, a place where a person could choose a favorite historical style and settle in with his fellow men to a cinematic vision of the good life.

I let the engine idle at the corner, hesitant to make the turn. It was going to take me a while to adapt to the fact that the place had been sold. I'd come to see the house as Brian's inheritance as well as mine, repayment for his constancy and late-night advice, a nest egg my father, when all was said and done, might have decided to pass on to us. That the buyers were a gay couple didn't help; I thought of them as understudies who'd lucked into our roles on opening night. My reverie ended when the cloying fragrance of frosted cake woke me to the here and now. I pressed the pedal and sped away.

After waiting a week or so for my father and Betty to settle in, I called to see how they liked their new home and reached a disconnected number. I checked with directory assistance to make sure 805 was the right area code for Oxnard, which it was, then scrutinized the remaining digits to make sure I hadn't mistaken the seven for a one. I punched the number again in case I'd misdialed, and again was greeted by the recording of a woman who said, in a voice devoid of feeling and inflection, "We're sorry. The number you have reached has been disconnected." *We're* sorry? Was she Pacific Bell's spokes-robot? The collective pronoun only emphasized the fact that no one but me was sorry in the least. Thinking my father may have accidentally transposed two of the seven numbers, I tried a few permutations, but to follow this process through to its logical conclusion, I'd have to dial seven-to-the-seventh-power variations, whatever gargantuan number that was. At this rate, reaching my father could take me the rest of my life, which, metaphorically, was what I'd been doing with my life up till then.

Below the phone number he'd scrawled, "Siesta Court," but there were no numerals to indicate an address, and I wasn't sure whether this was the name of the street or of the trailer park itself. The more I said it to myself, the more Siesta Court sounded fictitious, a location too bucolic to be true, like Cheever's Shady Hill or Levin's Stepford. It was as if my father had packed his bags and vanished into an imaginary landscape.

Cake or no cake, I couldn't help but think he'd done this on purpose.

"A phony number!" I grumbled to Brian. "I haven't thought about people giving other people phony numbers since I cruised the bars." Even back then, this breech of simple decency irked me, and it had happened to me and all my bar-hopping friends at least once. I mean, how hard was it to say you weren't interested in someone while the two of you were face-to-face? Why knowingly fan the flames of false hope? Anyway, it's one thing to get the brush-off from some guy in a bar, but from your own father? I felt as if I'd been abandoned on a stranger's doorstep. Except there was neither a stranger nor a doorstep, and I was pretty old as foundlings go, and the word *foundling* was completely wrong, since *lostling* was closer to what it was like.

What would I do if another week went by without word from him? Who could I contact? He hadn't spoken to his daughters-in-law in years. His former neighbors wanted nothing to do with him. Betty was the only person who might know where he was, and they shared a nonexistent number.

"Can you believe this?" I asked Brian.

"It still tastes pretty good," he said, scarfing down the last dry slice. He swallowed hard. "Even the frosting."

"Hello, Bernard?" The prodigal father. "Bernard?"

*That's my name,* we used to say on the playground. *Don't wear it out.* "Where have you been, Dad? I've been worried sick."

"I moved, remember?"

"The number you gave me is wrong. I asked information for Edward Cooper on Siesta Boulevard, Avenue, Place, Way. I tried everything Siesta!"

"The number's under Betty's name."

Of course; if you're going to antagonize a corporate monopoly, you might as well kiss their services good-bye. "I wish you had called."

"I'm calling you now. Would your phone ring if I wasn't?"

"It's just . . . I had no idea how to find you."

"How'd you like to have dinner with your old man?"

In my head I said, No! Aloud I mumbled, "When?"

"How about now?"

"It's two o'clock in the afternoon."

"How about an hour?"

"Tell me what's going on, Dad."

"For crying out loud! Where'd you learn to be so suspicious? Can't a father visit his son? I thought that's what you wanted."

An ambulance wailed down a nearby street, and a second later I heard its siren over the phone.

"You're in the neighborhood, aren't you?"

"Look. Do you want to get together or not? I didn't take the bus all the way out here so I could suffocate in some phone booth."

"You took the bus?"

"I sold the Caddy. They can use it for scrap metal as far as I'm concerned. Damn thing depreciates just sitting in the driveway. And the mileage, forget it! Guzzles money. Besides, the gal at DMV wouldn't renew my license due to my glasses. All I need's a new pre-scription. I've been driving a car since before she had eyes!"

"Is Betty with you?"

"No. And if she calls you and asks where I am, tell her you don't know. Tell her you haven't heard from me in weeks."

"I *haven't* heard from you in weeks."

"Good," he said. "Then you won't have to lie."

Whatever he was up to, it wasn't good. Oxnard is sixty miles north of Los Angeles, a daunting journey for a man my father's age, especially one who hadn't used public transportation since the 1940s, when Pacific Electric's Red Cars plodded along the down-town streets, sparks cascading from overhead wires. That he'd arrived here safely was a tribute to his grit when meeting a challenge, or his desperation when fleeing from one.

I was about to leave the house to pick him up when Betty phoned. "Your father and me had a fight," she blurted. Her voice was ragged. "He stormed out hours ago and I don't know where he is. He was confused worse than I've ever seen him. He'd been gone for almost an hour when I got in my car and went looking for him. He barely knows the area. There are lots of places around here a per-son could get lost, railroad yards and citrus orchards. You could walk a long way and not see a McDonald's or 7-Eleven. Every few miles I'd pull over to the side of the road, get out of the car, and stand there shouting my lungs out. I couldn't remember whether he was wearing his Miracle-Ear when he left. And who's to say he'd answer if he heard me? I drove and drove and hardly saw a soul. It might as well have been me who was lost. I could have sworn the end-time had arrived!"

As difficult as it might have been for me to imagine Betty's vision of the Rapture—believers abruptly sucked into the sky, their bodies rising heavenward in a great migration—it was even more difficult for Betty to imagine herself being left behind with the unrepentant, her cries unanswered in the desolate landscape. "If Ed found his way back here while I was out looking for him, I'm not sure he'd recognize our trailer without my station wagon parked beside it. The trailers in our court look pretty much the same. 'Cracker boxes' is what he calls them."

I told Betty not to worry, then failed my father by letting her know he'd called me from the corner. "Praise the Lord," she said forlornly. "Did he tell you the DMV revoked his license? He sold his Caddy the very next day. You know how proud he was of that car. He's usually shrewd about business, but he left it in front of the trailer park with a For Sale sign and struck a deal with the first people who came along. A young couple. Newlyweds maybe. And listen to this: he let them pay with a personal check! 'Good riddance,' he kept telling me. 'It's someone else's headache now.' What he'd done didn't really hit him until he figured out that he had no way to go to the bank and make the deposit. He asked if he could borrow my car, and when I told him he couldn't drive without a license, he said, 'What the hell difference does a piece of paper make? You think I'll drive any better with a piece of paper?' and I said, 'It's against the law,' and he said, 'Don't tell *me* about the law. I have more law in my little finger than most men have in their whole hand.'

"He called me selfish and yelled at me to get out of his house. *His* house. I couldn't believe it! I waved the deed to the trailer in front of his face so he could see both of our signatures for himself. He snatched it away and stared at it for a long time, checking to make sure his signature was his. His hand was shaking something awful. I said he better sit down and get a grip on himself, and he threw the deed on the floor, grabbed a couple of his things and left, but not before reminding me I wasn't his wife."

"I'm sorry," I said.

"He had every right to say it. I'm not his wife in the eyes of God. We pooled our money to make a life. No man has wanted that from me—a life together—in a long, long time. But we shouldn't have lied to that social worker, Mr. Gomez, about your father's mental health. Now we're being punished by the lie coming true!

"This trailer park is tiny and I'm sure the neighbors heard us yelling. I'm looking for steady work and I can't get work if people think I fight in my private life or if they hear that I tried to cheat an old man out of his mobile home. It only takes one rumor to ruin a reputation. The arguing, the accusations would be one thing if people thought we were husband and wife, but after all this time, he still tells them I'm his nurse!" Betty usually had comforting proverbs and Bible quotations to fit any dilemma, but none came to her now. "Maybe it's the medications and he can't help acting this way. I thought things would be different after . . . I thought once we moved . . . If he had a relationship with the Lord . . ."

"Betty . . ."

"If he knew the Lord through me, I mean, like the friend of a friend. What I'm trying to say is that I've worked at plenty of places where old folks can't feed themselves or tie their own shoes. They dirty their diapers and cry for their mothers. Old people, not a tooth in their head, crying for a mother who's never going to come. It has to be the most pitiful sound on earth. Half of them don't recognize their own children on visiting day; all they see's a stranger who claims to be kin. You can't hardly blame them for saying mean things like, 'I don't know you. Go away.' That's how bad I thought it had to get before an old person was a danger to themselves or someone else. You know me," she said sardonically, "always a step ahead of the doctors.

"I thought there was normal and then there was not normal. But not normal sneaks up on you. Not normal takes its sweet time. It was terrible the way your father looked at me before he walked out.

He recognized his signature on the deed but didn't remember signing his name. Either way it frightened him to death. And you know
what happens when your dad gets scared. He blames the nearest person. Oh, he didn't have to say it outright. I saw it on his face as plain
as day: if I had forged his signature, the deed would make sense; if I
was dishonest, then he was sane. Trusting other people was never his
strong suit. My mistake was thinking I was going to be the exception, the person he'd never turn against." She blew her nose and
took a breath. "The man's in trouble. There. I said it."

The reason for my father's unannounced visit, or so he claimed, was
to hand over a family heirloom he'd been wanting to give me ever
since he'd packed up the Spring Street office. A belated gift, to say
the least. This act of generosity justified his anger toward Betty—
how could she have refused a favor to a generous old man?—with
the added vengeful benefit that his disappearance would cause her
distress. By denying him the use of her car, she'd condemned him to
spend the rest of his days wandering through Oxnard on foot, a lost
tribe unto himself.

My father's mercurial love bounced from one ungrateful recipi-
ent to the next, and I knew enough to mistrust it, knew I'd stay in
his favor for only so long and always at a cost to someone else. Still,
he could have made up any number of excuses to explain his visit
to the city, and he made one up that included me.

Even before I spotted him squinting into a row of news vending
machines on the corner, I began clearing off the passenger seat,
plucking tape cassettes off the floor, and tossing empty water bottles
into the back. He'd often said my car was "a pigsty," but I wasn't
cleaning up the car to prove him wrong so much as I was trying to
impersonate the responsible adult pictured on my driver's license.

I found a parking space on my first trip around the block—a
small miracle in a city as crowded as this—and edged my car toward
the curb. My father looked up from the headline he was reading and
stared at me through the passenger window. He tightly clutched a

brown paper bag to his chest, as if someone might try to steal it away.
I waved hello and smiled as if everything was fine. I could tell he was
looking right at me because his thick prescription glasses magnified
his eyes, the trajectory of his gaze direct and unmistakable. The sky
was an ingot of afternoon light, everything distinct beneath it. I
motioned for him to open the car door and climb inside. Not a
blink. Not so much as a twitch of volition. Betty's phrase came back
to me, "Strangers who claim to be kin." We continued to stare at
each other, my father and I. With the windows rolled up, the world
surged by with barely a sound. He seemed to be sealed inside the
sunlight just as surely as I was sealed inside my car. I was afraid to roll
down the window, afraid he wouldn't respond to my voice, wouldn't
react if I called him Father. Stranded in the gap between silence and
speech, I could almost feel my own name loosen and peel away, leaving me raw and anonymous.

His eyebrows bunched in puzzlement when I lowered the window. The hum of the city flooded in.

"It's you!" he cried happily. "I couldn't see through the glare on
the glass."

"Didn't you recognize my car?"

He looked the vehicle up and down. "It's clean," he said. "So, no."

I walked around to the passenger side and opened the door for
him. "Thank you, sir," he said. I didn't know it yet, but medieval
chivalry would play a central role in this reunion. I reached out to
help steady him into the seat, but he kept his arms folded over the
paper bag, shifting his weight, unassisted, limb by limb.

We ignored the telephone ringing in the corner booth, probably
the operator requesting that he make another deposit. Cars flew
through the busy intersection, generating enough wind to blow
candy wrappers and want ads along the sidewalk. If I'd been told as
a child my neighborhood would one day teem with nonstop traffic,
I never would have believed it. Nor would I have believed that my
father would ride the bus through several outlying counties to meet
me on the same street where, long ago, he'd threatened to leave me
and drive away.

Back behind the wheel, I suggested we sit a minute and bask in the rarity of a convenient parking space. "Fine with me," said my father. "I'm not going anywhere." I slipped the key into the ignition, half a dozen others dangling from the chain. "You got a lot of keys," he said. "My philosophy is: it's better to get it down to one. That way you only got one to keep track of. If you lose it, though, you're up shit's creek." I remembered him in the living room, crawling on the white carpet, except that in the memory—so much for trusty recall—the shag was as tall as wild grass, a synthetic meadow I crawled through too, a son alongside his father, foraging for a key.

"It's a long haul from Oxnard," I said.

He shrugged.

"Are you feeling okay these days?"

"Whaddaya call okay?"

"Do you feel like yourself?"

"Who else would I feel like?"

No matter how tightly he clutched the bag to his chest, he couldn't steady the tremor in his hands, and so he beamed a munificent grin, as if to convince me that he shook with the excitement of gift-giving alone. I waited, but he seemed to forget that a gift is bestowed.

"Is it a cake?" I teased.

He examined the flattened bag, turning it this way and that. I hoped he understood the reference. What could be worse for a once-antic man than ungraspable banter? "Yes," he said. "A pancake."

He handed me the bag and, radiant with anticipation, watched me fold it open. The weedy scent of old paper wafted from its dark interior. I could make out the edge of a wooden picture frame, the gleam of glass.

"Go on," he said.

The first glimpse wasn't encouraging. An illustrated shield featured three stout bulls in silhouette, their tails arched above their backs. Realistic pink ribbons, or once-red ribbons faded by sun, festooned the picture's borders. Not ribbons exactly, for they were also like the tendrils of a plant that sprouted an occasional spade-shaped leaf. Above the shield hovered the kind of medieval helmet worn with a clanking suit of armor. A grate on the lower half of the helmet allowed a knight to breathe, although large rectangular eyeholes revealed that the helmet was empty. *Oh God,* I thought, *not something headless!* And then I thought, Now *there's* a prayer.

"You don't even know what it is," said my father, "and already you don't like it."

"I do!" I said. "What is it?"

"It doesn't look familiar?"

Printed at the bottom in a nearly unreadable Gothic font was the name Cooper, every letter barbed with serifs, even the *o*'s. Fluttering above the family name, a banner read *Frango Dura Patientia.*

"It means," said my father, "'I break hard things by perseverance.' All of us do. All of us Coopers. It's a whaddaya call it—a motto. You have in your hands our family crest! It used to hang in my office, remember? The bulls are for courage and there's a bunch of other symbolism. Read what it says on the other side."

A genealogical fact sheet had been glued to the back of the frame. "Heraldic symbols are testaments to the bravery, heroism, and meritorious deeds of our ancestors. They appeal to the pride of distinguished families today, just as the valiant deeds and self-sacrificing acts of contemporary persons would appeal to their ancestors." Along with this flattering description of anyone who valiantly plunked down a couple of bucks for a reproduction of his or her family crest, the armorial lineage of my family had been traced to its ancient seat in England. Specifically, to nine British counties including Northumberland, Dorset, Nottingham, and Shropshire. I knew that Cooper was an occupational surname for a maker of casks and barrels, but when I saw the identity of the ancestor to whom we supposedly owed our DNA, the tint of our skin, the slope of our noses, the very core of our character, I couldn't keep still.

"Dad, we are not related in any way, shape, or form to the Wee Cooper of Fife. You understand that, right?"

"Maybe not to him in particular."

"Not in general either. Not even remotely. Your parents and Mother's came from Russia."

"So?"

"So I don't think they passed through an Irish fiefdom or wherever the Wee Cooper called home."

He pointed to a passage tracing the earliest member of the family to a William Cooper, who traveled from Yorkshire to Bucks County, Pennsylvania, in 1699. "I grew up in Philly."

"But you were born in Atlantic City."

"You never know how far a person can go. I knew a judge who grew up without any advantages whatsoever. He had to fight tooth-and nail to sit on the bench, and that's where he sat for the rest of his life."

My birthright as a Cooper was to persevere. "I'm not talking human potential, Dad. It's a matter of history."

"This," he said, snatching the frame out of my hands, "is history."

On the wall of my father's waiting room there'd hung an etching of a barrister in a powdered wig, his chest puffed out as he pontificated to twelve jurors—all of them asleep in their seats. A brass statuette of blind Justice stood on the end table and balanced mounds of peppermint candies on her bobbing scales. Next to issues of *Life* magazine lay a book entitled *Laffs Galore,* one-liners to rival Henny Youngman's. Hadn't the family crest been displayed in the same spirit of levity, humor to soothe a fretful clientele?

Judging from my father's downturned mouth and sagging shoulders, the answer was no. He set the crest facedown in his lap.

"Dad," I said, "wasn't your father given his surname at Ellis Island?"

"He was a cooper smith. That's how he made his living."

"His name must have been changed to Cooper from something else."

"From what?"

"That's what I was going to ask you. You're the only person left who knows."

My father stared into the distance and moved his lips, silently shaping name after name. One among them might be ours. There came a soundless flood of appellations. Forty days and nights of names.

"Dad?"

His lips began to quiver. His eyes grew red.

"It's okay," I said. "Forget it."

"I did," he whispered.

A week later, my father sat beside me in the east wing of Saint Joseph's Hospital, in Oxnard, waiting for an appointment with a geriatric specialist, less than pleased to be there. He wouldn't have come at all if Brian hadn't known Dr. Montrose personally and vouched for her reputation. Despite Dad's mistrust for people in the medical profession, and whatever his misgivings about two men living together, he was proud that his son had snagged himself a doctor. Brian had a degree in psychology, not medicine, but a doctor was a doctor in my father's book, and he couldn't care less if an *M.* or *Ph.* preceded the *D.*

He turned to face me, his glasses flashing. "I don't want you to watch me grow old."

"Believe me," I said, "there are plenty of things worse than growing old."

"Such as?"

"Such as *not* growing old."

For a moment we were allied in silence, remembering Bob and Gary and Ron. Their deaths were done, but their dying survived them.

"Look at it this way," I said. "We're growing old together."

"It's happening faster to me."

"No, Dad. You and I are aging at the same rate."

"Time goes faster when you're older."

"It only *seems* to go faster. It can't go faster for you than it does for me." No sooner had I said this than I realized that Einstein had, in fact, proven time's relativity. I forged ahead anyway. "I know this is hard for you, but there may be a medical reason for your confusion . . ."

"Who's confused?"

"Well, I am, for one. I've been confused by several things you've done recently. Especially your trip into the city last week. Things I've chalked up to . . . your temperament."

"I got news for you: having a temperament doesn't make me a bad person."

A bedraggled man in a wheelchair rolled himself into the waiting room. A thin blue tube snaked from his nostrils to a portable oxygen tank.

"Your behavior may have a physiological cause," I continued. "It could be treatable. There's no harm in talking to Dr. Montrose."

"She sure as hell won't tell me anything I couldn't tell myself."

"She might be able to suggest a new medication or changes in your regimen." I didn't mention Alzheimer's or geriatric dementia, though these possibilities must have occurred to my father, too.

He leaned close. "Let me ask you something."

I wanted to be as frank as possible. If there was a medical ordeal ahead, maybe we'd have a last chance at attachment. I looked into his eyes. "Ask me anything you want."

"Why . . . ," he said, then hesitated.

"Go on." I urged him.

"Why are you reading the *Ladies' Home Journal*?"

"What?"

"Why did you pick that magazine out of all the magazines in the waiting room? There must be I don't know how many others to chose from and you picked that."

The March issue had been lying on my lap, opened to a double-page photo of the creamiest seafood bisque I've ever seen, a kind of culinary centerfold. I thought I'd cook it for Brian and was about to rip out the recipe. Even in a time of crisis, Dad found a way to goad me like a pro. "Nobody here cares if I'm reading a men's magazine or a women's magazine!" I glanced around the waiting room to see if I could spot a man reading *Today's Bride* or a woman reading *Popular Mechanics,* but where is proof when you really need it? "Ideas about masculinity and femininity are different now than they were in your day." I thought back to the hot afternoon I'd been cinched into my father's jumpsuit, drunk on rum punch and basted in my own perspiration, staggering through a backyard filled with dykes disguised as housewives who were really machines. "People today are more . . . flexible."

"I'll bet," he said.

The man in the wheelchair wasn't even pretending not to listen. His eyes met mine and glistened with interest. His posture improved.

I said, "You were trying to change the subject is what you were trying to do. Then we wouldn't have to talk about why you're here. Well, it's not going to work." But it had, of course, worked like a charm. Conversation between us ceased. We folded our arms and glowered straight ahead.

"Dad," I said, "I hate that one of us always has to be right."

"I'm not the one who always has to be right. You are."

A nurse hurried into the waiting room and glanced at a clipboard. People shifted in their seats and listened. She had to call for Mr. Hahn—the man in the wheelchair—twice before he managed to release the handbrake and propel himself forward.

Dad said, "You gotta hand it to the old bastard for getting himself to the hospital." Translation: *A son should release his father's handbrake and stand aside.*

"I'm sure someone brought him."

"You don't know that for a fact."

I tossed the *Ladies' Home Journal* onto a table heaped with magazines and fished a copy of *Men's Fitness* from the pile, a publication my father was pleased to see me "read." Looking at pictures of half-dressed men triggered one lustful detonation after another, and I was grateful they didn't make noise. An article about elderly athletes showed a group of fleet and happy geriatrics dashing through an obstacle course. Great, I thought, now old people can't just sit back, relax, and fall apart, they have to jump hurdles into perpetuity.

My father countered with faint snoring. He slumped in his chair, mouth hanging open, stomach rising and falling beneath his indestructible jumpsuit. I noticed that the collar had frayed, insofar as synthetic resin can fray. Here and there, the fabric was stained with a spotty chronicle of former meals. He hadn't given up on personal grooming entirely—he'd doused himself with Old Spice—but his long campaign of vanity had come to an end, both its failures and triumphs behind him.

When the nurse called, "Mr. Cooper," I thought for a second she meant me, and I wondered who would watch over my father when I was gone. His eyelids fluttered at the sound of her voice. I could almost see our family name sinking inside him like a pebble in a well, its ripples disrupting the waters of sleep, triggering his limbs to shift and his flesh and bones to unwillingly wake in the form of an aching, groggy old man.

"My apologies," said Dr. Montrose. "I'm running a little late." A fleshy, energetic brunette, she escorted us into her office and took a seat behind her desk.

My father landed heavily in the chair facing her and I sat off to the side. "The wait wasn't too bad," I said. Dad glared at me because he couldn't understand why I didn't protest what he thought was an unreasonably long delay for an appointment he wasn't keen on in the first place.

"What did you and your son do in the waiting room?" Dr. Montrose asked. She locked him into eye contact. And so the evaluation began.

"My son read the *Ladies' Home Journal* and I made the mistake of noticing out loud, for which I got my head chewed off."

She turned to me. "Were you reading the *Ladies' Home Journal*?"

I looked at my father when I answered. "It's not like I subscribe," I said.

Dr. Montrose took this as a yes.

"And do you recall what magazine you were reading, Mr. Cooper?"

"No."

I thought of intervening because I knew my father meant he hadn't read a magazine, not that he couldn't recall which one.

She leaned forward, elbows on her desk. "Have you been having any difficulty remembering things recently?"

"I'm fine."

"I'm sure you are. But if we test you today, we'll have a baseline to compare against future tests."

"Future tests?" He looked as if he'd tasted something sour.

"What about that upsets you?"

"What about what?"

"About what I just said."

My father went pale. "What was it you said?"

Dr. Montrose jotted a note. "I'm going to ask you several questions," she continued, "and I'd like you to answer them one at a time."

"How else would I?"

"How else would you what?"

"Answer them, for Christ's sake!"

"Calm down, Dad."

"I'll calm down when I'm good and ready."

"We'll be working from what's called the Mini-Mental State Examination," said Dr. Montrose, "and I'll score your answers as we go along."

Dad adjusted his Miracle-Ear. "So test me, already."

The doctor retrieved a sheet of paper from her desk drawer and began to read aloud. First, she asked my father to tell her the date. He got it right, whereas I'd silently answered along and was off by a couple of days. Was my lapse symptomatic of a larger cognitive problem? I scooted my chair closer. Now I had to prove to myself that there was nothing wrong with me by answering every subsequent question correctly. I also had to face the fact that I felt competitive with my father, as though we were opponents on a quiz show hosted by Dr. Montrose. She held the sheet of questions in such a way that light streaming through her office window turned the paper translucent, and I wondered if my father could read the correct answers from the other side. Then I realized there *were* no correct answers to this kind of test, only variable replies. Was there any way to cheat on a mental competency exam? None that I could think of, which may or may not have been a good sign.

"What country are we in? . . . State? . . . City? . . . Hospital? . . . Floor?"

Not until Dr. Montrose whispered, "Bernard," did I realize I'd been muttering answers under my breath. There was no way my father could have heard me from where he was sitting, so it wasn't as if I was prompting him. And anyway, I got them right. Dad, on the other hand, didn't know what floor we were on, but if *he* had been the one to push the elevator button instead of me, he probably would have known it was the third. The mechanics of recall are delicate, so iffy and contingent.

As for calling this hospital "Saint Sinai," if Dr. Montrose had thought about it for a minute, she would have realized that his answer combined the names of two major medical facilities, Saint Joseph's and Cedars-Sinai. His guess was as logical as it was wrong, but since the testee wasn't given credit for near misses or whimsical hybrids, why explain his error's fine points? Besides, I'd already been caught talking to myself, and Dr. Montrose must not have thought me the most reliable advocate for a man who's rapidly failing his Mini-Mental. Sensing he'd made a mistake, my father lowered his head, laced his fingers together in his lap, and stared at one hand meshing with the other. He had the shamed, inward look of a man who knows he's blundered but doesn't know how, and therefore can't correct himself or offer an excuse.

"Mr. Cooper," asked Dr. Montrose, "are you ready to continue?"

Still staring into his lap, my father nodded. His head seemed heavy, as if with answers that would soon elude him.

"Spell *world* backwards," said Dr. Montrose.

Dad looked up and unclasped his hands. His glasses slid down the bridge of his nose. "Why?" he asked, peering over the rims. "Why *world*?"

Because the world *is* backwards, I said to myself. Laws are repealed. Iron rusts. Logic unravels.

"I suggest you don't overthink the questions, Mr. Cooper. Just try to relax and let the answers come."

My father poked his glasses back into place. He deliberated on every letter. "*D* . . . *L* . . . *O* . . . *R* . . . *W*?"

She recorded his score. "Now, please repeat the following list of items in the order I read them to you: apple, penny, table."

Dad cocked his head and thought a minute. "Did I get it right?"

"You haven't repeated the items yet."

"Not those," he says. "*World*. Did I get it backwards?"

"Ask me at the end of the test."

"Suppose I forget?"

"We should move on to this next question," insisted Dr. Montrose. "It's important to administer the MME as methodically as possible. I don't want to rush you, Mr. Cooper, but once we've established the pace, digressions are only going to interfere with your concentration and skew the results. Now, kindly repeat after me: apple, penny, table."

"You can't tell me now?

"Penny, table, apple," she persisted.

Was it me, I wondered, or did she get the order wrong?

My father probably couldn't see well enough to read the spines of the books lining the shelves behind the doctor's head: *The Aging Population. Dementia and Its Consequences.* The titles would make me nervous if I was trying to prove my mental acuity.

Dr. Montrose waited, with perfectly calibrated neutrality, for my father to recite the list. She'd been schooled in being patient, had practiced it the way one practices the piano, striking every octave of calm, every note of analytic distance.

"Apple," he said at last. "The rest I forget." He dismissed his insufficient recall with a wave of his hand, but he looked at me to gauge how he was doing. I smiled noncommittally back.

Next, she asked him to repeat the phrase, "No ifs, ands, or buts." Without missing a beat, my father drew himself upright, gulped the necessary air, and spit out the words with a force that caused his face to redden like a fanned coal. He pounded his fist in his open palm.

He was good at ultimatums. Ultimatums were his forte. No ifs, ands, or buts about it, he was ready to resume.

"Can you tell me what this is?" she asked, holding up her pen.

"A ballpoint," he said. "Does it have your motto on it?"

Dr. Montrose informed him that men and women in her profession didn't, as a rule, have mottos. Then she noticed that there were, in fact, words printed along the side of the pen. She held it horizontally and squinted. "Hot Water Management Service," she read. "Where could this have come from?"

I suspected this question wasn't part of the test, but it was hard to tell where the Mini-Mental left off and idle curiosity began.

Dad said, "Pens are everywhere these days. People need pens to make lists, what with all the rushing and the doing and the coming and the going. What I'd like to know, though, is what the hell is a Hot Water Management Service?"

He'd posed a blunt yet provocative question, one resistant to statistical norms, to pre- and postmodern theory. Was the need to manage hot water greater than the need to manage cold or lukewarm water? Was it managed through a system of pipes and valves? Was the service a private enterprise, or government run? We hadn't a single answer among us, not a guess or speculation. The doctor continued to gaze at the pen, holding it at either end and slowly turning it between her fingers as though she might find still other phrases inscribed on its side. Beyond the hospital window, the sky above Oxnard deepened into dusk. A couple of pink clouds glided across the horizon and for a moment it seemed as if the building was revolving while the clouds stood still. As we tried to unpuzzle the message on the pen, the office's walls and furniture dimmed, our faces growing vague. A clock ticked loudly on the doctor's desk, and I felt a certainty down to my bones that the three of us, second by second, were drawn toward a vast and eventual forgetting. Nothing we could do or say would stop it. No matter where we turned we couldn't turn back. One day this room wouldn't ring a bell for anyone now sitting within it.

*    *    *

Dr. Montrose explained that my father's score revealed a mild-to-moderate cognitive impairment. She addressed Dad directly, telling him it would require several more tests, both physical and psychological, to discover whether his condition was temporary.

"You call this a condition?" he asked, moving his arms and legs as if his aspirin-enhanced mobility made further tests unnecessary.

"I think we should schedule an MRI for you later this week."

"I just took it!" he protested.

"That was the MME. There are so many acronyms in our profession. It's confusing, I know."

"It's ridiculous, is what it is. It's alphabet soup." If my father grasped the ramifications of scoring poorly, if he gleaned from Dr. Montrose's gentle voice her wish to buffer the news that his faculties might decline over the coming months, he didn't let on. He was as upset as he would have been had he lost a round of gin rummy, tossing his cards onto the table, ready to try his luck again.

Both my father and I had hoped the results of the examination would be somewhat definitive, if that's not a contradiction, but the consultation added yet another ambiguity to our already extensive collection. Dr. Montrose implied that my father's mental acuity could go either way, or any way, or every way at once, which, as my father had said in the waiting room, was something we could have told ourselves.

Night had fallen by the time we left Saint Joseph's. Arc lights in the parking lot tinted white cars yellow, red cars brown. The world lay before us in a new, deceptive spectrum. We'd both forgotten where I'd parked and we wandered across blacktop still soft from the day's heat, sure we'd spotted the right make and model, only to discover, once we came closer, that we'd made a mistake.

The central wing of Saint Joseph's towered above us, a monolith of lit-up windows. On every floor, people waited with a terrible impatience for recovery, visitors, morphine, sleep. My father had narrowly escaped the place, and by the time we finally found the car, I couldn't get out of the parking lot fast enough to suit him.

After negotiating stop-and-go traffic along the commercial strip, we passed fewer and fewer fast food restaurants and discount designer outlets, until we sailed through the outskirts of town, where distant lights lay scattered across the black landscape. The sky was more of the same, but higher.

I'd come by the trailer park earlier that afternoon to pick up Dad for his appointment and to drop off Brian for a private talk with Betty. The plan was that Brian would ask if we could pay her to continue living with my father until I could find a suitable retirement home or assisted-living facility. In broad day, the Siesta's trailers had been uniform in shape and painted drab industrial colors, sunspots glaring on their corrugated roofs. Not only were they similar enough to confuse a person with cognitive problems, they were similar enough to induce confusion in a person without cognitive problems.

Before Dad and I drove off to meet with Dr. Montrose, Betty drew me a map of the route between the trailer park and Saint Joseph's, and now, as my father and I returned after dark, he glanced at it repeatedly and warned me that her directions were wrong.

"They got us to the hospital," I told him. "They ought to get us back."

"You'd trust a bunch of chicken scratches?" Whether or not he could have pinpointed the source of his anger—Betty's refusal to let him borrow her car—it seized him each time he glanced at the map. "That woman couldn't find her way out of a paper bag."

"It's *fight,* Dad, not *find.* She couldn't *fight* her way out of a paper bag. Or—wait—is it *punch?*"

Whenever he recommended that I make a turn or continue straight ahead, I grunted in compliance, then followed Betty's drawing. I was pretty sure we weren't lost, but between the charade of obeying my father's instructions and the endless bolt of open road unfurling in my high beams, we could have been inventing the miles as we drove along.

*Siesta Trailer Park* was spelled out for passersby above the main gate, the sign's wooden letters all but invisible against the night sky. No matter how slowly I drove down the property's unpaved main road, a cloud of dust billowed behind the car. There wasn't a person in sight, yet every window jittered with light from a television. A raucous pack of dogs materialized in my headlights, their teeth bared, eyes incandescent. Once it became clear that I'd slow the car but wouldn't stop, they yapped a last, collective protest and bounded away.

"Home again, home again," said my father as we crept toward his trailer. "Jiggity jig." He asked if I remembered him reading me *The Three Little Pigs* when I was a boy. "That," he explained, "was why you decided to become a writer."

"So you *did* hear my acceptance speech?"

"Speech?" he asked, baffled.

I shrugged. "Nothing."

I put the car in park and told my father that Brian had stayed behind to discuss some important matters with Betty. Through the screen door to his trailer, I could see Brian and Betty seated across from each other at a small dinette table, talking intently. A neon fixture in the kitchen cast a bright, uncompromising light over the entire room. Brian leaned forward at the slant of active listening. Betty held a steaming mug with both hands, a wisp of damp hair clinging to her forehead. The glazed resignation on her face told me she'd grudgingly agreed to our plan, as ready as she'd ever be for the task ahead.

"What's to discuss?" asked my father. He squinted through the windshield, through the cloud of dust stirred up by our arrival, and waited for my answer. No sentence I'd written up till then had called for such treacherous, measured phrasings. I looked away so my face wouldn't betray me. *Your thoughts are no longer dependable. Plans you cannot change have been made.* The insolvability of it all must have made me thickheaded because it took me a moment to realize that my father hadn't just opened his door to get some air but had slipped out of his seat and was headed toward the trailer. He hoisted himself up the steps of a front porch that looked like a big aluminum stepping stool. I dashed from the car and caught the screen door an instant before it sprang shut behind him. Neon tubes leeched color from the room, and even now I remember the scene in black-and-white, like one of the images Brian had described from the The-matic Apperception Test, a picture whose story is imminent yet fixed. My hand forever reaches out but never touches my father's shoulder. I'll never restrain or calm him down. Wrenched from solemn conversation, Brian and Betty turn their heads, not know-ing for a moment who's barged through the door. My father stands within a glaring room and ceaselessly reads two startled faces: *Who are you*, they demand. *Where did you come from? What do you want?*

# This Side Up

When I gripped my father's shoulder, our misunderstanding, like a rusty machine, shuddered and started up again. He spun around at the touch of my hand.

"Betty is going to stay here with you, Dad."

"That's nice," he said warily. "Why wouldn't she?"

"Why wouldn't I," echoed Betty. "I'm his nurse." She carried her mug into the kitchen and rinsed it under the blasting tap. A pair of headlights swept past the windows, the raucous dog pack giving chase.

"In the meantime," I said, "we can start looking for a place where . . ."

"Did you offer Brian a cup of tea?" he asked Betty.

"No," she said curtly. "I offered him soda." She grabbed a bottle from the refrigerator and refilled Brian's glass. A head of foam hissed toward the rim. Brian chugged soda before it overflowed, coughing his thanks.

"And one for my son?"

"Maybe later," I said.

Betty glared at my father, then marched back into the kitchen and opened a cupboard door with enough force to send a vehement little breeze across the room.

"This place is certainly compact!" exclaimed Brian.

"You'd never know to look at it," remarked my father, eager to resume his role as the man of the house, "but there's storage galore."

"Built-ins," added Betty, handing me a glass. "The mess is hidden."

I couldn't blame her for mocking my father's expectation that we'd carry on as normal, though it wasn't clear if he wanted to avoid a confrontation with Betty until after Brian and I left, or if he had succumbed to what further tests would determine was dementia. For now, however, none of us could come up with a better plan than complicity.

"How 'bout a tour?" Dad asked no one in particular. Brian and I made enthusiastic noises and stood at the ready.

"I think I'll sit this one out," said Betty. She settled into her seat at the dinette table, but the trailer was so small that she essentially joined us without having to move an inch.

It seemed logical, I suppose, to start the tour with a few interesting facts about the dinette set since it was right there in front of us, waiting for explication. My father informed us that it was made of Formica and chrome and purchased by Betty at the Furniture Barn's liquidation sale. Betty shifted in her chair and gave us a perfunctory wave, as if she were on display in some absurd museum.

The tour resumed with a slow pivot around the room. Dad said, "That open space between the kitchen and the dining area is called a . . . a . . ."

"A pass-though," said Betty.

"Due to the fact that you can pass food and other items through it, on a plate or what have you, without walking all the way from the kitchen to . . . well, to over here." He paused. "It seemed like a selling point at the time. The agent called this floor plan . . ." He deferred to Betty. "A what did he call it?"

"A step saver."

My father snorted. "Not that your old man has many steps left!"

The mahogany breakfront so prominent in the former living room had been replaced by a hutch containing Betty's collection of religious figurines, including a sculpture of praying hands. Plugged into an outlet, the hands emanated a pious light thanks to the Oxnard

Department of Water and Power, which, according to my father, routinely sent "nuts" out to the trailer park to read the tenant's meters. And the meter for their particular trailer, my father insisted, was always "on the fritz." This explained the ominous pile of unopened bills I'd noticed on the kitchen counter, several from the DWP.

"And over here," he said, pointing to three cardboard boxes stacked against the wall, "you'll see the moving boxes we haven't unpacked." Various destinations—bath, bedroom, storage—had been scrawled across them. Emphatic black arrows indicated which end was up. Somebody (I hoped my father) had stacked the boxes in such a way that each arrow was aligned in the correct, ascending direction, like a child's blocks balanced one atop the other. Never had that simple injunction—*This Side Up*—seemed to me as meaningful. Is there anything more important than being oriented, in complete accord with the compass points, your feet firmly planted on the ground? Is there any knowledge sweeter than knowing whether you're coming or going?

The tour continued as my father guided us a few steps here, a few steps there, stopping to identify the trailer's standard features with an enthusiasm the average tour guide usually reserves for suspension bridges and natural rock formations.

Here is the linen closet.

The medicine cabinet's salves and tablets.

Here is the light switch.

The thermostat.

Up there you'll see the smoke detector.

Behold the phone jack.

We squeezed into a hallway that was really more of a vestibule with exits. My father opened the door to his "office" and stood at the portal, barring our way. Brian and I peered over his shoulders. The hidden mess Betty had spoken of was not, as I had first thought, metaphoric, but a Dumpster's worth of genuine refuse. The depositions and memos and old manila folders that had been gathered into stacks and piles at the former house now blanketed the floor, ankle-deep, sorted according to alphabet soup. A small wooden desk broke through the clutter like an island rising from a paper sea. On the last Friday of every December, at five o'clock sharp, people who worked downtown celebrated the new year by opening their windows and flinging outdated calendar pages onto the streets below, and my father, judging from the state of his office, had decided to continue this tradition indoors. The drawback to his version of the ritual was that he didn't rid himself of clerical excess but trapped himself within it, like a bird who gathers twigs and grasses to build a nest it can't fly out of.

Brian had always been able to discern, in a crowded public place and from a considerable distance, those seemingly ordinary people who turned out to be mad ranters, prisoners to tics and repetition, obeyers of demanding imaginary voices, and he'd developed a subtle grunt to warn me if one of them was headed our way. He made that sound now, and I leaned against him—I could hardly avoid it in those cramped quarters—for the solace of his body heat.

Dad stepped back and quickly shut the door. "Been busy," he said. "Swamped. Retirement is a full-time job."

At the threshold to the master bedroom, he again blocked our way, though this room was inaccessible for a different reason. Whereas entering the office would have meant tramping over layers of paperwork, the bedroom was almost entirely occupied by his old California king, the mahogany headboard blocking the lower half of the only window. I say the room was "occupied" by the bed but it would be more accurate to say that the bed "consumed" the room, which was cushioned like a playpen and yet as abject as a padded cell. It amazed me that he'd decided to take the bed with him to Oxnard, and I wondered what feats of strength and engineering had been necessary for the movers to cram so large a mattress through so small a door. A narrow, very narrow aisle ran along two sides of the bed, just wide enough for Betty and my father to sidle along it like people trapped on a window ledge. The door from the hall swung open less than halfway before it struck the edge of the mattress with a muffled thud. Bedtime preparations must have culminated with my father and Betty sucking in their stomachs and drawing themselves upright in order to squeeze the sleepy bulk of themselves through the door, inadvertently polishing the doorknob with the chamois of their pajamas. If the bedroom closet hadn't been accessible through sliding doors, their clothes would have hung there, as Betty might have said, till kingdom come. Not surprisingly, the bed was unmade, since one of them would have had to crawl across it to tuck the sheets in along the two sides flush with the walls, and then crawl back to dismount the mattress, leaving a trail of self-defeating wrinkles. No, for the two people who shared this room, neatness was a pretense best abandoned.

As we peered at the rumpled bed, I heard Betty pad up behind us. She placed her hand on my shoulder and left it there with just enough reassuring pressure to let me know she'd calmed down. My father was telling Brian that he'd owned the bed for practically half his life, that it was the only bed he could depend on for a good night's sleep, that its springs were of an enduring quality absent in the sorry excuses for a mattress they sold folks today. It may be an old bed, he said, but it was a hell of a lot better than sleeping on the floor. He also told Brian that my mother died of a heart attack in the bed, which was true, and that my brothers and I were born in it, which was false, and I didn't have either the energy or heart to set the record straight. The record was bent beyond repair. Exhausted as I was by the prospect of a long drive home, the "Lament of the Bed" seemed to me as elegiac in its failed longings as a story by John Cheever or a poem by James Merrill. It may have been the jewel of my father's oeuvre, a ballad on par with "Cooper & Sons" and "The Captive Bride."

"Now you've seen everything," said Dad, closing the door to the bedroom and concluding the tour.

Brian said, "You two have quite a place here."

"Yes," said my father, "I do."

Betty remained quiet, but her hand slid off my shoulder and fell to her side.

The hall was cramped and stuffy now that the doors to the office and bedroom were closed. We huddled there with the palpable self-

consciousness of strangers in an elevator who suddenly don't know
where to look or how to stand. I half expected to feel the hallway
descend and to hear a soft melodic gong when it slowed to a stop,
the doors swinging open upon an entirely different world or, short
of that, an entirely different trailer in a less depressing park.

"Shall we retire to the living room?" asked Dad. The formal
locution came out of nowhere, a snippet from an old movie or an
outdated book on etiquette. If his grandiosity was unintentionally
comical in the drab setting of the trailer, it was lamentable too, a
relic from the world of refinement to which my father had always
aspired.

"Let's," said Brian, and we jostled down the hall.


Betty told me that after Brian and I had left, she decided to establish
the new ground rules of their relationship by sleeping on the couch.
She said she was singing softly to herself as she lofted a clean white
sheet over the cushions. She owned half the furniture, had con-
tributed half the down payment on the place, and now she was making a refuge within it, a space that was indisputably hers. She was too
wistful to pay much attention when she sensed my father standing
in the hall, watchful, pensive. He asked her what the hell she thought
she was doing, a question she'd fully expected from him, and one she
would have answered in a more kindly tone if her exasperation from
earlier that night, from the whole futile move to Oxnard, wasn't
coiled in her voice. She told him she wouldn't think of depriving
him of *his* bed in *his* home, adding that *his* relationship with her was
going to have to change until I'd found another place for him to live.

"You can't kick me out!"

"Oh, Ed," she'd said, "I'm not kicking you out. We went over
this already, before the boys left."

"My boys?"

"Remember all of us talking at the table? It couldn't have been
more than an hour ago. Look at me, Ed. Are you listening? You and
me are going to sell the trailer and split the money. If we're lucky we

might break even. And don't waste your breath on accusations. I'm as honest as the day is long. Bernard is paying me to stay with you until he can find you another place to live." Betty remembered, too late, that the monetary part of our bargain was supposed to remain confidential.

"He's paying you to be with me?"

Betty couldn't have known it then, but by "be with" my father meant "love."

"Yes," she said.

I imagine him reeling at the idea that I'd been paying Betty to love him. *For how long?* he must have wondered. *From the beginning?* Was being in his company so abhorrent a chore? Wasn't he a joker, a generous man, tender when she didn't drive him up the wall? Had Anna also been paid to love him? Had his wife? His sons? Betty said he leaned unsteadily against the door frame. He looked chastened, maybe, but otherwise alert. In his head, however, the world ground its gears and turned in reverse. Not only had love been a bluff, but paternal concern, passing romance, fondness for colleagues, neighborly regard. Every connection came undone. A lifetime of practice shedding his past had prepared him for this moment of amnesia, the first of many. The reason he stood there suddenly unraveled. The hours scattered in different directions. Nothing existed outside his skin. There was only the black contraction of his birth. That's when Betty saw him open his mouth and wail like a baby.

# The Bill from My Father

My father showed up for his next appointment with Dr. Montrose at the right hour but a day early, so he wasn't, technically, late or unexpected. She'd been writing a report on the decline of another client when he walked into her office without knocking. He announced that he was carrying $5,000 in cash and wanted to hide it from Betty. According to the doctor, he whipped out his wallet and counted the money again and again, each time arriving at a different figure. She watched for a while, taking notes, then encouraged him to put his money and valuables in a safe deposit box. Finally, she dropped a paper clip onto the floor and asked him to pick it up. Although this was meant to test his motor skills and comprehension, the lag time she reported—"He took quite a while to respond to the instructions"—could just as easily be explained by his incredulity. *Pick it up yourself,* I imagined him thinking. *Do I look like a maid?*

The doctor called to tell me that my father's mental health had deteriorated enough to warrant a diagnosis of geriatric dementia. In the weeks since we'd first met with her, I'd been researching assisted living facilities—places either discouragingly expensive or, if affordable, as stark and lonely as holding cells despite promising names like Wilshire Manor and Sunset Village—but now she advised me to keep him at Saint Joseph's for a standard three-day observation

period, during which time the staff would determine whether he
should be released on his own recognizance or held at the hospital
for a prolonged period of medication and therapy. We agreed that
the latter possibility would be the most beneficial since his temper
flared uncontrollably. A neighbor at the trailer park had recently seen
him threaten one of the service men from the DWP with a potato
peeler. "I caught some stranger futzing with my meter!" Dad told
Betty in his own defense. Instead of exact change, he'd presented a
bus driver with a pair of tarnished salad tongs from the silver service
he'd long ago bought for my mother, crestfallen and then abusive
when the driver refused to accept them, or, as my father saw it,
insisted on a handful of "pitiful nickels" instead of certified sterling.
Later, when he couldn't find the tongs, he accused Betty of stealing
them. *They didn't just get up and walk away themselves!* Betty was at her
wit's end and asked me to intervene. I carefully suggested that he
might have left the salad tongs on the bus and reminded him that
Betty was there to "watch out for him." "Why should she watch out
for *me*?" he'd shouted. "*I'm* not the thief." In some strange way his
delusions were a windfall, since his best chance for medical care and
supervision—to be committed to the psychiatric ward at Saint
Joseph's—would be predicated on his worst behavior.

While I had Dr. Montrose on the phone, I asked if his insurance
would pay for a private room.

"As far as I can tell, his policy covers . . ."

A barrage of knocking interrupted our conversation. "You can't
just keep me here because you feel like it," I heard my father yelling.
"I'll sue you bastards from here to . . ."

Dr. Montrose ordered a nurse to escort my father out of the
room. A woman burbled assurances, and my father's voice receded
along with hers. I asked the doctor if she'd told him I was on the
phone, worried that, if she had, he'd think his confinement had been
my doing.

"Heavens, no! That would have made things worse. We'll watch
him closely and call you once we've had a chance to examine him."

Moments after I thanked her and hung up, the phone rang again.

"This is Lucinda."

"Who?"

Lucinda was the nurse who had managed to calm my father down. They were at a pay phone in the hallway outside the doctor's office. He'd insisted on talking to me, and since all he had on him was five grand in one-hundred-dollar bills, she'd lent him change and made the call. Lucinda handed my father the phone.

"Hey there." He sounded positively jaunty.

"Dad, I know this must be very hard for you . . ."

"What?" His hearing aid squealed. "I'm at the hospital." It took me a moment to remember that he didn't know I knew he was there.

"Are you sick?"

"I'm fine. Can you come and get me?"

"Maybe you need to stay there. Is that what Dr. Montrose thinks?"

"What?"

I repeated myself, yelling.

"Don't yell at me, you . . . !" A pause in which he checked his anger. He couldn't afford to offend me, and he struggled to stay calm. "Can you come and get me?" he asked again, the pitch slightly higher.

"It would take me a couple of hours to get out to Oxnard during rush hour, Dad. Maybe you should wait and see what the doctor says. I could pick you up on Monday."

"Monday! That's five days away."

"Three."

"Three, five, for Christ's sake. I'm asking you to come and get me."

"Betty can bring you anything you need."

"I left the trailer when she wasn't looking," he said. "She treats me like I'm her patient!"

"Listen, Dad. I spoke to Dr. Montrose."

"Did she think you were my attorney? I'm going to sue!"

"You're there for a reason. It's perfectly legal."

"Don't lecture me on legal. I was arguing cases before you could wipe your behind!"

"I can come and visit you, but I can't take you home."

"Talk louder, I can hardly hear you."

"Put Lucinda on the phone."

"Who?"

"The nurse."

"Hello?"

"Can you . . . I'll talk to you, and then you can tell my father what I've said. That way he might hear better."

"Okay!" She was yelling already. "I see what I can do!"

"Tell him he has to stay there for at least three days, but I'll come visit him first thing tomorrow morning."

I stared out the kitchen window as darkness settled on Hollywood, the receiver gripped in my fist. My father could hear Lucinda, but he couldn't understand her Thai accent. He barked at her to slow down and asked what the hell language she was talking; words, like everything else, were slipping beyond his comprehension. Finally, he grabbed the phone out of her hand. "Forget it," he said. "Don't come and get me. You don't owe me a goddamn thing."

When I was twenty-eight years old, my father sent me a bill for his paternal services. Typed on his law firm's onionskin stationery, the bill itemized the money he'd spent on me over my lifetime. Since he hadn't kept tabs on the exact amounts he'd doled out over the years, expenditures were rounded off to the nearest dollar and labeled *food, clothing, tuition,* and *incidentals.* Beneath the tally, in the firm but detached language common to his profession, he demanded that I pay him back.

The total was somewhere in the neighborhood of $2 million. I remember being impressed by the amount, though this may have been a defense that allowed me to feel more worthy than worthless; what an expensive life I'd lived! I was shocked and insulted too, of course, not only because my father had made such a calculation, but because my life could be added up—or reduced—to a single figure. To see your existence in the form of a bill gives all your loves and fears and struggles about as much poignancy as a check for a cup of coffee.

The bill was a Proustian experience in reverse; one glance and the bygone extravagance it allowed me to recapture was purely quantitative, a bunch of numbers that yielded little in the way of memories. I saw my life as a mathematical "problem" whose constituent parts—*clothes: $72,000,* for example—brought to mind not a soft yellow shirt from my boyhood, but a warehouse crammed with shirts and pants and jackets past.

The millions of dollars I supposedly owed my father didn't strike me as a specific sum so much as an abstract, unpayable enormity, especially given the amount then in my checking account. The salary I earned as an adjunct teacher was nothing compared to this Everest of debt. No bar graph or pie chart or table of weights and measures could have better illustrated the fact that I earned a pittance. In short, the bill was having the effect my father had probably intended.

I can't for the life of me remember what had prompted my father to send me this bill in the first place, and as long as I can't remember, I risk sounding as though I'm leaving out some blunder or ingratitude on my part for which this bill was retribution. A discerning reader might understandably wonder if I am *choosing* to make myself appear more innocent and put upon than I actually was. But can't it sometimes take *one* to tango? Don't undeserved blows often come out of the blue?

The truth, as best as I can recount it, has me going about a routine Saturday—I lived at the time in an apartment on Mansfield Avenue, the living room warm with afternoon light—when a letter fell through the mail slot, one among others. It surprised me to see my father's return address; our occasional contact tended to take place on the phone or in person. I noted that the salutation, "Bernard," wasn't preceded by "Dear," but this formality seemed fitting for an official document.

There came a point during the literal and metaphorical unfoldings of the letter when I thought, simply, *Oh, an invoice.* Perhaps my father was sending it along to me for some reason the text would make clear. And so I read on:

> Your obligations to your father (the party of the first part) are considerable and the only way to impress upon you (the party of the second part) the necessity of compensating him for the fiscal burdens he bore on your behalf is to make his sacrifices evident in the form of the following, recorded herein as a legal and binding document. Should you fail to make payment in full, this matter will result in actions for which I advise you to hire counsel.

That my father, swept up in lawyerly omniscience, referred to himself in third person only added to my confusion, not to mention the detached sensation that I was gazing upon the letter, and myself slumped in a chair as I read it, from a stratospheric height.

I double-checked the signature. It was his, all right, the letters rich with loops and convolutions. *Go ahead,* I thought, *let him dun me. See if I pay. No parent in his right mind asks his child to reimburse him for that child's life! I didn't ask to be born,* I thought melodramatically. Besides, had I known I'd be charged for my boyhood, I might have eaten fewer snacks, been easier on my shoes, more frugal with my allowance.

Suppose I actually *would* need to hire a lawyer to fight this in court? The first candidate who sprang to mind was none other than my father. In other words, as I sat in my sunny living room, utterly stunned, my image of him would not shift from Dad-as-lawyer to litigant-as-Dad.

I couldn't help but dream up a doozy of a counterclaim, its itemizations even more preposterous than my father's: *chronic insecurity—$90,000; narcissistic wound—$75,000; oedipal complex—$15,000.* Of course, because these damages were psychological in nature, it was both difficult and whimsical to assign them a monetary value, but the punitive spirit of this counterclaim was gratifying. For a while at least. Then the whole petty endeavor depressed me and I thought,

*Is this what people are to each other, a flurry of demands that can't be met, hurts for which there's no restitution?*

By ignoring my father's letter, I risked his vengeance, and though I seriously doubted that he'd have the audacity to take me to court, the letter proved him capable of who knew what. To answer back, to acknowledge his claim in any way, was to give it credence. Still, I couldn't help but wonder if his demand *did* have credence, especially if I thought of the debt as familial rather than monetary; he was my father, after all, the man who bore my "fiscal burdens," and every son owes his father something. Are we not, from conception till death, the spermatozoa launched by our fathers and flailing our way through the world? I slipped the bill into my desk drawer, resolving to calm down and allow some time to pass before I figured out how, or whether, to respond.

During the days and nights that followed, I couldn't settle on a convincing or comprehensible reason to explain why my father had sent me the bill, though I suspected the catalyst might have had something to do with his offer, a few months earlier, to buy me a new car. He'd made the offer on a day I'd come to visit him. As I pulled into the driveway, he was watering the birds-of-paradise in his front yard. Back then I drove a Fiat whose paint had oxidized to the overall color and texture of rust. The car sputtered as I shifted into park, coughing a cloud of noxious exhaust. Just a year after I'd purchased the car with money from a small inheritance left by my mother, it began to fall apart with vengeful rapidity. The vinyl upholstery flaked off the seats in sticky black patches. Soon they were nothing but lumps of raw foam that crumbled like stale sponge cake. One of the rear windows no longer rolled up. My apartment didn't come with a garage, which meant that I parked on Mansfield Avenue; despite the wide open window, the car's condition made it unattractive even to thieves. If it rained outside the Fiat, it rained inside as well. On cold nights a stray dog made the backseat his home, leaving behind a legion of fleas to feast on my ankles. It was humiliating to be seen inside the car, especially in Los Angeles. When idling at a stoplight beside a purring sports car with rear stabilizers, anodized hubcaps, and a leather interior, I had to force myself to remember that an automobile does not a man make, and that I was a writer who placed a higher value on words than on material possessions. Which is to say that I cultivated a hollow sense of superiority around new cars. I couldn't afford to fix the Fiat and, having failed auto mechanics in junior high, couldn't repair the car myself. With all this in mind, I parked on the shady side of my father's driveway in the hope he might not notice what a rattletrap my car had become.

My father sauntered toward the Fiat as I got out, peeking though the open window despite my attempt to block his view. A rare tenderness lit him from within and stirred my allegiance like daybreak stirs a bird.

"Hey," he said. "Looks like you could use a new set of wheels." The phrase "new set of wheels" was an affectionate flourish meant to make him sound, in the parlance of his own youth, palsy-walsy.

"I can't afford a new car," I told him. I distinctly recall facing my father and shaping my tone so that I sounded neither pitiful (I'm too poor) or petulant (I'll never be able to buy a new car).

Before I knew it, my father and I were cradled in the plush bucket seats of his white Eldorado, gliding toward a Toyota dealership in West Covina whose ads he'd seen on TV. He pointed a stubby finger at his chest. "Let me handle this," he said. "I've bought plenty of cars in my life and I know how to deal with these bastards. You watch; I'll beat them at their own game. They won't know what hit them."

On one hand, Dad's braggadocio made me feel invincible, as though I were in the company of a seasoned pro. On the other hand, it relegated me to the role of admiring onlooker and suggested that I was too incompetent and naive to buy my own car. Which was entirely true. I floundered when it came to the treacherous etiquette of negotiating a major sale, a feat that required, it seemed to me, a keen mistrust of one's fellow men coupled with a barely sublimated bloodlust. As far as I was concerned, getting gypped out of a few bucks was simply a built-in fee for avoiding confrontations with strangers. I'd watched my father often enough to know that such transactions excited him into what can only be described as a rapture of antagonism; he didn't mind yelling threats and pounding desks and generally hurling himself bodily into the arena of commerce. Still, if a new car required me to be embarrassed by his aggression, bring on the blushing; and if it required a few hours of my infantalization, I was more than willing to comply. Besides, his intent was generous. The Caddy whizzed past slower traffic, as regal as a motorized mansion.

As we walked across the asphalt lot of the Toyota dealership, colorful plastic pennants rippled and snapped in the breeze. I thanked Dad in advance and told him that I didn't need whitewalls, an air conditioner, or a radio. Basic transportation would be fine. He nodded and forged ahead. Secretly, I hoped my modest expectations might endear me to him even more; maybe he'd close the deal that very day. Before his mood changed. Before I said something that would inadvertently set him off. Before he said *crap* or *bastard* to the dealer. My excitement was indistinguishable from panic. I wanted a beautiful new Toyota more desperately with every step. I wanted an end to the self-consciousness I felt on the road, an end to the shameful sense that the thunderous rumbling and rank exhaust were coming from my person rather than my car.

The showroom felt bracingly cool after the heat of West Covina, the air thick with the deliciously medicinal perfume of new upholstery. In the center of the room, a sleek new convertible turned around and around on an enormous platform, as if swooning to the Muzak. The second we entered, salespeople, sensing prey, rose from their desks and converged. It occurred to me that we would be the prize for the fastest walker, the one whose handshake greeted us first. The victor was a skinny man whose snug black suit lent him an eel-like iridescence, or perhaps I was just seeing him as my father might: slippery, unctuous, not to be trusted. Dad shifted his weight to meet the man's gaze, his posture erect. He walked up to a minivan on display and kicked a tire as if to gauge, through his knowing toes, the vehicle's overall quality. He squinted at the sticker price.

"John," said my father, reading the salesman's name tag. "Firstly, I'm an attorney. Secondly, when it comes to cars, I'm not some idiot off the street. A cousin of mine is fleet manager of a Cadillac dealership in San Bernardino." A complete fabrication as far as I knew. "If we cut through the crap, you just might make yourself a sale. My son here—I'm buying the boy a car—doesn't need any bells or whistles."

"I'm Bernard," I said to the salesman. He shook my hand without taking his eyes off my father.

"Well, Mr . . . ?"

"Cooper. Edward. Attorney at law."

"I gotta hand it to you, Mr. Cooper. It's nice to meet a customer who knows what he wants and comes prepared to do business."

My father shot me a sidelong glance as if to say, *Watch and learn.*

"I'm going to make this painless," said the salesman. He spun on his heel and walked toward the glass door that led to the lot. We followed him outside to a veritable poppy field of new Tercels until we reached a red two-door that John claimed was the least expensive automobile on the lot. "This is the cheapest?" asked my father. His synonym for *least expensive* was meant, I suspected, to cast aspersions on the merchandise—*That's nothing more than a metal shell with some baked-on paint*—and therefore place him at a strategic advantage. Though it pains me to do so, I must add that my father's gold Star of David had loosed itself from the humid interior of his shirt to glint conspicuously in the afternoon light, the sight of which, given my father's unabashed haggling, caused a chord of shame to vibrate inside me. I felt compelled to explain to the salesman how my father had worked hard for everything he owned; he was a hoarder, a scrimper, a seeker of bargains who could never take his solvency for granted, and in this respect he was like thousands of people who'd grown up poor and endured the Depression, Jewish or not.

But that was a lot to explain to a salesman, especially on the cusp of a deal that would better my life. Certainly my father would have chastised me, and rightly, for making an excuse on his behalf, especially one coming from a young man who'd had it comparatively easy and for whom both money and automobiles were mysteries on par with astrophysics. To put it bluntly, if my father was conforming to the cliché of the cheap Jew, I was that cliché's beneficiary. I peered at the car, feigning disinterest. Quite a performance considering how I coveted that little red Tercel.

"Mr. Cooper," said the salesman, "I know a shrewd man when I see one, and I'm going to do something that could put my job on the line. But before I tell you what it is, Mr. Cooper, I want you to promise that you won't say a word to my boss."

I'd once heard that repeating a person's name is a way to make them feel important, to win them over, and John, it seemed, had heard the same. Each time he invoked my father's name, I felt myself lean closer, progressively mesmerized because I was a Cooper, too. My father, however, was immune to customer seduction. It wouldn't have mattered if the salesman were Rasputin, Dad wouldn't budge. "Let's hear it," he grumbled, folding his arms.

"Mr. Cooper, I'm going to let you drive out of here for a mere two hundred dollars over the factory price. I'm going to scratch my commission on this. Frankly, I need the sales points more than I need the money, and if we can lock up this deal pronto, it'll be worth my while. And of course, worth yours."

"You've got to be shitting me, John. I know you can give it to me under factory. I'm not paying a penny more than factory. Period."

My heart misfired, mouth went dry.

"As I said, Mr. Cooper, I don't mind giving up my commission but I can't *lose* money on the deal. I'm giving you the best price you're going to find in L.A. County."

Other customers were milling uncomfortably close to my Tercel and succumbing to the persuasion of salespeople. I wanted to turn to my father and blurt, *Why would he lie?* But it would have been disastrous to say anything, especially if I seemed to be siding with my father's black-suited adversary.

"I'm not buying it," my father said. It took me a second to realize he meant the dealer's story, not the car itself. "I know how this game is played. And I'll play along up to a point. But we've reached that point, so let's see what kind of a deal you can give me."

"Shop around if you don't believe me, Mr. Cooper. Then come on back. The offer still stands. Better act quickly, though, 'cause this baby isn't going to stay on the lot much longer."

My father gave John the once-over, then turned to me. "Let's go," he said. "We're taking our business elsewhere."

The salesman curtly thanked my father and walked away.

"I think he's basically an honest man," I mumbled.

"Honest my ass." My father looked at me with something like pity; I'd never catch on, would forever remain a sucker, a rube. We trudged across the lot toward his Caddy.

The drive back to Los Angeles took a good forty minutes. My father still fumed from the encounter with the salesman, his ears and neck flushed with blood. He'd been unmanned by having his deal rebuffed in front of his son. I tried to bolster him by praising his efforts on my behalf, telling him he was a gutsy negotiator. My joviality, however, couldn't have been convincing; the Fiat kept careening through my head, leaking oil and molting upholstery. Sensing my disappointment, Dad insisted that the deal was far from over. "The guy's playing hardball, but you watch. The phone will be ringing when we get back to the house. It'll be him and he'll say . . ."

My father launched into an imitation of John cooing *Mr. Cooper this* and *Mr. Cooper that,* his interpretation making the salesman appear more obsequious than he'd actually been. I'm positive Dad used the phrase *tail between his legs,* because it colored their struggle with a certain zoological ferocity. My father promised that when the call finally came, John would apologize for being too hasty and lower the price. I'd have my car before I knew it.

One day passed. Two. Three. Each day I called my father on a transparent pretext and attempted to find out whether he'd heard anything from the salesman. On the fourth day, I steeled myself and asked him outright.

"Keep your pants on," grumbled my father. "I said he'd call, didn't I?"

In the meantime, I'd researched the prices at other Toyota dealerships around town and discovered that John's offer was the best of the bunch. And so I called my father in a last-ditch effort to own the car.

"Dad," I said. "I've done some comparative pricing."

"So?"

"I think we should go for the Tercel before it's sold. And if it's a matter of not wanting to pay more than the factory price—and who can blame you?—I'd be happy to contribute the extra two hundred dollars myself." The proposal had about it the pleasing hue of team-work, and I wished I'd thought of it days ago.

"It's not about the two hundred bucks," shouted my father. "It's a waiting game. He's holding out so I'll come running back and throw my money at him. If you can't sit tight for a while, if you have to have everything you want right when you want it, you might as well forget the whole damn thing." Before he hung up, he said, "And don't pester me anymore. I'll call *you* when the car is ready."

The bill arrived after a month of silence. By then I'd given up on the car, resigned to drive the Fiat until it broke down completely or until I could afford to make payments on a new car, whichever came first. Losing that Tercel was a substantial disappointment, but one swiftly eroded by the grind of daily life: grading papers for my fresh-man comp classes while trying to figure out how to earn more money and still have time to write. If I had any energy left over to fret about a car, I'd fret about the one I owned. Our visit to the Toyota dealership might have ended up being one of many aggra-vating but forgettable misunderstandings I'd had with my father—stepping on the other's toes: that's how the two of us knew where we stood—if not for the letter.

I suspected my father might brood about our day at the dealer-ship, but I wasn't prepared for the extremity of his reaction—if in fact the bill *was* a reaction. Whenever I tried to make a connection, the machinery of cause and effect began to break down. Perhaps my father had been offended by my offer to supplement the cost of the car, thinking I'd implied he couldn't afford it, couldn't pull off the deal on his own. Yet, even taking into account the full force of my father's volatility, it seemed unlikely that my offer of $200 would result in him suing me for two million.

As the month wore on, my longing for the car grew dimmer while my father's no doubt deepened, thrusting him back to the deprivation he knew as a boy. The salesman's refusal to call must have undermined his notion of how the world worked, how bargains were struck by men like himself, men possessed of wile and nerve. What had happened, or failed to happen, defied his every paternal assurance, his promise that the phone would ring, the salesman buckle, the car become mine. How humiliated he must have been to know that I awaited his call. That he'd *asked* me to wait must have made it worse. My father's refusal to be in the wrong meant that I'd have to wait forever.

Twenty years have passed since I opened that bill, and for most of those years I'd taken it for granted that at some point during our afternoon in West Covina, my father had given the dealer his telephone number. But I've sifted through that trip a dozen times, squinting against the glare of new cars, breathing the icy air of the showroom, and I can't recall my father handing over one of his business cards, or filling out a form of any sort. Even if my father had been right, the salesman wouldn't have known where to reach him.

Before she officially admitted my father to the psychiatric ward at Saint Joseph's, Dr. Montrose drove him to his trailer and then to a nearby Bank of America, where she helped him acquire a safe deposit box. He carried the $5,000 in cash and his important possessions in a grocery bag, which he kept in his lap. Dr. Montrose sat beside him, and as he paused at each blank in the application, she whispered his Social Security and Medicare numbers, the statistics before her in his open file.

That night, she phoned at 11 P.M. to tell me he'd complained of stomach pains that had worsened in a matter of hours. She'd finally sent him to the Intensive Care Unit, where the staff suspected internal hemorrhaging. Tests were being run, she said, and an internist would consult me in the morning. "Your father's been unusually agitated, but it's probably the pain." She told me he'd hurled a pitcher against the wall, swearing a blue streak at Lucinda, who up until then had been able to keep him relatively calm—as long as he understood what she was saying. But whenever fatigue or exasperation thickened her accent, he demanded to speak to Betty, who he'd kicked out of his room just hours earlier for "talking his ears off."

The following morning in the lobby, the buttons for the elevators wouldn't light up no matter how firmly or often they were pressed. People milled around, holding bouquets and sipping Styrofoam cups of coffee. I checked and rechecked the piece of paper on which I'd jotted my father's room number, unable, in my dread, to commit it to memory, which committed it to forgetfulness. The broken button, I warned myself, was only a hint of malfunctions to come. I took a deep breath and tried to both acknowledge the future and hold it at bay.

When an elevator finally appeared, it opened up to reveal Betty. The only passenger, she stood against the dim rear wall, her metallic blond hair like those gold-leaf halos encircling the heads of saints in Renaissance paintings. With her shoulders thrown back and chin uplifted, she stepped into the morning light, her eyes fixed on mine. She looked every inch a heavenly messenger come to deliver momentous news. Tears slid down her cheeks, skin glistening where a layer of face powder had been washed away. She opened her arms, cinched me inside them. I couldn't, and didn't want to, resist. Her bulky lavender sweater smelled pungently of floral sachet, and remotely of Old Spice, the faint, valedictory trace of my father lost to the antiseptic odor of the hospital as soon as I took my next breath.

"It's a miracle!" she exclaimed, pulling away. She dug into her shoulder bag and handed me Kleenex.

I dabbed at my eyes. "What are you saying? Are you saying he's okay? When I saw you crying, I thought . . ."

"He's regained consciousness! He's talking!"

"Are you sure? Last night Dr. Montrose told me . . ."

"Go and see for yourself!"

When she stuffed the package of Kleenex back into her bag, a gilt-edged Bible caught the light. Deathbed conversions couldn't be all that uncommon at Saint Joseph's (Brian, who'd been raised in the pragmatic United Church of Canada, referred to these eleventh-hour transformations as "cramming for the final"), and I hated to think that my father might have accepted Christ's salvation while insensible with pain and fear, like a prisoner who finally relents and signs a false confession. Had Betty come here on a mission? Had my father felt it necessary to change who he was, and worse, to disavow who he'd been, that a higher power might spare him from death, or let him die in peace? Better he should dial the prayer line in Texas just to kill time. Better he should defend a headless chicken, proclaiming it a sign from God for the benefit of all mankind.

And so the sight of Betty's Bible stirred me to a revelation: the father I had was the one I wanted, even if I was destined to spend my life perplexed. Of course, I still had qualms about him and always would, but relatively speaking, and for the time being, I'd come as close to qualmlessness as I ever got.

Betty and I were dry-eyed by the time the next elevator arrived. She wrote down the number of the Oxnard apartment she'd moved into with her cousin. We said our good-byes and I crowded in with people headed toward other sickrooms on other floors. I was eager to reach my father while he was still aware enough to notice I brimmed with appreciation.

I had to wait in the anteroom of the ICU for Lucinda to buzz me in. The door opened on a swarm of sounds. A suction pump wheezed. Beeping heart monitors drifted into and out of synch, strangers' pulses briefly allied, then divided. Lucinda, every bit as diminutive and efficient as I'd imagined, introduced herself and turned to lead the way. I followed her glossy black hair, the heavy length of it swaying with her gait. We had to dodge doctors and nurses who spoke in code and moved from one curtained enclosure to the next, all of them responding to a set of demands I could percieve only as an overall blur of emergency. We were halfway across the room when Lucinda stopped in her tracks. She explained that my father's kidneys were failing and warned me that I'd find him unconscious. "From sedation," she said, "and losing the blood." She clutched the edge of the curtain and waited until she saw some sign that I'd registered the gravity of his condition. Then, despite my look of dire surprise—had I misunderstood what Betty had told me?—Lucinda yanked the curtain aside.

My father sprawled in the bed as if sinking into his own impression. His eye lids flickered with the urge to open. With his dentures removed, his lips caved into a mouthful of darkness. Lucinda announced that he was being hydrated intravenously and fed through a catheter inserted directly into his stomach. She'd planted the catheter herself, and before I could stop her, she tossed the blanket aside to show me her handiwork, a thin plastic umbilicus trailing from a scarlet incision near his navel.

For the next week, every time I entered the room, I found him sprawled in the same position, jaw lax, lungs heaving. According to Lucinda, he often woke late at night after the sedation wore off, certain she'd stolen his money. Or else he feared he'd forgotten where he hid it, or whether he had money hidden at all. Soon he believed she was stealing his clothes. Stealing the water that filled his glass. Stealing dirt from the potted plant. This endless succession of thefts enraged him, though even he, a former lawyer, could never prove she'd taken a thing. An old hand at dealing with dementia, she took his accusations in stride. Fearing he might harm himself or another patient, Lucinda sedated him when he grew unruly. But even after a dose of morphine he'd try to wrench the tubes from his flesh, claiming he was late for work, and she had to strap his arms to the bed.

When my father took the first wet breaths of pneumonia, sedation was no longer necessary—a fevered weakness kept him in check. I'd squeeze his shoulder: nothing. I'd insinuate my face into his but discover I was invisible, no one's son after forty-eight years. Now and then a reflex fired down his spine, legs twitching for half a minute.

My father's hearing aid had been removed, and one afternoon I apologized for my part in the misunderstandings we'd had over the years. There were plenty to choose from, but I mentioned the car and bill in one breath, as if this, at last, confirmed their connection. I apologized for his part too, since I wanted to believe he would if he were able. I had no illusions that my father heard me or understood a word. There had been so many times, especially later in his life, when he gladly switched off his hearing aid; like a child who closes his eyes and believes the world has disappeared, he moved through a hush that silenced the earth. I wished him that muted refuge now.


A month after my father died, I visited the Oxnard branch of Bank of America to open his safe deposit box. I wasn't expecting to discover much of value; during the last days of his life, he'd been badgered by a small but persistent battalion of bill collectors. "They're the ones who're strapped for cash," he'd told me. "It's their problem, not mine." My father had come to believe that paying even the smallest bill might make him appear weak or defeated, whereas debt, rather than humiliating him, proved his triumph over the importunings of authority, and finally over the great green tyranny of money itself. In any case, the contents of the safe deposit box constituted the bulk of my inheritance, and I had no idea what I'd find inside it.

With its decorative borders and official seals, my father's death certificate bore a remarkable resemblance to money, though of course it was signed by the county coroner instead of the secretary of the Treasury, a document nonnegotiable in every sense. The bank manager checked it against an entry in her ledger, then escorted me though a security door and into the windowless vault, whose walls were like those of a mausoleum, hundreds of numbered cubbyholes reaching from floor to ceiling. Since my father's box was on the top row, she had to climb a metal stepladder, teetering on her high heels while she inserted the key Dr. Montrose had given me. She slid the narrow safe deposit box from the wall, and as she handed it down to me, I noticed a piece of adhesive tape stuck to the bottom. "Mine," it read in my father's crimped, arthritic scrawl, a penmanship that came with old age and bore none of its former flourishes. He must have thought this label would prevent what little he had from being stolen, or prove it belonged to him alone, a hedge against destitution.

The manager led me to a small private viewing room and closed the door behind me. I set the safe deposit box on the table, lifted the lid.

This was my inheritance: $5,000 in one-hundred-dollar denominations. Heaped in a blue velvet jewelry box were a few gold rings my father had bought for my mother, rings she'd worn so infrequently they barely held a sentimental charge. Wedged in the very back I found an old sheet of onionskin stationery from my father's law office, the same letterhead on which he'd typed my bill. On it he'd made dozens of computations in pencil, numerals meant to figure out, once and for all, how much money he had. Yet my father trusted none of his solutions; the problems were repeated several times, the numbers smudged.

The modest contents of the safe deposit box came as no surprise. Long ago I'd given up on inheriting my childhood house or any portion of the savings my father had squandered on the business schemes and lawsuits—motivated, I understood now, by burgeoning dementia—that left him bankrupt. I stuffed the jewelry into one of my coat pockets and cash into the other, feeling a weight that the things I carried couldn't quite account for. I left the key inside the empty safe deposit box, the strip of tape still stuck underneath. Soon the manager would slide it back into the wall, my father's claim forever asserting itself in the Oxnard branch of Bank of America.

Once inside my car, I counted out the cash once again. While thumbing through the money, it occurred to me why, just a month ago, my father had tallied these same one-hundred-dollar bills over and over in Dr. Montrose's office, why he kept his calculations locked in a vault. Counting can be a form of consolation, a clarifying prayer; you utter numbers and believe in reason, in the steady progression from one thing to another, in the prospect that things will finally add up. That three follows two is a certainty, as inevitable, my father would have said, as taxes and death.

# Afterlife

Soon my father's afterlife began. Which is to say that the repercussions of his death assumed a life of their own.

Late one night, while Brian lay beside me and enjoyed a routinely peaceful sleep, I began to wonder why, according to Betty, my father had regained consciousness in her presence but not in mine. "Dad," I imagined saying, "maybe there was a reason you didn't regain consciousness when I came to the ICU. Maybe you were still angry I hadn't come to get you out of observation. Or maybe you still thought I'd paid Betty to love you."

*Listen to yourself! A person doesn't decide to be unconscious! You don't need a motive to go into a coma! Ask your mental-doctor friend!*

I'd wrongly supposed that as I went on living and my father didn't, my tendency to invoke his voice, to engage him in the old heave-ho, would simply fade away. But as the weeks turned into months and the months turned into a longer bunch of months, his brusque rejoinders and knotty logic thrived inside me. Picking up the slack in his absence, I played Dad's part with increasing conviction. I still thought of him as irrational, but now that I was better at being him, I thought of myself as irrational, too. Thus formed the bonds of father and son. Too late, perhaps, but unbreakable.

\* \* \*

The day Betty had appeared like an apparition in the hospital lobby, tearful over Dad's sudden recovery, I'd stumbled upon indisputable evidence that she *had* tried to proselytize him, whether he'd been conscious or not. After Lucinda rushed me through the ICU and pulled back the curtain, I stood immobilized at the foot of his bed, unable to bridge the abyss between the groggy but talkative man Betty had led me to expect and the thin, intubated figure lying before me, gasping for air. Shunts needled their way into his veins. Glucose dripped through his IV tube like sugar water through an eyedropper. Beneath the scent of rubbing alcohol, he exuded a sourness that some animal part of me recognized as the scent of fear. I moved closer, as if he'd called out to me, though he hadn't made a sound. That's when I noticed a videotape lying on his nightstand. Addressed to *Resident,* it had been sent to the trailer park from the Trinity Broadcasting Network, home to Betty's favorite show, *This Is Your Day.* How attentively she'd watch the afflicted limp toward the spotlit Reverend Hinn, his hands a conduit for the Lord's glory. The video, still encased in its cellophane wrapper, hadn't been opened. The address label obscured its title, though a photograph of orange-and-yellow flames flickered across the box in an ominous conflagration.

Only once, as a young boy, had I stolen something that belonged to my father; I snatched a handful of change from his dresser. He didn't miss it, though for days the fear of getting caught hovered above me like a thunderhead. Years later, when he billed me for my life, I expected to see that petty theft added to my tab. And yet I stole the video without a moment's hesitation. Intuition told me not to let him see it, whatever it was, and so, when my visit came to an end, I scooped the box off his nightstand, parted the curtain, and walked away.

Several freeways later, I eased my car into the garage and headed up the back stairs to the kitchen, video in hand, my curiosity mounting. Late morning sun shone through the windows, but I flicked on the glaring lights regardless. I put on my reading glasses, the lenses almost as thick as my father's, and found myself in a

crystal-clear face-off with a man identified on the back of the box
as Dr. Maurice Rawlings. In the color photograph, his gray hair
was brittle, his skin so wan and chalky he could have passed for a
plaster statue. Transparent cellophane provided no protection whatsoever from the doctor's stony—brimstony—visage. Actually, his
gaze was aimed a little to the side, which gave it the menacing
potential to shift without warning and incinerate anyone standing
in its path. Forget airbrushed authors' photographs or glossy Hollywood headshots. His burgundy tie and jacket may have matched,
but that was his last concession to the camera. He was squint-and-
grimace from the Adam's apple up. I hate to be ad hominem about
it, but from every indication, scolding the masses was Dr. Rawlings's bread and butter, and he'd either been born with, or had
earned, precisely the face to get the job done.

Removing the cellophane wrapper required a sharp object. Still
dazed by the sight of Dr. Rawlings, I absently reached into the
kitchen drawer and pulled out . . . a potato peeler. An odd coinci-
dence given the fact that a potato peeler had been my father's
weapon of choice when confronting the DWP's meter reader. I'd
never given much thought to the potato peeler's relative benignity.
Gripped in my fist, it weighed next to nothing. Granted, Brian and
I owned a really old potato peeler, one so dull it could hardly peel
potatoes let alone pierce an enemy's flesh. It seemed especially flimsy
when compared to the handguns and automatic assault rifles that
were wreaking havoc on high school campuses across America. The
comparison wasn't meant to excuse my father's actions, but to
acknowledge the possibility that he may have grabbed the utensil as
thoughtlessly as I. And if he'd picked it up on purpose, I'd like to
think that choosing to defend himself with a potato peeler instead
of, say, a twelve-inch knife, was at least an indication of his ambivalence about harming a fellow human being. It's a stretch, I realize,
but isn't absolution composed of such stretches, such makeshift revi-
sions? I broke the plastic seal and peeled it off the box, revealing the
title beneath the address label:

## TO HELL AND BACK

Up until now, there have been virtually no descriptions of "bad" near-death experiences. Has anyone ever been to Hell and returned to tell about it?

The answer was yes, and Dr. Rawlings had recruited five unfortunates to tell their cautionary tales. Together, these stories would show that the usual reports brought back from angelic realms of white light and peaceful music gave a distorted view of life after death, a view that had become popular because it gave false comfort to complacent atheists, and also to Christians who resisted the principle of eternal damnation. The copy advised using the video as a "witnessing tool" for unsaved friends and loved ones, and suggested that its message may change viewers' lives. Their afterlives, too.

That every "Hell" was capitalized spoke theological volumes. For Dr. Rawlings, Hell wasn't just some five-alarm fire, but a furnace fueled by the flesh and bones of the unconverted. Why should my father listen to a man who thought of him as kindling?

As for the scarcity of "bad" near-death experiences, the two or three people I knew who'd nearly died had nothing *but* bad things to say about it. The nearer to death they'd come, the worse their experience. In fact, the only thing worse than the near-death experiences I'd heard about were the near-life experiences—merely going through the motions of being alive, every taste and color blunted, libido flagging, zest at an ebb—that were commonly reported in Brian's consultation room, and in regular rooms across the country.

How had Dr. Rawlings found so many people who had gone to hell and lived to tell about it? Did he cater to a sinful clientele? The mere idea of a doctor who sought out the formerly dead was enough to give me an arrhythmia.

Had you asked me back then if I considered myself what fundamentalists like Dr. Rawlings disapprovingly called "a moral relativist," I would have said, *It depends.* I've rarely been able to form an opinion without also considering several contradictory opinions until I arrive, through the process of elimination, at another opinion I retain the right to revise at any time. And now I couldn't help but wonder: if Dr. Rawlings and his patients had read *Gulliver's Travels* as devotedly as they read the New Testament, might I have been holding a video entitled *To Lilliput and Back*? Isn't one's vision of the afterlife shaped by the very drives and passions that shape one's life?

Which brings me to Betty. She'd left the video behind knowing that it might be her last gift to a man she'd loved and toward whom she still felt concern. No doubt she bestowed it with good intentions, specifically those that pave the road to hell. What kind of gift is it to warn a man that the suffering he's accrued throughout his lifetime will go right on accruing after he's dead? I don't know about you, but I'd want my last gift to be soothing and useful, like a pair of flannel pajamas. My father didn't need a preview of doom. My father needed to yank out his tubes, slip into his jumpsuit, and resume the delusion that, temporarily detained by failing kidneys, he was running late for retirement.

I stared into the flames and dared myself to pop the tape into our VCR. Then I vetoed myself because watching it would remind me of the insidious ways in which people make other people feel like sinners. Then I overrode my veto because I was curious to see a low-budget dramatization of hell that might include, if I was lucky, writhing amateur dancers.

By absconding with the video, I'd hoped to save my father from being saved. He was in intensive care and in no condition to withstand a tongue-lashing from an ashen, wrathful cardiologist. All things being relative, however, I also understood that I'd denied him the opportunity to see the video for himself and make his own decision. In either case, right and wrong were beside the point. He never regained consciousness. At least not with me.

After my father died, I kept *To Hell and Back* in my desk drawer, but every time I opened the drawer to get a pencil or a postage stamp, the flames startled me as if they'd burst from the box at that very instant, fed by in-rushing oxygen. I winced at the thought of my desk catching fire, computer melted to a bubbling puddle. Still, I didn't want to throw the tape away. Despite the trouble already caused by writing about my father, I'd begun to contemplate making him the subject of an entire book, and I thought there might come a day when I'd need to refer to Dr. Rawlings's video, if I could ever bring myself to watch it.

Brian refused to watch it with me. He preferred *Jeopardy!* He preferred *National Geographic* specials like *The Secret Life of Caves* or *Galapagos, Land of Dragons.* He even preferred talk shows where the guests made shocking disclosures and then ripped off their clothes, private parts censored with flickering pixels. At hell, however, he drew the line.

"Please," I wheedled. "From a sociological standpoint, it might be educational."

"Hell isn't edifying," he insisted. "You don't learn from your mistakes in hell. You pay for making them."

Recruiting a friend to watch it with me proved just as futile. My ex-girlfriend, Lynn, told me she'd had the wages of sin pounded into her during Catholic school. "I've had enough hell to last a lifetime," she said. "I won't go back unless I'm dragged." Monica said she couldn't possibly add Dr. Rawlings's video to the already long list of films she was obligated to watch for her class. "A Feminist History of Film" was now "A Post-Feminist History of Film," and it required a whole new syllabus that included recent female buddy pictures, women-in-sports documentaries, erotica written and directed by women, and videos by performance artists such as the Guerrilla Girls and the Lesbian Avengers. "Right now," she said, "hell is way at the bottom of my list."

And so the video stayed in my drawer.


Brian and I drove out to the trailer one afternoon to sort through what was left of my father's possessions. Once we entered Oxnard, the sky turned misty from sprinklers dousing rows of green crops on either side of the highway, an occasional stunted rainbow hovering in the spray. I'd loaded the back of my car with cardboard boxes and garbage bags and, in case those weren't enough, an empty suitcase. Since I'd last been to the trailer, his small chaotic office pushed at the edges of memory, growing steadily larger and more promising until I thought of it as an unexplored geological site that might yield torn ticket stubs, stereopticon slides of the grandparents I hardly knew, a sheaf of old letters he'd sent to my mother, rich with the endearments I'd never heard him utter aloud. These finds were unlikely, but some unconditional wishfulness, some hunger for history, made me eager to search through the rubble for clues to my father's lifelong silence.

Motley dogs, timid in the daylight, watched from a distance as we unloaded the car. Balancing boxes in our arms, Brian and I mounted the metal steps. I was too encumbered with stuff to turn around and check, but I heard what sounded like screen doors creaking and window blinds raised in the nearby trailers. The Siesta's residents must have been accustomed to the sight of neighbors vacating the premises at all hours of the day and night—these were homes on wheels, after all—and here we were, two strangers with grave faces come to strip the trailer of everything but echoes, then pack up the salvage and drive away. As I bent down to find the key Betty left for us beneath the mat, aluminum siding shimmered in the periphery of my vision, as if the last place my father called home was built from a substance as fugitive as dew.

He'd amended his will with handwritten codicils nearly a half a dozen times in the month leading up to his hospitalization. Either Betty or I would be named as beneficiary—until the next pendulum swing of his allegiance. One of us always loved him more, and thus the other, loving him less, proved themselves undeserving.

Because he and Betty had argued about the missing salad tongs on the day he made what turned out to be the last revision to his will, her name had been stricken and replaced with mine. I became my father's heir by default, though I'd done nothing special to earn my position as beneficiary apart from being too far away on a certain day to be fingered for stealing the family silver. Betty *had* been there, and I thought it only fair that she receive compensation for sticking with my father during a period when he most needed, and was quickest to challenge, her sincerity, a test of endurance even for a woman devoted to ailing bodies and lost causes. I phoned Betty at her cousin's and offered to sign over my father's share of the trailer; as the sole owner, she could either move back there or sell it and keep the proceeds. I was certain that my father, in his right mind, would have wanted me to do this for her. Betty thanked me, her throat clenched against welling emotion. "It's sad," she managed to say, which just about said it all. Eulogies tend to idealize the dead, and I'm not about to gild my father's flaws, but in the pause that followed, I pitied the man his alienating rage, a burden he'd been helpless to temper or change, and I looked back on his outbursts with a mixture of awe and fondness.

"This is silly," said Betty, "but I still expect him to come walking through the door."

I know, I wanted to say. I still expect him to push me through it.

"I'm starting to see how moving here was a mistake God wanted me to make. He's led me to a whole new life! Not that your father was a mistake. I didn't mean it that way. No, your father was . . . he was my . . ."

"The two of you were like husband and wife."

"*Like* is right," she sighed. "Living in the trailer would be hard after all that's happened. If I sell it for a fair price, I can afford an apartment sooner than I thought!" One blessing begat another, and Betty happily counted them aloud. Just when it had seemed she couldn't generate new clients through word of mouth, the home care service she'd worked for in Los Angeles was able to assign her a number of jobs in and around Oxnard, where an influx of retirees and the construction of low-cost convalescent homes had invigorated local growth. "Old folks go for trailers in a big way. Less rooms and doodads. Let's face it," she added cheerfully, "the Golden State is aging!"

At several points during our conversation, I was tempted to ask her about *To Hell and Back*. Had she really expected my father to switch lords at the last minute? By now, though, it seemed small-

minded to express my displeasure, especially about a gift I made sure
he never received.

I'd like to claim that my call to Betty was inspired by sheer generosity. In truth, I was glad to get rid of the trailer; once I signed it
over, there'd be no reason to visit the dusty, somnolent land of Siesta
ever again. I'd come to think of Oxnard as the seat of my father's
undoing. As far as I was concerned, his destitution's one and only
saving grace lay in the fact that its prominent landmarks—the hospital, the trailer park, the fields through which he'd wandered to
prove his independence—were a far cry from the city where he'd
made a living. Los Angeles would always represent his years of striving, whereas Oxnard would always be the wall against which his
years of striving collided. I hoped that some unruined version of
him might be easier for me to preserve at a geographical distance,
his bankruptcy and madness kept separate by ninety miles of seaside
towns and inland counties, gas stations and fast food franchises growing like reeds along the banks of the interstate.

A blast of heat came at us as I shouldered open the door. The
power had been turned off and trapped air simmered within the
trailer's walls. We cranked open every window in the empty living
room, T-shirts clinging to our sweaty skin. Betty had moved her
belongings to her cousin's. Gone was the hutch, the dinette set, the
hands lit up in prayer, the sofa she'd slept on while undergoing her
transformation from my father's lover back into his nurse.

Brian and I carried boxes to the threshold of my father's office,
its floor hidden beneath layers of paper. Important documents and
family artifacts would be taken with us so I could comb through
them more carefully at a later date. The rest was destined for land-
fill. Grimy, uneven light from the window mottled the walls and
highlighted a small photograph hanging in a Plexiglas frame above
the desk. Intrigued, Brian ventured into the room, nearly slipping
on loose sheets of paper as smooth as shale. "Have you seen this?"
he asked. He stepped aside as I approached, giving me a head-on
view of a snapshot neither of us had noticed last time we were here.
It showed Dad wearing madras shorts, a thin summer shirt, and a

nautical cap with a black visor. A camera hung from his neck like a pendant. Shot against an arid, glaring background, he'd drawn himself up to full height and squinted into the distance. In his fixity and anticipation, he rivaled the gazers of the ancient world: Ulysses leaning from the prow of his ship, Penelope scanning the sea at dusk. Beside him stood a figure swaddled from head to toe in dazzling white robes. "Must be from his honeymoon in Greece," I said, and just as I did, I realized that the robed figure beside him wasn't a figure at all, but a figure's absence. Anna had been scissored out of the scene. Given the tremor in his hands, he'd excised his second wife with surprising precision, leaving only a telltale sliver of her dark arm. It was as if he'd gone on their honeymoon alone.

I asked Brian why he thought my father would hang the photo right out in the open where Betty could see it. "He's warning her to watch her step. She could be snipped from a picture, too."

"Bingo, I think." I threw my arm over his shoulder and thanked him for never making me feel expendable.

"I promise to love you uncategorically," he said, "as long as you agree to a few conditions . . . "

I braced myself, waited.

"That was a joke."

"Oh."

We opened the window and basked in a meager breeze. We decided that the best way to proceed would be to start at the far end of the room and work our way toward the door. We each cleared a place for ourselves on the floor, then sat there and procrastinated. It was one thing to look down at the paperwork a man has accumulated over the course of his life, and quite another to sit within it, surrounded on all sides by records of what he'd earned and owed, accountings come to nothing and close enough to touch.

There was no way to begin other than to reach out and grab the nearest file. A quick scan of the contents told us whether it should be placed in the save or toss pile—two piles virtually indistinguishable from the other piles rising all around us.

"I don't trust the whole idea of *closure,*" I told Brian. "TV and radio shrinks say you can get over grief by following specific steps. One, two, three, and the sadness is over."

"Dividing a complicated process into simple steps is comforting to people. They're less overwhelmed. It gives them a sense of control." He held up a faded takeout menu. "Toss or save?"

"Toss."

"How constructive would it be," he continued, "if I told a grieving client that no matter what steps he takes, he'll miss the other person for the rest of his life."

"What *do* you tell a grieving client?"

"I tell them there's no timetable."

"So you don't believe in closure?"

He glanced around the room. "I believe in cleanup."

The task was disheartening for Brian as well as for me. The previous year, his own father died of heart failure in the family's Wingham, Ontario, home.

"Do you think about your father?" I asked.

"Every day."

"Do you feel like he'll always be with you?"

"I feel like he'll always be dead. That's why I miss him."

Before long, we began comparing documents plucked from the rubble. Most pertained to what had become the animating force of my father's old age. File after file had been gathered toward a single, obsessive end: ten years separated Gary's death from Ron's, but weeks after each of them died, my father brought lawsuits against their respective wives. The suits demanded that Sharleen and Nancy repay him "any and all monies" my brothers had borrowed since becoming his partners at the Spring Street office. Every check of his they'd cashed, he contended, had been a loan. Canceled checks were strewn throughout the room. Along with funds to help them with an occasional house or car payment, I found canceled checks ranging from $25 to $50 and dated on my brothers' birthdays and wedding anniversaries. These too, he'd insisted, were loans.

Sharleen and Nancy had been more than ready to cut their losses and settle out of court; the sooner they were free of a litigious father-in-law, the better. Their eagerness to reimburse him was an insult he didn't take lightly. How dare they offer to meet his demands! He then informed them that he'd been charging 10 percent interest on the loans (a rate my brothers would never have agreed to). Since several checks had been cashed ten or twenty years earlier, the interest was often disproportionately greater than the loan. He refused Sharleen and Nancy's offer to make monthly payments. Only one crushing sum was acceptable, a reparation that would leave them broke.

The basis of these suits may have been ludicrous, yet he'd retained contacts at the Hall of Justice, and by juggling bits of evidence and wording depositions just so, he managed to take both Sharleen and Nancy to court on seven separate occasions. With dismissals, continuances, and a host of postponements, he averaged about one hearing per year. Filing an eighth suit would have constituted "malicious prosecution," entitling his daughters-in-law to countersue, and so he seethed within the legal limit. He knew, of course, that once Sharleen and Nancy repaid him in full, they'd sever all connections. He sued to prolong their obligation rather than to settle his claim. He held them in a monetary thrall. As long as he engaged with them, he engaged with Ron and Gary.

I knew that asking him to drop the suits might touch him off, but I went ahead anyway. "Look," I said one night at the Brass Pan, "about the suits; do you really need the aggravation?" I hadn't planned to say it this way, but once I had, it seemed a fortuitous choice of words because *Who needs the aggravation?* was the phrase he used when enough was enough, and it let him know I was worried about him. Which was true in the overarching sense that I was also worried about my sisters-in-law, and even worried about my brothers, who were beyond worry, though I did my best to fret on their behalves.

"Don't lecture me," he warned, shifting his weight in the red leather booth.

"I just meant to—"

"Lecture me, is what you meant to do."

He knew that I'd maintained contact with both Nancy and Sharleen since my brothers' deaths, and by further campaigning for clemency, I'd be seen as a traitor, a double agent working for their side, which might lead him to disown me yet again. But estrangement was also possible if I did nothing; every time he mentioned the lawsuits, I felt sorry for my sisters-in-law, and my fondness for him was compromised.

"Well then," I said, clearing my throat, "I think it would be best if I didn't discuss the legal proceedings with anyone involved. Just to be, you know, impartial."

Dad shrugged at my apparent refusal to take sides. "Fine," he said. "If that's what you want." If he felt betrayed, he didn't show it. Perhaps he needed a break from the demands of antagonism. His reaction had also been softened by the vodka tonic I'd urged him to order, and into which the bartender, recognizing Dad as a regular, poured a payload of ninety-proof.

Still, I couldn't ignore the very real—or rather, the very unreal—possibility that if my father could sue Ron and Gary's wives, he might decide to go after Brian. By then, Brian and I had lived together for seven years, and I wondered if the legalities of common-law marriage applied to us automatically, even though the legalities of marriage were automatically denied. The palimony suits filed against Rock Hudson and Liberace by their . . . *pals* had redefined traditional divorce. If palimony made it easier for common-law couples to sue each other, did it also make it easier for a common-law in-law to sue his child's common-law spouse?

During a recent bout of insomnia, I'd thought I'd found an effective way to protect Brian from a possible lawsuit. I'd leapt out of bed, run downstairs to my study, and torn a sheet of paper from one of the yellow legal tablets on which I wrote first drafts. I chose a fountain pen (more formal than a ballpoint) and set out to create a "legal instrument" attesting to the fact that neither Brian nor I had ever borrowed money from my father, and in the event of my death, Brian should not be held responsible if my father filed suit. Until I had the time and money to hire an attorney and draw up a proper will, this document would have to do. I'd read somewhere that leaving a person one dollar makes it impossible for them to contest a will, since they haven't technically been omitted. To my father I bequeathed a buck. On the scale of fiscal insults, a dollar is admittedly harsh. It's like leaving one's parent a lousy tip, though tipping one's parent is an insult in itself. Stinting my father may sound like a way for me to get back at him for sending me a bill for my upbringing (in which case it would have done quite nicely and cost me almost nothing), but sparing Brian was foremost in my mind; I couldn't die in peace if I thought he'd have to face a costly, protracted legal battle once I was gone. And so I took the necessary step. Dad wouldn't know a thing about it unless he tried to sue my spouse. I recorded the date, drew dotted lines for our signatures, and, recalling Bob's license to carry a gun, added my thumbprint should the document's authenticity ever need to be verified.

The following morning, thinking how pleased he was going to be, I handed Brian the sheet of paper. He looked it over. And over. He registered no expression whatsoever. He said, "If it makes you feel better, I guess there's no harm in signing it." His forbearance hit me like a brick. In the disillusioning light of day, my affidavit looked about as legitimate as play money. No, not even as legitimate as play money, which is at least printed by a toy company. Mine was homemade and therefore *counterfeit* play money.

I unbit my lip and asked, "Was this a totally insane thing for me to do?"

"No," he'd said. "Not *totally.*"

The two of us continued to make our way across the paper land-scape. Several bloated garbage bags filled the empty living room, while the boxes and the suitcase contained scarcely anything worth keeping. Neither of us had thought to bring a flashlight, and we raced against the arrival of night. Every time we glanced out the window, afternoon edged closer to dusk. The sun's reds and oranges were magnified by currents of air blowing inland from the Pacific. Windblown grit pattered steadily against the trailer, a sound like faint, abrasive static. Even as the temperature dropped, the office walls radiated the day's heat, making the topmost layer of paper warm to the touch. Our judgment declined along with the light; what was important and what was not were harder and harder to tell apart.

Page after page made reference, in capital letters, to RICHARD COOPER and RONALD COOPER. I wasn't sure whether this was a legal formality or, like Dr. Rawlings's uppercase *H,* a stylistic quirk. I must have been bleary from examining so much stuff, because my brothers' names took on a third dimension, a life of their own. At times they bobbed to the surface of the text. At others they hovered above it. I can't remember whether Sharleen and Nancy were men-tioned in caps. I recall only that my brothers' names were of another order, greater than the sum of their syllables. RICHARD and RONALD recurred like a chant, an incantation. From where I sat, I could see my father's IBM Selectric dwarfing the desk. The electricity didn't need to work for me to remember the typewriter's rumble when it was switched on, how the print ball leapt up and smacked the platen, every letter leaving its sting. The metal casing—thick enough to with-stand a hammer—vibrated with such force that the whole machine would blur with motion and threaten to shimmy across the desk. To lay your fingers upon the keyboard was to savor earthquakes, speeding trains. When my father sat down to prepare his greatest case—*If it please the court, I ask that history be retracted, that spent money flow back to its source*—power must have coursed through his fingers. His first son's death had been death enough. He refused to let the next deaths take hold. He replaced grief with a full-time vendetta. Shapeless rage was divided into files. For incalculable loss, a quantity of dollars. Instead of silence, nights of typing. Necromancer, demigod, my father hit the shift key and conjured sons from nothing.

A few months after we'd cleaned out my father's trailer, I sat at the desk in my downstairs study and browsed several Web sites where, for a nominal fee, the visitor could search for information about his or her ancestry. The idea had been suggested by Lynn and Monica, who'd become so computer-savvy over the years, they referred to themselves as "techno-crones." The two of them were of the opinion that a person couldn't fully know herself unless she knew her history, which they had formerly called "herstory," and which I currently called "mystery." The number of ancestry sites surprised me; out of the initial dozens, Google yielded about eight pertinent hits. One site featured an animated American flag waving in the vacuum of cyberspace. Another droned a listless rendition of the National Anthem. Every site required the user to fill out a questionnaire. With no idea what the family name had been before it was changed, with no idea where in Russia my paternal grandparents had come from, I had scant information with which to conduct a search. I figured the best bet was to start with my father's name and work as far backward as the database allowed. But first, I needed to make a short list of potential sites.

When I opened my desk drawer for a pencil, I was flabbergasted to discover that Hell was gone. Its absence was alarming. Its absence was gigantic. Had I grown so blasé about the sight of flames leaping up every time I opened the drawer that I failed to notice their disappearance? I reached deep inside the drawer and, except for pencil shavings stuck to my palm, came up empty-handed. After systematically inspecting every other drawer in the desk, I ducked beneath it to rummage through the wastebasket and pat the shadowy floor around my feet. Could I have dropped the video or thrown it away by accident? I had no recollection of moving it to a different place, or any clue as to why I would have moved it, if in fact I had. Hellfire isn't easily overlooked, and it was troubling to think of myself as a person who could lose track of something so significant.

Lapses of memory on this scale never failed to trigger panic; they marked me for my father's fate, brought me closer to the chaos of his final days. Forgetfulness was untenable.

I burrowed through a hutch in my study where I kept my health and car insurance records, stubs from utility bills and school paychecks, all meticulously filed away as a hedge against the day when bill collectors and repo men would track me down like wild game. As often happened when I scrambled to locate lost keys or a misplaced wallet, each dead end, each indication that the world refused to yield the missing object, only added fervor to my search. I ransacked the shelves, fanned accordian folders. Miscellany rained to floor. *A videotape,* I said to myself, *doesn't just get up and walk away!*

Seconds later (I had to reassemble the events of that night on the following day), I stood amid the papers scattered at my feet. Was I still at the trailer? I slumped into my desk chair. On the computer screen there blinked a long, very long, possibly endless list of people with the surname of Cooper. During a blip of lucidity, I realized I must have accessed an ancestry site with my credit card. I possessed just enough presence of mind to wonder how much I'd charged to my account. If one was charged on a per-name basis, I'd be broke by morning. It occurred to me that I should walk upstairs, wake Brian, and tell him that something strange was happening, but just as I gripped the armrests of the chair, my reason for standing evaporated.

As I'd suspected in what seemed like a previous lifetime, both the names Edward and Cooper were too common to narrow the search, and so, with a couple of rubbery jabs at the keyboard, I typed in "1906" and hit return. Endless mutations swelled the ranks: Edward

Coopersmith, Everet Coombs, Emma Koestenbaum, Ellen Kincade. Mutations of my father's name were dredged from the nation's telephone books, census reports, immigration records, ships' manifests, and, for all I knew, from the data banks at the Library of Congress. As I scrolled down the page, half the population of America flew upward at a blinding rate.

The rapid motion strained my eyes. I closed them for a moment and dimly remembered that Dr. Montrose had been kind enough to prescribe sleeping pills without my having to drive all the way out to Oxnard to meet with her. This memory was hitched to an even dimmer memory in which she warned me over the phone that one of the side effects of the drug might be a brief phase of amnesia. I wondered what she'd meant by brief, in the sense that I had no idea how long I'd been in this indefinable state of mind. My state of mind is often indefinable, and for a person accustomed to a fair degree of ambiguity, the equipoise between consciousness and dream didn't, at first, seem strange.

Returning from the pharmacy that morning, I'd uncapped the bottle and gazed longingly at the little cylindrical pills at the bottom, a spellbinding blue. Throughout the day, I'd imagined how deliciously soporific it was going to be when I finally popped one into my mouth: the tender weight of it on my tongue, the draft of tap water washing it back, peristaltic contractions coaxing it deeper and deeper into my stomach, where it would dissolve in a bath of gastric acid and saturate my bloodstream with one irrepressible message: *Sleep.* Which is another way of saying that I'd imagined taking the pill so often and with such vivid anticipation, I wasn't sure if I actually had.

For legal reasons, I'm not at liberty to give the name of the sleep aid or the pharmaceutical company that produces it. I can say, however, that the usual lullaby of brand names—Ambien, Restoril, Halcyon—doesn't begin to describe the physical effect of the drug, which was like being whacked over the head with a velvet sledgehammer.

When I willed my eyes to open, I looked across the room and saw, just beyond the door to my study, cracks in the wall of the stairwell.

I hadn't noticed them before, and I went to take a closer look. Paint flaked onto the stairs as I ran my hand along the plaster, and it seemed that only a slightly greater application of pressure would send the wall crumbling down around me. I was certain that the cracks had been caused by our automatic garage door opener, an antiquated mechanism whose rusty chain strained with effort and shook the house. Had I been wrong all these years to think that my father had gone overboard by suing his next-door neighbors because he believed the tremors from *their* garage door had damaged his living room walls? Or was I, like Dad, prone to focus on cracks in the plaster?

Everything Brian and I had retrieved from my father's trailer had been packed into cardboard boxes and stored in the garage; could I have put *To Hell and Back* with the rest of his stuff? I needed to get my hands on the tape right away, otherwise I'd lie awake all night and worry that, if I'd placed it in the garage and didn't remember, I was turning into my father. If it *wasn't* there, I'd also lie awake and worry that I was turning into my father. But wait! Insomnia was no longer a problem! I had sleeping pills! I trudged upstairs to the kitchen—the steps were steep and many—and tapped a pill from the bottle. As the pill dropped into the center of my palm, it triggered a wave of déjà vu. Not your average dawning of familiarity. I had déjà vu of having déjà vu of having déjà vu, followed by several et ceteras. I was lost in a loop of eternal return. I swallowed the pill.

The garage door loomed before me, looking especially heavy and impenetrable until I realized I was holding the . . . the . . . clicker. I raised my arm, aimed, and clicked. I'd been eager to return home from work or errands many times since we'd lived in that house, but never had the sluggish opening of the garage door seemed as auspicious. The mechanism lifting the door was fitted with a light socket on a ten-minute timer, and the interior of the windowless garage, built into the hillside, blazed with light. I'd recently replaced its burnt-out lightbulb with the only unused bulb we had in the house, an amber bug light that, for reasons only entomologists know, repels insects. To human eyes, however, especially ones as dilated and sleep-deprived as mine, the light was anything but repellent. Our cars gleamed like mobile gold bricks. Exposed pipes were gold-plated. The walls were gold bullion stacked to the rafters. I'd discovered Eldorado in my own home, its gate rising before me and spilling twenty carats of light into the dark suburban street. Cars parked along the curb were burnished. Every shrub and mailbox in sight was transmuted into precious metal.

While standing unsteadily in the middle of the street and gazing straight ahead, I went to sleep on my feet. The next thing I knew, I lurched to attention, muscles clenched to prevent a fall. Awed all over again by the Midas light, I walked—no, was drawn—into the garage. Cardboard boxes were stacked against the back wall, a corner of my father's jumpsuit sticking out from beneath a flap. It was the one article of his clothing I'd kept (Betty had given the rest away to a local charity, which, I later found out, was the Oxnard chapter of Benny Hinn Ministries). Its polyester was destined to outlast me, a synthetic blend so durable it could probably withstand Armageddon.

I was opening one of the boxes when the gold air went black, tripped by the timer. Not so much as an afterimage tarnished the dark. Heat poured in through the open garage, but the summer night was moonless and the neighbors had long ago turned off their lights. I thrust up my arms to feel my way outside and struck my hand on the side of my car. It's a good thing I dropped the clicker because the noise of shattering plastic woke me from another plunge toward sleep. The crickets nearby abruptly ceased. Then resumed in unison. Or else it was blood pulsing through my ears. I took another step and began to buckle. I crossed into another country where the body is seized like contraband. I landed softly, padded, it seemed, by my willingness to fall. The concrete floor felt cool against my cheek. The surface of the world was too hard for sleep, and yet I slept deeply. I dreamed I was my father, searching the dark for misplaced possessions, and though he sensed their presence nearby, he'd forgotten what he wanted, and why.

Starless and immense, night was visible beyond the wooden joists of the roof. When I blinked away sleep, I realized I wasn't looking into

the sky after all, but at sheets of tar paper stapled to the ceiling. I'd
fallen asleep in the narrow space between our cars. A glance right
and left revealed dim glimpses of each car's undercarriage and the
zigzag tread of radial tires. I was like a man who wakes on a two-
lane highway, grateful he hasn't been flattened by traffic. My neck
was stiff, feet tingling with pins and needles. It required concentration to lever myself into a sitting position. Once I was sitting, it
required concentration to stay that way. Through the gaping garage
door, I could make out the vague gray geometry of our neighbors'
houses and, less distinct still, houses rising on the hills behind them.
It was dawn, what Sylvia Plath called "the blue hour," a time before
the city stirs, before silence drowns in the din of daily business.

Perhaps I would have been more upset by my predicament had
I not felt so rested. I hadn't slept for long, but a brief reprieve from
insomnia left the perpetually restless part of my brain (which is to
say the entire cranium) refreshed and ready to get back to work.
Overnight I'd become a neophyte of sleep, a convert to its cause.
Brian probably dozed through the whole episode, and if I snuck
back into bed now, he'd never guess I hadn't slept beside him. It
would have been a shame, though, not to take advantage of the early
light and search for the video one last time. I got to my feet, brushed
off the dust.

What a relief when I spotted flames in one of the boxes! My neck
and back relaxed. I grabbed the video and returned to the house,
greeted by the sight of papers scattered over the floor of my study.
It didn't take long to remember rummaging through the hutch, not
desperate to find the video so much as desperate not to lose it and, by
extension, my mind. I was about to slip *To Hell and Back* into my desk
drawer when I had to brace myself against the wall. This residual
drowsiness promised a few more winks if I headed up to bed, but it
also offered the ideal state in which to finally watch the video. I was
alert enough to pay attention and padded with just enough pharmaceutical armor to brave a visit to hell by myself.

I mounted the stairs. Slid the tape out of its sleeve and into the
VCR. Adjusted the volume and lay back on the couch.

The ministry's logo spun on the screen: a white dove radiating spokes of light and perching upon a gold cross. The credits rolled to mournful organ music, though any little ditty played on an organ usually sounds like a dirge to me. What a shock when Dr. Rawlings parted the curtain and shuffled onto the set through clouds of dry ice! His shoulders were stooped and narrow. What had been the stern rock face of his features in the photograph wasn't as nearly intimidating on video; the corners of his mouth sagged forlornly, the pouches beneath his eyes making him look preternaturally sleepy. Sleepier than me. He turned and faced the camera. The incinerating glare I'd braced for wasn't much hotter than a ray of winter sun. "Good death experiences?" he asked. "They're a dime a dozen. You never hear about the Hell experiences because the Hell experiences are embarrassing. It's an *F* on your report card. A slap in the face."

I had to force myself to stay awake while each interviewee discussed losing his moral bearings and wandering down a wayward path (drinking, stealing, gambling, etc.) until an illness or accident temporarily ended his life and gave him a firsthand taste of Hades. "The only thing keeping me alive," said one man, "was that I didn't want to die." Another prefaced his story with a tearful disclaimer, saying he was unable to divulge the ugly details of what Satan's minions, who had fooled him by dressing in hospital scrubs, did to him once they lured him down a smoke-filled hallway. Then he proceeded to describe "tearing, biting, tearing, scratching, gouging, ripping, and biting." Still another told of seeing both his mother and stepmother walking toward him, but their dresses had no pockets, and he remembered the phrase, *You can't take it with you.*

The five men who had returned from Hell were Caucasian and in their late fifties, leading one to conclude that either Hell's population is suspiciously homogeneous or that these men were not a representative cross section of the damned. Notable too was their shared clairvoyance; they each claimed to have known, as they hurtled toward a fiery pit, the principal sin committed by the screaming souls they were about to join. In every case it was precisely the sin about which the interviewee himself was most troubled. So, Hell is hellish either because it's a big roiling psychological projection or because it's divided into Dantean sub-Hells such as Alcoholics' Grotto or Fornicators' Molten Core.

Hell looked like—because it was—stock footage of rising flames. To represent each man's journey to the underworld, he (or the actor who played his younger, unconverted self) was superimposed over flickering orange fire while twisting in torment. Special-effects-wise it was a mistake to show the same wall of flames over and over; with each repetition, it seemed less burning and unbearable, a condition one could gradually adapt to like the temperature of a hot tub.

The tape was almost over and the sun was coming up. Light stretched across the carpet, defined the walls. The house slowly resolved around me, becoming, as it had every morning for seven years, a place I remembered from the night before. I could hear Brian, up for the day, brushing his teeth in the bathroom. He passed by the door, surprised to see me up so early.

"I'm watching a documentary about hell," I told him, nodding toward the TV.

"Oh," he yawned, "I wondered what you were up to." Then he staggered off to make coffee.

When I looked back at the TV, Dr. Rawlings had changed from his suit into a white coat. A stethoscope hung from his neck. "Once you're dead," he said, "there's not a thing you can do about it. But God has given us the power to restart the heart and get the lungs working before clinical death sets in." He made a distinction between resuscitation and resurrection, and as he did so, the camera pulled back to reveal a female mannequin that lay atop a gurney and stared insensibly toward heaven. The mannequin wore a red, white, and blue jogging suit, her ample blond hair shining like gossamer.

"We said we'd show you how to start somebody's heart up again, and you do it with your bare hands." Dr. Rawlings looked at the mannequin and managed an expression of halfhearted alarm. "So, immediately, you see if she's all right." He cleared his throat and shouted, "Hey, lady! Did you faint?" Then into the camera, "Maybe she's intoxicated and she'll talk to you. Or she just bumped her head." He walked toward the gurney without a hint of urgency. So calmly, in fact, I thought he'd walk right past it. He instructed the viewer to listen, look, and feel if her chest was moving.

"If we can catch people before they die," he said, "we give them the option of accepting Jesus Christ as their personal savior. If they die like this"—he nodded toward the woman—"we don't have to question where they went. But those that die on the street, where did they go?"

*At least hell's got a fire to make the place homey. If you don't believe in the afterlife, you can't light a match, a candle, nothing!* Or so my father—May he rest in peace—would have answered back.

Dr. Rawlings pinched the mannequin's nose between his thumb and forefinger and pried open the retractable jaw, exposing the scarlet cavity of the mouth. For all his medical training, he seemed a little squeamish about placing his lips over a strange woman's mouth, even for educational purposes, even if she was inanimate. But once the doctor set his personal feelings aside, he bent over, inhaled mightily, and blew a gale of air into the patient. The chances of reviving a mannequin are slim, of course, however skillful the mouth-to-mouth, yet the utter futility of the task made it all the more heroic. Our host shifted his head this way and that until he and his subject were tightly sealed together, sharing an airway. The exhalation was a superhuman feat; Dr. Rawlings was like one of those opera singers who can hold a note for so long you start to wonder if their diaphragms are connected to an air hose. When his breath finally gave out, he pressed his fingers to the mannequin's neck, said "Boom, boom, boom," and leaped back into action. He pumped the chest with a vigor just shy of violence, the heels of his hands sinking into the springy sternum again and again. The mannequin's running shoes jumped with every thrust.

I figured I might as well use this opportunity to learn CPR. I sat up and followed along with Dr. Rawlings. In with the good air, out with the bad. Count the seconds. Compress the chest. And if the victim doesn't respond, if the heart ceases beating or the lungs collapse, if the body resists resuscitation and the soul refuses to be redeemed, take another breath and try again.

# Rest in Peace

Before the new owner took possession of the trailer, Betty phoned to ask if I wanted my father's bed. "I wouldn't feel right taking it with me when I move, and I thought you might like to have it as a keepsake."

"It's kind of big for a keepsake," I said, "but thanks anyway." I told her Brian and I already had a bed that was, to quote Goldilocks, just right. What I didn't tell her was that I could never rest in a bed where my father spent so many hours of his life. A bed in which he'd had sex. From which he'd been banished. Where he'd possibly been assaulted in his sleep. Where he'd read *TV Guide* and listened to scripture. A bed where he tossed and turned past midnight, weaving his clients' misfortunes into a story that, like many on my syllabus, laid bare the course of a failing marriage.

In Cheever's "Reunion," the son says of his father, "I knew that when I was grown I would be something like him. I would have to plan my campaigns within his limitations." I'd pretty much resigned myself to this relay race of fate, but there were certain campaigns I was determined to wage on a fresh, untrammeled mattress of my own. Namely: sex, reading, and sleep. Each was my idea of heaven, especially in that order.

"We could always get a new mattress for it," said Brian. He didn't want the bed either; he was playing devil's advocate.

"It's not just the mattress. My father is embodied in the whole bed. His likeness might as well be carved into the headboard."

"That's . . ."

"I know," I said. "It's primitive. It's superstitious. But I hid in that bed when I was frightened of the dark as a kid. My mother chain-smoked in that bed, blaming herself when her sons were sick and her husband was seeing other women. I was born in that bed!"

Brian looked doubtful.

"Well, according to lore." My father probably meant to say that I was conceived in the bed, not born in it. Still, as a son to whom little history was handed, I grabbed at even the misremembered bits.

"When you went back to Canada for your father's funeral," I asked, "did you sleep in his bed?"

"He'd been dead less than a day!" said Brian. Then he grew quiet. "I considered it, then I slept in my old bed. I was worried his sheets might still be warm. Or might have grown cold."

In what turned out to be my last conversation with Betty—once she'd moved to her new apartment, she seemed eager to start over, and we had little reason to stay in touch—she told me she'd placed my father's bed on consignment at Rags to Riches, an Oxnard antiques shop. California may have been booming with new housing for the elderly, but several retirement villages and nursing homes consisted of single rooms that came with a bed, a chair, and a dresser, like college dormitories. Someone had to buy the furniture the elderly were leaving behind. It was highly unlikely, but not impossible, that a few belongings auctioned off in estate sales or sold at secondhand stores would miraculously gravitate back to the houses from which they came. To give my father's life more resolution than it actually had, I liked to imagine his bed returning to the house on Ambrose Avenue after the new owners, who just happened to be antiques hunting in Oxnard one day, found the mahogany headboard of their dreams. "Wait till you see it," they'd tell their friends. "It looks like it was meant to be here."

The bed had been purchased from a department store on Wilshire Boulevard in 1940. Once the deliverymen drove away, my parents sat on opposite sides and bounced on the mattress to test its firmness. Then they lay back and stared at the ceiling. They'd lived together for fifteen years. All three sons were still alive, the fourth unborn. They stretched their arms toward each other and found that their fingers barely touched. The bed seemed larger than it had in the store. It sprawled beneath them like a continent.

They'd bought the bed thinking it was just a big soft slab upon which a person either slips into or resists slipping into unconsciousness. But to say a bed is a thing to sleep on is like saying the sea is a drop of salty water. Below the cotton quilting lay a hidden world. Wooden braces keep the mattress from collapsing. Inner springs coil when pressure is applied, twanging each time we shift in our sleep or flail to find the ideal position, searching for the lost aquatic comfort we knew long ago in our mother's womb. However tame or acrobatic, sex takes its toll on the foam padding, lust grinding it down to powder, the grains sifting earthward night after night. Microscopic colonies of mites wait for the falling manna of our skin. Dreams sweep across the surface like seasons. Fevers and night sweats drench the sheets. A bed is a lectern, a pedestal, an altar, a rack, a boxing ring, a cavern of blankets, a spotlit stage, a trampoline, a nest, a grave.

# Last Words

We hit a stretch of the I-5 where Griffith Park's scrub brush and rocky outcroppings gradually thinned into the manicured green hills of Mount Sinai Memorial Park. Brian was only slightly more cautious behind the wheel of a car than my father had been; if counseling clients required him to keep his reactions in check, the road was a blank canvas on which he expressed his every impulse. That day, though, he was solemn and cautious, hands positioned on the steering wheel at ten and two o'clock. He stuck to the speed limit despite the mammoth trucks and SUVs looming up in the rearview mirror and following inches away from our tail. When Brian refused to yield the right of way, they'd veer into another lane and hurtle past us like missiles on wheels.

I glanced at my watch, a not-so-subtle hint for him to step on the gas. I often asked Brian to drive when we were running late; his dependably breakneck pace and disregard for solid objects always made up for lost time. "Relax," he said, eyes on the road. "This isn't a race."

Going to visit my father's grave also meant visiting the graves of my mother and three brothers, all buried in a family plot whose last available space was reserved for me. Dad had acquired a total of six plots when he'd made funeral arrangements for my brother Bob, in

1964, though he didn't mention the purchase to anyone in the family for nearly a year.

"I bought plots," he announced to my mother and me one morning at breakfast, apropos of nothing. I was in my first semester of junior high. Ron and Gary lived in apartments near the Spring Street office.

*"Plotz?"* said mother, setting her coffee cup in its saucer. A spoonful of corn flakes was suspended near my lips. My father slathered his toast with jam.

"Plots. Like in a cemetery. Now we each got a plot of our own. Next to Bob, *olev hasholem*. It's all taken care of."

"You could have let me in on this!" she cried.

My father glared at her. "I told you about it just now! Was I talking to myself?"

"After the fact is not *letting in on*."

Had my father only left well enough alone, or apologized for not consulting her. Instead, he added that Mount Sinai's funeral director agreed to sell him six graves for the price of five. "Consider the savings!" Recounting his riposte isn't easy, because my parents warned me at a young age that many non-Jews believed we had horns, were cheap, and killed Jesus Christ. (These faults, I assumed, went from least to most egregious. Had *I* arranged the list, horns would have come last. As for Christ, I would have remembered killing someone's savior.) My father wasn't boasting about his clout as a negotiator so much as he was defending his decision to grab the land while the grabbing was good. In some respects, Mount Sinai was similar to the new subdivisions that were being bulldozed into the Hollywood Hills—vacant lots bought for their promise of peace, an investment with long-range benefits.

Still, any father who brings up, at breakfast, the eventual death of his entire family should probably expect everyone seated at the table to ponder, at least fleetingly, their own mortality and the mortality of others. But my father was (a) surprised that his news put a damper on the meal and (b) miffed that my mother wasn't quicker to appreciate his foresight. "You want I should've left the matter up to chance? I thought you'd be pleased." Panic tinged his voice, the panic of a man who, beyond haggling with a mortician, signing contracts, and writing a check, had nothing left to say or do. His business was finished. A row of trenches were reserved in the dirt.

He looked so miserable I almost blurted, "Thanks for the grave, Dad," but merely thinking it made me feel jinxed, and I only got as far as an intake of breath.

Mother said, "I suppose I should be grateful you told me now instead of letting me find out about it when I'm dead. A mother deserves some say in these things. A wife too, in case the word should ring a bell."

"What's that supposed to mean?"

She cinched her bathrobe, rose to her feet, and made a show of clearing the table. Our plates were still full.

"You don't want me to take the initiative? Fine. I'll cancel the contract. *You* go to the graveyard and pick out plots. But do it soon, because we sure as hell can't change our minds once we're in there."

Mother dumped scrambled eggs into the garbage disposal, a dire act for a woman who, hungry or not, ate scraps from our plates on principal rather than letting food go to waste. She rinsed a fistful of cutlery, then paused to calm down. "Is there a view?" she asked, clutching a bouquet of wet utensils.

"Sinai is a mount, Lil. Of course there's views. You got Burbank and Studio City right at your feet. Everywhere you look is a panorama. Bob is close to the top of the hill, don't you remember?"

"I remember the ground," she said, drying her hands on a dish towel. "I remember the grass as we walked up the hill. When we got closer, I saw that the walls of the grave were moist and flat, the corners as sharp as they are in this room. I was glad—*glad,* can you imagine?—that it was like a room and not just a hole in the ground. The mound of soil next to the grave? I think they put a tarp over it so you almost believe the grave will never get filled, will always stay open to the air and light. After Kaddish, Rabbi Kaplan lifted a corner of the tarp, and I remember him handing you a shovel, Ed, and when you were done, he gave it to Ron, then Gary, then Bernard.

He had to lay his hand on each of your shoulders and look into your eyes, nodding his head to let you know that God thought it was all right. It wasn't, though, was it?"

She looked at us as though she'd just realized we were sitting there. "Were there stones in the dirt—is that why the sound was so loud? Every shovelful made that loud hollow sound and scattered across the lid of the coffin. It was like a dream, each of you taking your turn and walking up to the grave with a shovel, and I wanted to shout to stop you from falling in, but as soon as I heard that sound I didn't care how sad or frightened you seemed, how close you stood to the edge. All I thought was, *How can they do this?*"

My father and I began to stammer in our own defense, but Mother raised a hand to shush us. "I meant, how can they *stand* to do this? I know you had to. No one else should have. No one. It has to be done by the ones who are already broken and can't break anymore because of one shovelful of dirt. I was angry anyway. Who else was I going to blame? God? My son's blood? The men who'd made the grave so straight? None of it makes sense. I'm just telling you, these are the things I remember, not the view."

The next minute got stuck in its slot. No one knew how to pry it loose. Finally I said, "There was a man I read about in *Ripley's Believe It or Not* who spent a week underground in a special coffin. They fed him through a tube and everything. People could see his face in a little window and they got to ask him questions about what it was like to be buried."

Mother returned to the table. She lit a cigarette and leaned back in her chair. "He could say what it was like to be buried *alive,* maybe, but that's not the same thing."

My father said, "Not by a long shot."

"Houdini promised he'd come back from the grave," she continued, "and look where that got him."

"Where?" I asked.

"Dead," said Mother. She blew a stream of smoke toward the ceiling. It hovered over our heads like weather.

"Be that as it may," said Father, "he didn't say *when* he was coming back. People are probably waiting for him as we speak, like they are for the second coming. Take it from me: whoever gets back first has a big advantage. It's no good to be the *second* person to invent the wheel."

"Cheating death isn't something you invent," corrected Mother. "It's something you do. If you're lucky." She recounted a story she'd read in *Life* about a "mystic yogi" who, through the power of his mind alone, could keep his heart from beating and didn't need to breathe. Soon, the Miracle Chicken reared its headless neck. My father used its plight to illustrate the pros and cons of coming back. On the one hand, you're alive; on the other, you have to die all over again.

There arose the tempting idea of living forever. I said I wanted to.

"It *sounds* good," my father warned me, "until you read the fine print."

"What your father means is that the price for eternal life is having to grow older and older." Mother gently stroked her neck. "Older than anyone we've ever seen."

"Older than a redwood," I said.

"It's no picnic at fifty," said my father, "so multiply that by a couple of centuries and see how you like it. Unless," he reconsidered, "they figure out a way to arrest the aging process."

"Who's going to figure *that* out?" Mother wanted to know.

"The people whose business it is to take care of these things."

We switched philosophical positions at will, one of us a champion of resurrection or an advocate of extended longevity, the others finding loopholes, casting doubt. The point wasn't to debate the issues with consistency. The point was to dodge a foregone conclusion, to leap from one diversion to the next. After losing Bob, we'd had our fill of death. We were sick of its grim contingencies.

Brian signaled well in advance of the Forest Lawn exit. I couldn't stop thinking about how insistently my parents and I had willed the topic off course that morning at breakfast, our evasion as tangible as the sensation of Brian's car banking around the off ramp. We sailed along Forest Lawn Boulevard, the concrete channel of the Los

Angeles River to our right. At night, taggers climbed over the
cyclone fence and spray-painted the names of their gangs on the
steep walls, loyalties trumpeted in brash colors. A Santa Ana was "in
effect," as the weathercasters said, the wind wicking moisture from
everything it touched. Drought had left the river basin empty except
for pools of standing water whose only current was the skyward pull
of evaporation. It would take days of drenching tropical rain to turn
these shallows into the murky torrent one saw on the nightly news
whenever a careless child fell in and was either rescued by Caltrans
workers or swept downriver to his death.

On our left, the wrought-iron fence bordering Mount Sinai
Memorial Park ran for a good half mile, its pickets tipped with
ornamental spears. The technical distinction between a memorial
park and a cemetery is determined by the presence of headstones.
The Glendale branch of Forest Lawn is a cemetery renowned for its
Carrara marble bas-reliefs, a stained-glass reproduction of da Vinci's
*Last Supper,* a scale replica of Michelangelo's *David,* and a popular
"museum store" that sells every sepulchral souvenir you could imagine short of an ashtray shaped like a cremation urn. Forest Lawn
epitomizes the theme-park atmosphere envisioned by morticians of
1950s Los Angeles, whereas its sister institution, Mount Sinai, is
characterized by a lack of tombstones and thematic statuary, a condition that stems, in part, from the Talmudic prohibition against idol
worship. Instead, the dead are identified by evenly spaced grave
markers flush with the earth and surrounded by a carpet of hardy
Bermuda grass. Nothing distracts the eye from absence.

Today was the eleven-month anniversary of my father's death,
the last day his grave marker could be unveiled according to the
Jewish laws of mourning. That I'd postponed the unveiling till the
last possible minute may seem like negligence on my part, which it
was, but I also had reason to procrastinate. It's believed that this waiting period gives those close to the deceased enough time to reckon
with the bleakest and most immediate phase of grief, which will
better prepare them to see the intimate's name inscribed on a bronze
plaque, to take in the dates of birth and death—a span as brief as the

dash between them—and to understand that, even though the body lay below the earth, moldering in its cocoon of burial clothes, the person to whom the body once belonged has been recollected from every angle, in every cast of light, scored into the survivor's heart so often and with such painstaking intensity that, over time, the deceased has become miraculously animate and has taken up permanent residence in mourners' memory. The longer I put off the unveiling, the more time my father had to settle into the chambers of my brain, to hang up his jumpsuit and make himself at home.

Not until Brian pulled up to the information booth did I begin to see the flaw in my logic. My father was already as entrenched in my memory as he would ever get, and what I perhaps should have done was arrange for the observance to take place nearer the thirty-day mark instead of the eleventh month. The eleventh *hour*, really, for I'd waited so long to call the mortuary and plan my visit that the cutoff date for this preliminary period of mourning, measured from the time entered on his death certificate, was an hour away.

The Jewish laws of mourning are less prescriptions than sugges-tions, and I knew that no spiritual punishment awaited me if the unveiling didn't take place precisely within the given time frame. No burning bush would lecture me on punctuality. Rabbis wouldn't cart me off in handcuffs. My grave wouldn't be turned into a planter or be repossessed. The problem was, I still feared disappointing my father, providing him with definitive proof of my irresponsibility. He may not have been sentient in a strictly physiological sense, but he was alive enough to speak his mind: *Eleven months and you're too busy to throw on some decent clothes and honor your old man?* Guilt and superstition are a volatile mix. I was really in a rush to get this done.

I gave the guard my father's name. He disappeared inside the information booth and emerged a minute later, arms folded across his chest, taking his time. "Turn right and park in front of the administration building," he said. "A receptionist in the lobby will give you a map with directions to the grave site."

As we drove off, I told Brian I thought the guard knew about my father's unusual epitaph.

"What makes you think he knew?"

"It wasn't anything he said or did, exactly, but we're dealing with a group of people who probably go through a training program where they learn to stay poker-faced in any situation." Although I'd searched their faces for signs of amusement, pity, or reproach, I hadn't been able to tell what, if anything, the employees of Mount Sinai thought of the two sentences my father had asked to have chiseled on his grave marker. Had his epitaph become a part of mortuary folklore, or were strange last wishes par for the course?


The day my father died, a woman named Traci Hirsch had called to introduce herself and tell me that before he'd moved to Oxnard, the two of them had met to discuss his "funerary welfare."

"Funerary welfare?" This was the first I'd heard of Ms. Hirsch, or of my father's posthumous plans. The conclusion I jumped to proved I was my mother's son as well as my father's: I wondered if their discussion took place in a hotel room over watery highballs. My suspicion was dispelled when Ms. Hirsch identified herself as a "pre-need counselor" on staff at Mount Sinai Memorial Park, where the hospital had sent his body. With her silky phone persona, she explained the nature of her work: helping clients "customize a burial service to suit their budgets and personalities." The plans are kept on record so a client can rest assured that, when the time comes, their wishes will be met to the letter. "Your father knew what he wanted and spoke his mind," she told me. I recalled Dad's brio at the Toyota dealership and pictured him slamming a coffin lid to see if it was well constructed. Ms. Hirsch added, a little ominously I thought, that the men and women of her profession considered it the height of kindness for people such as my father to make difficult decisions in advance so that others wouldn't have to. I agreed with her in theory—it *was* considerate—but I couldn't get past, for starters, the fact that her phone call came as a total surprise. Out of the blue was the last place from which I wanted information about my father, and the first from which it usually came. Mr. Delaney at

Pacific Bell, Mr. Gomez at Adult Protective Services, Dr. Montrose and Lucinda at Saint Joseph's Hospital had all contacted me—in the sense that lightning contacts a tree—out of the blue. And like Ms. Hirsch, each of them implied that my father was irascible while at the same time commending in him a certain charm they had a hard time putting their fingers on. I was sure that Ms. Hirsch's comment about Dad's kindness was offered to counterbalance whatever flabbergasting revelation she had in store for me. When I asked for the details, she said it was her policy to speak with relatives in person whenever such a meeting was "geographically feasible."

In the hours between the call from Ms. Hirsch and going to meet with her at Mount Sinai, I tried to second-guess what kind of rites Dad would have taken the time and trouble to prearrange. By a quirk of metaphysics, second-guessing him effectively assured that my various guesses would be wrong *because* I'd thought of them, which didn't stop me from trying. By midnight my mantra was, *How bad can it be?* I'd heard of people in New Guinea who paid to have coffins built in the shape of sports cars, a red Porsche with racing stripes the most requested model. In Atlanta, a traveling salesman's last wish was to have an exact replica of his battered valise carved in granite and used as his headstone, too heavy to tote through the afterlife. The world's most lugubrious jewelry may have been crafted by the Victorians, who wove locks of the loved one's hair into pendants and brooches to go with their mourning garments, memento mori worn close to the heart. I had no idea what state of mind my father had been in when planning his funeral. For all I knew, I might find myself standing at his grave site while a portable tape recorder (the one I'd used to interview him for the book I'd never written) blared "The Trolley Song" across the park, a few bereaved and clinging families turning from their services to shoot me angry looks.

The next morning, in the lobby of Mount Sinai's administration building, Traci Hirsch greeted Brian and me with her firm, unhurried handshake. She led us from the lobby into her office, a place made dour by velvet curtains and Federal furniture. She smartly folded herself into one of several chairs at a circular table and nod-

ded for us to follow suit. Ms. Hirsch produced a black leather-bound
ledger, and once she set it before us, she laid her hands guardedly
over the cover. Her every gesture had about it a cautious grace, as if
clumsiness or haste might wake the dead. She was all ceremony, the
air oppressive with impending disclosures. Compared to her formality, an unscheduled sniffle or hiccup would rip through the room
with the force of an explosion, and I started tamping down my reaction to Dad's last wishes before I'd even found out what they were.
"Please accept my condolences," said Ms. Hirsch, opening her
ledger. The binding cracked like cartilage. She turned to Brian.
"Were you the deceased's physician, Dr. Miller?"

"I'm Mr. Cooper's partner."

"I see," she said, jotting a note. "Deceased's business partner."

"No," corrected Brian. "I'm Bernard's partner."

"We live together," I explained to Traci. "We're a couple."

"And Dr. Miller is here to offer moral support? Isn't that wonderful. You know," she said confidentially, "these things are just a part
of life, aren't they? You needn't feel at all self-conscious about it in
front of me."

Brian and I looked at each other. By "these things" did she mean
homosexuality, or death? Was she telling us it was okay to kiss, or to
drop dead in front of her?

"Let me begin by saying that we at Mount Sinai want our pre-
need clients to feel that any sentiment they choose to express on their
bronze marker is entirely up to them. Our job is to honor the client's
wishes. We do whatever we can to help him or her find that special
phrase or inspirational quote that will best represent who they are
and will continue to touch the hearts of their loved ones for years
to come. You may be surprised to learn that many people find it an
enormous responsibility to choose just one memorable sentence . . ."

"I wouldn't find it surprising at all," I interjected. "You're asking
them to compress an entire lifetime into a few words."

Stiff to begin with, Traci stiffened further.

"He's a writer," explained Brian.

I said, "It's quite a challenge, is all I meant."

"A challenge we here at Mount Sinai are more than prepared to meet."

"Oh, I'm sure . . ."

"You might perhaps be pleased to know that ours is one of the first mortuaries in the country to develop a photo brochure featuring examples of the kinds of plaques people have created over the years. We also offer a wide variety of visual symbols one can add for emphasis, such as a menorah or Star of David. I can assure you that the majority of our clients leave their pre-need session with no complaints whatsoever about the statement they've decided upon. And of course, it can be revised at any time before the client dies. I can assure you I'd be the last person to underestimate the importance of one's final words. Certainly, as a writer, you must know that the Greeks had a name for composing commemorative remarks, *epitaphion,* from which we derive the word *epitaph*?"

"No, I didn't."

"You didn't? How interesting. They considered it one of mankind's most noble and demanding arts. You see, Bernard— may I call you that, rather than Mr. Cooper? It cuts down on the confusion—as I was saying, pre-need may sound like a very up-to-the-minute development in the funerary profession, but in fact it dates back to ancient civilizations, who, judging from the hieroglyphs they left on cenotaphs and inside tombs, were quite meticulous in their preparations for the hereafter. The memorial parks of today, however, are limited in space and regulated according to strict local zoning codes and industry-wide regulations, one of which calls for the standardization of grave markers. And that's as it should be. We wouldn't want to play favorites. Why should we require one client to keep it short while we permit another to inscribe a lengthy farewell address? Brevity plus quality. That's our approach." She waited, unsmilingly, for us to nod. "Your father, as I'm sure you'd agree, was . . . he was . . . an individual."

The room grew smaller.

"May I cut to the chase, Mr. Cooper?"

"Please," I begged.

She consulted the ledger. "'They finally got me.'"

"I'm sorry?"

"'They finally got me.'"

"Are *you* saying that, or are you telling me what *he* said?"

"I'm telling you that's what your father asked to have inscribed on his marker. Unless you have any objections. And I should tell you now to prevent any future misunderstandings that seeking amendments to his pre-need contract would require you to obtain full power of attorney and to assume, in writing, responsibility for any additional fees incurred beyond the one thousand dollars your father entrusted to us."

I assured Ms. Hirsch that I wanted him to have whatever he wanted, and that whatever he wanted done should be done in exactly the way he'd wanted it done, no deviations. "Excellent," she said, briskly closing the ledger. "I'm sure he'd be pleased to hear you say this. Now, if you'll excuse me, I'll make sure the viewing room is ready. The county coroner requires verification on the part of a relative or friend, but you're free to spend as much time with your father's body as you feel necessary."

*Your father's body.*

"In the meantime, let me leave you with some material to peruse. Your father left funds toward a casket but he hadn't decided on a particular model at the time of his death." She handed me a casket price list and paused to look fawningly at Brian and me. Such bright piety glistened in her eyes that I nearly felt jilted when, instead of saying, "I respect your lifestyle," she let go of the list and disappeared.

My head was reeling. Brian and I scooted our chairs together and flipped through the numbingly long list. I picked the first casket that sounded decent. "What about the Bedford?" I suggested. This model was described as "Eighteen-gauge steel. Blue finish. Blue sand pebble crepe interior with matching overlay and sunburst in head panel."

"That's a woman's casket."

"There are men's and women's?"

"You'll see what I mean when she takes us to the showroom."

I ran my finger down the page. "What about this one, the Majestic? 'Brush natural smoky gray shading with pinstripe. Gray cloud velvet interior. Solid bronze.' That sounds manly." The thought of velvet and gray clouds made me sleepy, plus the room was overheated and nodding off would have been better than waiting to see my father's body.

"The Majestic is over six grand," said Brian.

I turned to another page. "Look. This one's a lot less expensive. The lamb's wool sounds nice."

"That's a children's casket." He pointed to a parenthesis that read, "Twenty-one-inch stillborn."

I rubbed my temples. "Well, you choose one."

"Here's a perfectly good one made of fiberboard. The Kent."

I wrenched the list out of his hands. "Fiberboard!"

"It has silver ventura fabric and the interior is madrid crepe," he said defensively.

"You don't know what ventura fabric and madrid crepe are any more than I do! The Kent is just a step up from"—I squinted at the small print—"a metal-gasketed transfer case."

"It says the transfer case is for shipping only."

"Oh."

Brian gripped my hand and held it. "She's going to try to sell you the most expensive coffin," he said. "Take it from me, it's a business. They're out to make a dollar like any other business. The money he left won't go very far, and you'll end up owing the rest. This may sound crass now, but you'll be relieved when the bill comes."

"For Christ's sake," I said in the voice of my father, "and your people think *our* people are cheap."

I was laughing when Ms. Hirsch opened the door, but it was hilarity under pressure, heavy on the bobbing shoulders and shortness of breath, and maybe, just maybe, it passed as grief.

Which it shifted into as soon I stepped across the hallway and into the viewing room. "Do you want me to . . . ?" asked Brian, and then he and Ms. Hirsch were waiting on the other side of the closed door. The room, a dim ivory cube, was empty except for a gurney positioned in one corner. Directly behind it, another door led to the chamber where bodies were cleansed, injected with preservatives, and arranged for presentation. I smelled a medicinal odor tinged with rotting fruit: perfumed embalming fluid. A sheet had been draped over the gurney, leaving his shoulders and head exposed. I quickly glanced at the floor, focusing on the black wheels, the silver axles. Any minute I would lift my eyes and look. But first I had to renounce my faith in reconciliation. First I had to tell myself that souls are better spent than saved.

His eyes were closed. Slack flesh hung from the armature of his bones. Succumbing to its own weight, the bulk of him was caving in. Once I'd looked, I couldn't turn away, couldn't sever the gaze that held us together. As I approached, I could have sworn the freezing air wasn't a condition intended to preserve his body, but a force emanating from it. In death he radiated cold just as surely as, alive, he'd radiated heat. Cold issued from him like a warning, and it was impossible not to take heed. Gooseflesh tightened my skin, muscles contracting against the drop in temperature. I drew close enough to see the back of his neck sagging toward the metal table, his earlobes stretched and pendulous. Blood was settling like silt in my father's body, turning it an otherworldly blue. Not the human blue of eyes or veins or bruises. *Cobalt? Sapphire?* My throat constricted and names escaped me. When I'd stood beside his hospital bed, there'd been things I'd wanted to say, and I'd said them in the hope that he might somehow hear and understand. Now language couldn't bridge the distance. Language was a vacuum, unspoken, recanted. Silence interceded for us both.


Brian and I pulled into a parking space in front of the administration building. "Keep the motor running," I told him. "I'll get a map of the grounds." I raced across the parking lot and into the building's recessed entry, the glass doors parting biblically before me. Arrangements of carnations and roses lined the display window of the on-site florist's shop. Moisture beaded at the corners of the plate glass, spilling cool, leafy light into the lobby. The whole place was as still as a terrarium, impervious to the world. No receptionist sat at the desk. I peered around corners and investigated hallways, searching for someone in charge. I considered asking one of the occasional passersby if they knew where I might find a map, but it wasn't easy to wrest their attention. Men and women alike might as well have been wearing veils, so remote were their expressions, so inward their submission to grief.

Everyone I saw wore black and gray and navy. At least I'd dressed appropriately. Sort of. My jeans were the saturated blue of new denim, and with them I'd worn a relatively unwrinkled white shirt. While I wasn't exactly a fashion ad, neither was I slovenly. After all, does it really honor the departed to get so done up that, from their vantage in the afterlife, they couldn't pick you out in a crowd of mourners?

"Sir?" The receptionist had returned to her desk. "How may I help you?"

She typed *Edward Cooper* into her keyboard and scanned the screen, which lit her pretty, noncommittal face. Whir of microcircuitry. "Goodness," she said. "That must be one of our most common names. I show a total of six Ed or Edward Coopers. Shall I go through them one by one?"

I startled us both with my *No!* Opening the files of deceased strangers seemed as ghoulish as exhuming graves, all that musty information brought to light, plundered as though from a cyber-tomb. My father's death was complicated enough without having to learn the identities of his half a dozen graveyard namesakes. Besides, I was running out of time to pay proper homage.

"When did he pass?" she asked.

"Two thousand."

She hit Return and scavenged the database. Hanging on the wall behind her was a framed photograph of an astronaut wearing a space suit and holding his helmet under one arm. A placard identified him as Ilan Ramon, the Israeli crew member who died in the explosion aboard the space shuttle *Columbia*. Ramon possessed the vigilant,

unchanging gaze one sees on the faces of stone lions and wary
caryatids—an ideal sentry for this outpost of mortality.

"Your father!" exclaimed the receptionist. "He's here!" I spun
around to look behind me, half expecting a repeat of Dad's appearance at Kennedy Airport.

"Edward and Hilda Cooper," said the receptionist triumphantly.
"They're located in Maimonides, one of our loveliest sections. Properties 4418 and 4419."

Hilda? I would have brought this error to her attention sooner
had I not been sideswiped by the thought that Hilda, a woman I'd
never heard of, was in fact the person beside whom my father had
asked to be interred, and whose existence, or former existence, I was
only just now learning about. Hilda might have been his wife, girlfriend, housekeeper, nurse. I'd seen enough *Herald Examiners* in my
life to know that bigamy, and its industrious cousins polygamy and
adultery, were practiced far and wide.

"My mother's name was Lillian, not Hilda."

"Apologies," said the receptionist. She removed her sweater and
hung it over the back of her chair. This was going to take a while.
"Mother's maiden name?"

"Harrison."

She spelled it back for confirmation. "I do show an Edward and
Lillian, but they're in a multiple listing along with—"

"Yes," I said. "The other three are my brothers."

"All right!" she exclaimed, giving me a thumbs-up. She removed
a map from her desk drawer, uncapped a fluorescent yellow high-
lighter, and drew a line leading not toward Maimonides, but toward
Moses, a section farther up Mount Sinai Drive. Midway, she stopped
drawing and looked up at me. "That sounded awful, what I just said.
I'm sorry for your losses."

"You live," I said. "Things happen. You go on." This had a familiar ring, but not until hours later would I remember that my father
had said this to me in his living room, explaining, or explaining away,
three years of estrangement.

The receptionist handed me the map.

"When I get to the site, will the plaque be covered with something?"

She cocked her head.

"For the unveiling. Is there something I'm supposed to take off the plaque? Or should I have brought something along to put on the plaque so I could, you know, take it off?"

"There is no *unveiling,* technically. Unless you made special arrangements. Some people have ceremonies. Maybe a rabbi or a family member says a few words. Our maintenance staff makes sure the plaque is in place on the appointed day." She hugged herself against a chill. "I hope you aren't disappointed?"

"I'm relieved," I said. "It's one less thing I can do wrong."

"You can't do sadness wrong," she said. "You either do it or you don't."

I shook her hand, and when I stepped outside, squinting against the sun and the wind, I felt almost ready for the task ahead. Perhaps it had been foolish to take the idea of the unveiling literally, to anticipate lifting some sort of ritual cloth off my father's plaque. Part of me, I suppose, yearned to uncover a mystery at the last minute, a revelation that would enrich or reconfigure what little I knew about him. The plaque held no mystery, in the sense that I'd been forewarned about his epitaph. Yet as always with my father, a mystery remained.

"Who is *they?*" I asked Brian as I climbed back in the car.

"Who is who?"

"On my father's plaque. '*They* finally got me.' Who do you think the *they* is?"

He shifted into reverse. "Paranoia was an innate aspect of your father's personality, and it intensified with age. Remember the business with the silver? I'm not sure it's worth interpreting something as illogical as paranoia."

"Why is it any different from interpreting something as illogical as dreams?"

"I'm not sure dreams should be interpreted either. They're probably just a buildup of random electrochemical sense impressions that are discharged during the REM stages of sleep."

"That's a romantic way to look at it."

"It is," he insisted, "because if dream interpretation is a dead end, then I can skip it and move on to more effective ways of helping my clients."

I stroked his thigh. "I love you," I said.

"See," he said. "Skepticism is very romantic."

We turned onto Mount Sinai Drive. If there are peak hours at a memorial park, we came early enough to avoid them. We drifted by a parked hearse, the reflection of Brian's Toyota, dark as carbon, creeping along its length. We passed the Court of the Psalms and the Court of the Proverbs, two wings of a mausoleum whose enormous double doors were open to skylit spaces where crypts held the ashes and bits of bone, the grit of cremains. Sealed compartments lined the walls from floor to ceiling, reminding me of the safe deposit boxes at the Oxnard Bank of America.

"I think *they* is a composite character," I told Brian. "It's Mr. Delaney from the phone company, and it's the gas company's meter reader, and it's all the doctors and nurses and social workers who dared to interfere. It's the people whose offers of help he found demeaning, or people he decided were too inept and insensitive to help him in the right way. He might have thrown Betty and Anna into the *they* for good measure. And maybe even my mother, given how much the two of them fought. And me; I'm a *they*, no doubt about it. When you get right down to it, my father was a *they* magnet. He attracted adversaries real and imagined."

"They're so close together," said Brian.

"The real and the imagined?"

"No," he said, "the graves."

He was right. The markers we drove by divided the slopes into narrow, alternating strips of green and bronze. Beneath Mount Sinai there existed another, hidden mountain whose contours echoed the landscape all around us except that, instead of a wide morning sky suspended overhead, smothering black soil pressed down on regiments of the dead. As the car climbed higher, we rose not only upon a road, but upon a rotunda of human remains, a subterranean city of mitered pine and lead casket linings. We rose upon crumbling bolsters of silk upholstery and keepsakes of all kinds—photographs, letters, cameos, and lucky coins—possessions gripped by indifferent hands. On the ridge above us were clustered what the map identified as the Gardens of Tradition, the Gardens of Heritage, the Gardens of People of the Book, interconnected open-air courtyards where meandering walkways and stone benches existed solely for the sake of a reverie whose hush fell on the summit like snow.

Numbers stenciled along the curb indicated the range of "internment spaces" within a particular lot. The family plot turned out to be higher than I remembered. (The memorial park wasn't a place I visited unless I had to; I paid homage by sitting at my desk, where memory and prose led parallel lives.) Once we neared the right section, Brian pulled over to the curb and parked, wrenching the handbrake tight against the incline.

Poised at the perimeter of Moses, each of us held one end of the map to steady it against the wind. We had to look from the hillside to the map and back. With no upright landmarks, it was difficult to find correlations between a page crowded with schematic drawings of coffins and the undulating land in front of us. Once we felt sufficiently oriented, we set off to search in different directions.

Names and sentiments that had been illegible from the distance now clarified underfoot. Despite my urgency about observing the ritual on time, I have to admit that, step by step, inundated by the names of strangers—Hershel, Shirley, Boris, Estelle—I almost lost sight of the reason we'd come in the first place. Brian began to call out phrases with which the dead had memorialized themselves, or that their loved ones had chosen to remember them by. "Beautiful soul," he shouted. "Source of love." His lips moved, and then his voice, carried off course by the wind, would reach me after the briefest delay, like a warm belated breath. As he moved farther and farther away, I took his lead and read aloud. "Always with us." "Full of life." These declarations belonged to the earth and the air as much as— no, more than—to us. In this way we ranged over graves.

I couldn't help but notice that I took pains to step over the plaques, whereas Brian felt no compunction about stepping right on top of them, as if they'd been set there to pave his way. He might have done this in defiance of graveyard piety, or else tramping on the dead didn't strike him as taboo. In either case, his heedlessness, our call-and-response, the sun boring down on our balding heads—all this was exhilarating, and since exhilaration was the last thing I expected to feel that day, it was completely in keeping with my father, which is to say consistent with his unpredictability.

It had been more than a decade since the editor from New York had called to ask if I'd consider writing a book about my father, and my stockpile of biographical facts was as meager now as it had been then. His last breath carried him beyond comprehension in a way more literal, more definitive, than I could have imagined during his lifetime. I hadn't been able to find any mention of him in historical records or data banks, hadn't been able to locate a single one of his relatives or friends to press for information. Now that he was gone, our family name was untraceable, along with whatever legacy came with it.

My knowledge of my father had always been confined to what I'd experienced in his presence, including the flood of hunches and deductions that his smallest gesture—lifting an eyebrow, folding his arms—set off within me. I don't think I would have been nearly as alert to the minutiae of his behavior had there been more information, more clues to choose from. So this limitation also defined him, gave him outlines. For however long I remained capable of recall, he'd fit within my memory like a man within his skin. For the moment, this was knowledge enough.

I bent over to examine a few plaques. Each bore its lament in raised letters. Each was framed with beveled edges. I straightened up when I heard Brian shouting in the distance. He waved his arm to hail me over, his clothes rippling in gusts of wind.

And there it was, the family plot—my parents, my brothers, the allotments of land they'd vanished into. A row of tarnished rectangles gleamed dully in the sun. As terse as the epitaphs were, I couldn't take them in all at once. I started with Ron's on the far end.

My brother's marker was cool to the touch, conducting the temperature of the soil below. I ran my hand across the Braille of his name, but instead of apprehending the man to whom the name referred, what I read was something like the darkness at the heart of a cave, or the mineral bitterness of water dredged from a stone well. His red hair, the cramped hand holding a paintbrush, the senses that wrestled scale and perspective: particulars dimmed, obstructed by the dense metal of the epitaph itself. And so it went on down the line. *Loving Brother . . . Devoted Mother . . . Beloved Son.* With all due respect to those who chose them, these were ready-made phrases, sentiments expressed in a banal graveyard jargon, platitudes stamped across the landscape.

I mourned for language as well as family. Only painstaking phrases could restore the dead—not to life, but to the living. Only through certain arrangements of words could one envision departed people instead of their leaden commemorations lying at one's feet. How a writer can revive the world through language had been as unshakable a preoccupation, and as much of a conundrum, as the man whose plaque I'd come to unveil. For the first time in years, I thought I'd give that book another try.

At last we reached my father's grave. I stared down, weary at first, then stunned by what I saw. Brian noticed the discrepancy first. "It's not *they*," he said faintly.

I knew exactly what he was referring to, the word (and world) of difference between what we'd thought my father's epitaph said and what it really did. Yet so untrusting was I of my own eyes that I heard myself ask, "What does it say?"

"'*You*,'" said Brian. "'*You* finally got me.'"

"*You?*"

Brian began to laugh, a little crazily, I thought, for a psychotherapist. "It's not you personally, if that's what you're worried about."

"I wasn't until you mentioned it!"

He squeezed my shoulder, sparking an audible shock of static. "Really, it's not."

"I think *you* is God."

"Probably."

"How could both of us remember it wrong? Did that woman misinform us?"

"Ms. Hirsch was a micromanager. Her type wouldn't make that kind of mistake. I think I thought it was *they* because, after we met with her, you said she said it was *they*."

"But when I said she said it was *they,* you didn't contradict me."

We stared at the plaque, as if its message might change yet again.

I wondered if my father had given a great deal of thought to this epitaph. Had he considered other punch lines? *I forgot my hat. Where's the flashlight?* It took discernment to choose a single sentence that would allow him to thumb his nose at piety—in the most inappropriate context, no less—while at the same time admitting that his adversary (that would be *you*) had finally outwitted him in the long skirmish to stay alive. My father's death was a laying down of arms. Once he surrendered himself he surrendered utterly and forever, a defeat he'd put off only after testing every means of resistance he had within him, every form of avoidance, trickery, and physical force, until the Powers That Be bore down upon him from utility companies, collection agencies, and social service organizations, until God Himself eventually caught up, my father having given Him a run for His money. *You* or *they.* God or man. It's the same either way. It's both ways at once. It's a masterpiece of paradox.

I pointed to a patch of grass beside my father. "That gap must be mine," I told Brian. "It doesn't look like I'd fit."

"You will," he said.

I swung around to face him. "Are you this blunt with your clients?"

"Yes," he said. "What will your plaque say?"

"I want to be cremated. Maybe I could sell my plot to these people on the left."

"Seriously, what would it say?"

When I was young, before any of my brothers died, death seemed very far away—another country—which allowed me to be as melodramatic about it as I pleased. I wrote poems clogged with overwrought sentiments about death. With what adolescent stamina I could daydream about the huge crowd of mourners at my funeral, or imagine the amazing things I might say with my last breath, provided I died in such a way that allowed me the time and presence of mind to say something memorable while someone was there to write it down. Now that I was in my forties, the idea of drumming up a quote for my headstone seemed too great a concession to death, the inevitability of which I found more difficult to grasp than ever, except in tiny disheartening doses. The memorial park blazed with midday sun, and I realized that I'd miss the light if I were dead, though I'd possess no sentience with which to miss it.

"Ms. Hirsch was right," I told Brian. "It's hard to plan your last words in advance."

Gary had said, "Turn off the TV." He cursed the used-car salesman who straddled a bristling camel and rode it across the lot. Gary had had enough absurd splendor. He turned to Sharleen, beside him in bed. "Now I've seen it all," he said. Ron sank to his knees as he climbed the stairs. Nancy, on the floor below, heard only an "Oh" as his head came to rest on the upstairs landing. His unseeing eyes remained wide open as heat slowly leaked from his hands and feet. Bob lay strapped in an ambulance, red light spinning beyond the window. "Please," he said through a bubble of blood, and my father asked the paramedics not to use the siren, afraid the noise might frighten his son. Bob died exactly as he'd lived: quietly gliding through city streets. My mother swallowed her heart medication. "See you in the morning," she said, and my father nodded absently. She cinched her bathrobe and shuffled off to bed without any idea that this night was her last. She reclaimed each morning like a watch from a pawnshop. Why would tomorrow be any different? Only the names of the days were different. Otherwise they were hard to tell apart.

It was getting late. I had a class to teach that afternoon. Brian had clients. "So?" I said, and we walked into the wind. If all the last words that have ever been spoken were uttered at once, they'd gust past us and fan out across Burbank and Studio City, sweeping smog over the ridge of the San Gabriel Mountains, stripping every cloud from the sky. Before us was the view my mother had hoped the family plot would have, and I took it in as we neared the car. Stretching from one end of the valley to the other were movie studios, apartment houses, multilevel parking structures, hospitals, and retirement villages, most of them new. The Golden State Freeway had been repaved, and if the snarled traffic ever eased up, commuters would sail to their destinations with the frictionless speed of a dream. From this height, I saw the slopes of the memorial park descend to the valley floor below and level out, the city its continuation, scoured by a wind that took history with it.

## About the Author

Bernard Cooper has won numerous awards and prizes, among them the PEN/Ernest Hemingway Award, an O. Henry Prize, a Guggenheim Fellowship, and a literature grant from the National Endowment for the Arts.

He has published two collections of memoirs, *Maps to Anywhere* and *Truth Serum,* as well as a novel, *A Year of Rhymes,* and a collection of short stories, *Guess Again.* His work has appeared in *Story, Ploughshares, Harper's, The Paris Review, The New York Times Magazine,* and in anthologies such as *The Best American Essays* and *The Oxford Book of Literature on Aging.*

He has taught at Antioch University, Los Angeles, and at the UCLA Writers' Program, and is currently the art critic for *Los Angeles* magazine. He lives in Los Angeles, California.